FILMED THOUGHT

FILMED THOUGHT

Cinema as Reflective Form

ROBERT B. PIPPIN

The University of Chicago Press CHICAGO & LONDON

The University of Chicago Press, Chicago 60637
The University of Chicago Press, Ltd., London
© 2020 by The University of Chicago
All rights reserved. No part of this book may be used or
reproduced in any manner whatsoever without written permission,
except in the case of brief quotations in critical articles
and reviews. For more information, contact
the University of Chicago Press, 1427 E. 60th St., Chicago, IL 60637.
Published 2020
Printed in the United States of America

29 28 27 26 25 24 23 22 21 20   1 2 3 4 5

ISBN-13: 978-0-226-67195-6 (cloth)
ISBN-13: 978-0-226-67200-7 (paper)
ISBN-13: 978-0-226-67214-4 (e-book)
DOI: https://doi.org/10.7208/chicago/9780226672144.001.0001

Library of Congress Cataloging-in-Publication Data

Names: Pippin, Robert B., 1948– author.
Title: Filmed thought: cinema as reflective form / Robert B. Pippin.
Description: Chicago: The University of Chicago Press, 2020. | Includes bibliographical references
and index.
Identifiers: LCCN 2019014786 | ISBN 9780226671956 (cloth) | ISBN 9780226672007 (pbk) |
ISBN 9780226672144 (ebook)
Subjects: LCSH: Motion pictures—United States—History and criticism. |
Motion pictures—Aesthetics.
Classification: LCC PN1993.5.U6 P53 2020 | DDC 791.430973—dc23
LC record available at https://lccn.loc.gov/2019014786

♾ This paper meets the requirements of ANSI/NISO Z39.48-1992 (Permanence of Paper).

For George & Mark Wilson

CONTENTS

Cinema as Reflective Form

ONE

Cinematic Reflection

I

The ways in which thought about film and philosophical reflection might intersect are various and have begun to be explored more and more in the last few decades.[1] At that intersection, there are various philosophical questions that emerge in thinking about the meaning of, primarily but not exclusively, filmed fictional narratives, or movies. There are related questions about photography and other types of recordings of movement or figuration: documentaries, art videos, and nonrepresentational avant-garde films, for example. But both Hollywood (by now a general term for commercially produced narrative films, but sometimes restricted to "classic" Hollywood films of the 1930s, 1940s, and 1950s) and art cinema, considered as new art forms, have drawn the most attention.

The most natural philosophical attention to film or movies has been as a

Some of the following is drawn from longer remarks in my "The Bearing of Film on Philosophy" (Pippin forthcoming) and are discussed in more detail in Pippin 2017: 1–11.

1. There are several good surveys of these developments, up to and including the current divisions. See especially Wartenberg 2015, the first chapter of Wartenberg 2007: 1–14, and the introductory remarks in Sinnerbrink 2011: 1–11. There are also a number of readers and anthologies. See the list in Sinnerbrink 2011: 208. More than anything else, changes in the technology of film viewing have made possible a studied attention to film without great expense and investment of time.

subdivision of aesthetics, or philosophy of art. This is also the case with film theory, or just "theory," as a subdivision of film and media studies. There is the obvious question of what kind of an art object a filmed narrative is and so how it bears meaning and compares with plays, paintings, and so forth—a question that now must include not just celluloid recording but digital recording and projection, and narratives made for television. (So "film" is now often used to refer to any and all such technologies, not just celluloid recording.) This is sometimes called the problem of film "ontology," and a great deal of anglophone aesthetics concerned with film is occupied with that question. There is also the question of the specific character of the cinematic experience, whether the ways in which we understand what is happening are connected to our cognitive processing of events in general, and if so, how. In what ways is our relation to what we see and understand connected to what we see and understand in the real world? If there is that connection, how is the connection made and maintained? This is also relevant to our emotional involvement. Why do we care about fictional characters as much as we do, recoiling in fright, or weeping in sympathy with what befalls them, but in no way that prompts us to do anything about their fates, fictional as they are? I will discuss in several of the chapters that follow the question of our understanding these narratives *as shown to us*, purposively displayed, made for an audience. This raises the question of the "narrator" of the film. (Who is showing us what?) Is there an "implied narrator" of events in the film world (and what is a film world)? Is the narrator primarily the director, the so-called auteur, or is the whole apparatus for the production and distribution of the film, as well as the performers, the collective "agent" responsible for the product? Can that agent be said to have "intentions" that bear on the meaning of the film?[2]

But thanks largely to the work of the Harvard philosopher Stanley Cavell—and, from a different tradition, the French philosopher Gilles Deleuze—a distinct intersection has evolved, one that in some circles is now designated "film-philosophy." (There is an online journal with that name.)[3] This "style of philosophizing," one could call it, sometimes occurs within film studies

2. There is of course no reason that the maker of a film could not have reflective interests in just this question, that the philosophy at issue in some film could not be questions like: What is a film? What is a commercial film? What do people expect from a film? See Mulhall 2008, especially chap. 5. I argue in the following chapter on *Rear Window* that this is the central issue in that Hitchcock film.
3. Or even "Filmosophy," as in Frampton 2006.

or in philosophy departments, a fact that raises another issue too large for an economical discussion: the relation between "film theory" and "film philosophy," as practiced in the two departments. The idea I want to explore in the chapters that follow is one that has gained currency in recent years: that film can be itself considered a form of philosophical reflection, given a capacious enough understanding of philosophy, one not limited to the marshaling of arguments in support of explicit theses, nor one that is wedded to a notion of philosophy as committed to "problems" for which definitive "solutions" are to be provided.[4]

It remains, of course, extremely controversial among philosophers to suggest that the proposing of theses, defended by arguments, engagement in defense of such arguments against counterexamples or charges of ambiguity, of vagueness, of question-begging and so forth, are not simply constitutive of philosophy as such; rather that that is an approach suitable only for some controversies but not others. I count myself in the following among those who believe that such an approach does not exhaust philosophy as such, broadly understood as the non-empirical exploration of meaning and value (where that exploration is itself not limited to the "possibility of meaning and value," but to substantive matters of significance and worth themselves). There is a great deal to be said about this in "meta-philosophical" terms, but ultimately any such suggestion will be judged by the readings of films that purport to show what the meta-philosophical position claims to be able to show, whether a new way of looking at or thinking about a quandary in moral theory or philosophical psychology or political philosophy can credibly emerge from a reading of a film. No such result will be definitive. Compellingness, credibility, "seeing" the limitations of a traditional formulation or way of thinking, can never be dispositive considerations, but at the most significant registers of philosophical reflection, which is often the highest bar one can aspire to reach, and it is high indeed.

Moreover, while anyone committed to philosophy has a great stake in

4. One of the clearest statements of the claim is that by Mulhall 2008: "In other words, I do not look to these films as handy or popular illustrations of views and arguments properly developed by philosophers; I see them rather as themselves reflecting on and evaluating such views and arguments, as thinking seriously and systematically about them in just the ways that philosophers do. Such films are not philosophy's raw material, nor a source for its ornamentation; they are philosophical exercises, philosophy in action—film as philosophizing" (4). I am not sure about "just the ways," but one takes his basic point.

the question of just what philosophy is, it is also the case that a great deal of energy and heat can be expended over the issue of whether a film could be considered "philosophy" or not, without all that much hanging on the classification issue. I am happy enough to consider films just as such as a contribution to philosophy, and as philosophy, but if someone prefers to call films forms of reflective thought that illuminate something of general significance about the philosophical issues of self-knowledge, knowledge of others, the limits of moral appraisal, the relations of dependence and independence in a social form of life, the poisonous effects of unequal and arbitrary power on oppressed and oppressor alike, the role of fantasy in romantic life, vehicles to show us the limitations of conventional assumptions about intentional agency or individual responsibility, or the relation between individual and community, and any number of other issues that will come up in the following, and that this contribution is substantial and genuine even if not conveyed in the form of discursive argumentation, I can't see much point in insisting that that contribution should or should not itself be called "philosophy."

Not being constricted in one's conception either of philosophy or what can contribute to philosophy is probably a good idea in itself since most of the deepest issues traditionally addressed by philosophers simply are such that they do not lend themselves to definitive solutions in articles or books, even if philosophers keep proposing such solutions in the full knowledge that no consensus will ever form around their arguments. Many of the most familiar philosophical questions require a great deal of discussion before it is even clear what issue is being raised, and the issues themselves are differently inflected in different sorts of societies at different historical times, always requiring extensive qualification. (If the question is the "best" or most distinctly "human" form of collective life, it seems a completely different question once a wage-labor and private capital system are instituted, and different again once the primary economic activity becomes consuming and intense stimulation to consume.) Some way of getting the relevant factors and qualifications in view is clearly necessary, even if it is true that there is also a deep continuity across historical times in many basic questions themselves. And, as just noted, there are certainly many significant philosophical questions that have to be posed at such a high level of abstraction, and require such close, detailed, and often technical work, that they are distinct from any connection to this thick texture of a human life at a time. But with many important questions, the best we can hope for is some illumination about the dimensions of the issue, and some credible sense of what various responses to it would be like in a human life at a time. In such endeavors, it might be better to rely on the power of the imagination of great artistic geniuses than the toy examples some philosophers seem fond of. The generality of any such representation would then not be a matter of the abstraction of some common set of features and so the postulation of some vague principle, but a generality more characterized by illuminating exemplarity ("a perspicuous representation," a "concrete universal" as such exemplarity has been called); illuminating at a level of generality, but in a way not incorporable in a "theory."

So in these terms, the strongest claim is not that film might inspire a viewer to pose philosophical questions or that film can serve as examples of philosophical problems (like moral dilemmas, for example), or that they pose "thought experiments" that prompt philosophy (although films can certainly do all of these things very effectively, and we might want to know what is distinctive about cinematic means for doing so), but that film, some films anyway, can have philosophical work to do; they themselves need to be considered modes of reflective thought.

This sort of discussion would be considered "immanentist" rather than contextualist, focused on readings of films themselves, rather than what the film might tell us about the society in which it was made and received, its gender relations, family dynamics, power relations, and so forth.[5] But like most dualisms, this one can be misleading. Many of the films discussed here are, on such an immanentist approach, actually also reflections on such sociohistorical issues, thematize them and amount to expressions of dissatisfaction with some way of life. (This is particularly but not exclusively true of chapters 5, 6, and 10.) And this sort of contrast has its own problems. Some such contextualist approaches presuppose a relatively unproblematic access to something like "the movie," and then proceed to ask what such an object would mean for some audience, or for women, or for men, or in what way it operates ideologically, or psychoanalytically, or what "code" it invokes (or that all of this just *is* what it *is* to be that movie, to mean what it means). This is also possible and can be valuable. But there are movies that present us with a number of elements that are very hard to take in and process on a first viewing. Such a taking in of and responding to a movie can be initially confusing and incomplete, with only a dim initial sense of how the elements might fit together. This is not restricted

5. See, for example, the way Dyer 2000 sketches the relevant distinction.

to following details of an intricate plot. We might be quite puzzled about the point of being shown this or that episode, character, or even by means of this or that camera position or camera movement. "The movie" is not something "given" for subsequent subjection to a categorical or a theoretical framework, any more than in trying to understand an action, "what she did" or "what she was trying to do" are simply "given" empirically. This is because, so my suggestion goes, such movies embody some conception of themselves, a distinct form, such that the parts are parts of one organic, purposive whole. Just in the way that a bodily movement in space can count as an action only by virtue of the self-understanding embodied in and expressed in it, an artwork, including any ambitious movie, embodies a formal unity, a self-understanding that it is always working to realize. Such a formal unity (something like the "point" of making and showing the film) requires investigative work focused on the details of the film, both stylistic and substantive, covering as many details as possible. In fact, the movie, one has to say in an ontological mode, *is the movie it is* only by means of this emerging, internal self-conception, a dimension we can miss if we too quickly apply some apparent formal unity, like a genre designation or a sociohistorical concept, or if we simply attend to the plot.[6] In ambitious films—and such a category is by no means limited to "art cinema"—such a self-conception is unmistakably philosophical, and so what it asks of us is a kind of thought and writing that we are just beginning to explore.

---

6. I am making this point in a way I have elsewhere, in terms of reflective self-awareness that is not simply self-observational or self-interrogative, but in film theory there are several good analogues to this way of putting the issue. One very useful one is that sketched by Yacavone 2015 in terms of the duality between the "world in the movie," on the one hand, and the "world of the movie," on the other, what we see and attend to as depicted, and our sense of it being depicted in a way, or the "movie world" as a selection, highlighting, focusing, and, in its cinematic way, commenting. To use an example from an essay that follows, "Chinatown" in Polanski's film is a world in the movie, the world depicted, the denoted world, what the characters feel and believe about what they call Chinatown, and what we see as they see it. It is not just that area of Los Angeles. That is not what they mean. Rather it is also their ironic sense of their own world; trying to comfort themselves by isolating the corruption and mystery of a lawless world somewhere else, but aware or half aware that official LA is hardly more transparent or honest. And then there is Polanski's filmic world, *Chinatown*, what he lets us see and feel by the moody soundtrack, the mise-en-scène, the sepia tones. He ultimately lets us see that the world of Chinatown presented in the movie world of *Chinatown* is *much worse* than even the most cynical characters can appreciate. The two worlds coincide for a moment, as Jake realizes what the audience has come to realize, after the concluding horrific events. See also the phenomenological approach by Dufrenne 1973 and Frampton 2006.

In just this sense, there can be a coincidence between interpretive work and philosophical interrogation. We want to know why in *Talk to Her* Benigno's rape of the comatose Alicia is somehow folded into a shocking and morally disorienting account of her reawakening, and that question seems inseparable from a general question about the status of moral judgments, their decisive or qualified authority. When in *Rear Window* Lars Thorwald enters Jeff Jefferies's apartment and asks, "What do you want from me?" if we have been noting the constant analogy between Jeff's position and movie watching, we know the question resonates with the larger question of what we think we want from movies, and that the film has been suggesting how badly we understand the depth of that question, and its connection with non-cinematic issues, like adopting a spectatorial position with respect to other people. When in Polanski's *Chinatown* Jake's colleague encourages Jake to "forget it" because "it's Chinatown," we have to ask: What is he being encouraged to forget and why is that a reason to do so? Is it a question that suggests the futility of any expectation of justice? When Dix Steele tells Laurel in *In a Lonely Place* that she can see into his apartment, but he can't see into hers, we want to know how that line is embedded in the story of what appears to be a potentially redemptive but ultimately doomed relationship, and we want to know why it is doomed and what that has to do with our ability to know and trust others. In the Dardenne brothers' *The Son*, why is there so much emphasis placed on Olivier's uncertainty about what he is doing and why? *How* could he be doing what he is doing without knowing why? What view of agency must be behind such a depiction?

II

The major premises for all of what follows are Hegelian. This is not just because so many of the films deal with issues of self-knowledge and intersubjective relations with others (and the deep link between the two issues). And it is an influence in spite of Hegel's own anxiety, which was considerable, about efforts by his contemporaries (like Schelling and Schlegel) to blur the distinction altogether between philosophy and art. But there is no question that Hegel thought the "content" of art and philosophy were the same, and so that while art embodied a distinctive affective-sensible modality of knowledge, it was certainly a mode of knowledge of philosophical significance.

The full story of philosophical attention to artworks is a long one, beginning with Aristotle's claim in his *Poetics* that tragedy is more philosophical than history. That claim opened the discussion that Plato seemed to want to close off: In what sense *is* tragedy philosophical at all, such that it can be more philosophical than history? And that tradition did not end with Hegel. It arises in Schelling's claim that art is superior to philosophy *as philosophy*, in the claims of the German romantics, in Schopenhauer on music, Nietzsche on the ancient tragic poets, Heidegger on Hölderlin, the plastic arts, and painting, and in the contemporary work of philosophers like Richard Rorty and Bernard Williams. But I am starting with the Hegelian assumptions that I have tried to defend elsewhere.[7] It is that what Hegel called "fine art" (*schöne Kunst*; and I am assuming that great Hollywood as well as European art cinema must be considered a "fine art") is an indispensable form of collective human self-knowledge across historical time. This all involves much more than the way any artwork might be said to be "taking the temperature" of a society in an age with respect to its "spiritual health" or gender dynamics or class relations, although all of that and more might certainly be involved. In his *Lectures on Fine Art*, Hegel noted that human beings—understood as collectively like-minded beings, what he called *Geist*—are always struggling to realize or actualize (*verwirklichen*) some normative conception of themselves, and in having attempted such an actualization, having "externalized" such a self-conception (created some social or political institution, collectively acted in some way, debated and passed some law, engaged in some marriage practice, educated their children in some way), they are then, and only then, able to understand much more fully and concretely *what* they took themselves to be committed to in such a merely provisional and tentative self-conception, and thereby what it was they actually did. This is Hegel's famous notion of "retrospectivity" (*Nachträglichkeit*) in self-understanding.[8] In his terms in the *Lectures*, human beings must "double themselves" (*sich verdoppeln*)[9] not only to understand themselves, but *to be themselves*, given their distinct mode of being, as self-realizing beings. That is, the mode of self-knowledge distinctive for such beings is self-constituting as well as self-reflective, as human beings struggle to become who they take themselves to be. Art is understood as a distinct modality of such self-understanding, "externalization," and self-realizing. It is

7. Pippin 2014.
8. Pippin 2008.
9. Hegel 1975: I: 31.

for Hegel an affective and sensible mode of self-understanding and is counted as just as indispensable as representational modes (religion) and conceptual modes (philosophy).

This is a crude sketch, of course, and still highly metaphorical. The notions of like-mindedness, collectivity, actualization, and a distinctly aesthetic mode of understanding would all have to be worked out in detail before this could even be an adequate proposal in any philosophy of art. But it at least provides the essential framework for understanding how attention to artworks can have philosophical work to do without simply being philosophy as the tradition understands it. We could call it an aesthetic mode of understanding, or an aesthetic perspective on what philosophy traditionally tries to pursue at the more conceptual level. The most ambitious and controversial claim would be that philosophy as traditionally understood would be impoverished without such an aesthetic perspective, but any such claim is best shown rather than simply asserted, and that is what I attempt to do in the following essays.

III

I have divided the discussions below into five sections that comprise discussions of nine films. In a collection like this, a natural first question before beginning is why these films and not others? There can never be a completely adequate answer to such a question. There are always other films, other filmmakers who come to mind. If these, why not these others? But the films discussed all exhibit a feature characteristic of any aesthetic object, but especially prominent. A fictional world is presented, the world as understood by the characters; what they attend to, ignore, are afraid of; what institutions are powerful in that world; what presuppositions about rectitude and responsibility and so forth are clearly accepted or actively disputed. But our attention is also drawn in these films, more prominently than in many others, to *the way* that world is cinematically depicted; what is cinematically highlighted, ignored; why the camera moves and frames events one way rather than another; to what end a musical score signals something sad or ominous; and above all, in many of the films discussed, various figurative and expressionistic means are invoked to suggest that everything we see depicted is not as it seems, must be interrogated, thought about. This goes beyond puzzles about the plot, involving issues of meaning (in the sense of significance or importance), self-worth, self-knowledge, willful ignorance, manipulation, unfreedom—all not attended to as such or in an honest way by characters, but prominent for the attentive viewer. A general name for this feature would be irony, and that is explored in many of the chapters below. But it is this general feature—cinematic, reflective form, a film's being inevitably about itself, in at least the sense of its own self-conception being realized—that characterizes the choices made. These films seem to me simply exemplary instances of this feature.

In this first section, in addition to these general reflections, I have included a discussion of Alfred Hitchcock's *Rear Window* since that discussion best exemplifies the approach defended in this chapter. As just noted, it has become a commonplace that Hitchcock wants to set up a parallel, a kind of allegory, presenting Jeff (James Stewart) in the position of a movie watcher, isolated and immobile in his apartment, laid up with a full leg cast, endlessly watching his neighbors across the courtyard (all of them framed by their windows as if little movie screens), often in the dark so he won't be seen in turn. But it is also often assumed that Hitchcock does this to show us how "sinful" we are, how prurient movie watching can be, how voyeuristic it is. That is not the case, I argue here. The problem Hitchcock is posing concerns not cinematic viewing as such, but an inadequate way of watching movies, Jeff's (and very likely ours). This is posed as the difference between a purely spectatorial mode of viewing, as if the film is just there for us to watch and enjoy, and a more involved mode of engagement with the film, in which what it asks of us (mostly attentive, interpretive *effort*) is as important as what we expect from it. Not only is Hitchcock, in effect, complaining about the way people watch his films (as if Raymond Burr's character when he enters Jeff's room and asks, "What do you want from me?" is an avatar of Hitchcock addressing his audience), but he is tying that issue to something more than the ethics, the norm, of aesthetic attending. He shows that it is of the same family of ethical issues as are raised by our involvement with others, especially in romantic relations. The dialectic of spectatorial and involved plays out again here, and these intertwined plots raise all sorts of further questions about how the film can be said to exhibit its own self-consciousness, why everything Jeff sees, his films, seem to be about himself and his own anxiety about marriage and domesticity, how Jeff's position and limitations come to seem an exemplar of what is wrong with the isolated and alienated state of his neighbors, each locked in to what Claude Chabrol called their "cages." What Jeff's girlfriend, Lisa, calls "rear window ethics" turns out to have to do with much more than their worry about being Peeping Toms.

In the second section, "Moral Variations," I want to show how a cinematic treatment can greatly complicate the basic distinctions we need in moral philosophy, but which can become misleadingly abstract without a way of thinking about them informed by the shadings and ambiguities and hard cases that cinema not merely presents, but "works through" in certain ways, not necessarily to a "resolution," but to some sort of understanding not limited to the particular characters or situation involved. Of course, every serious moral philosopher realizes that morality requires some form of casuistry, that abstract distinctions can be extremely difficult to apply in hard cases, and that no theory can anticipate and provide a "decision procedure" for all complex cases (in spite of what some ambitious utilitarians and some statements by Kant might seem to suggest). The question is not whether this is so, but what the form of reflective thought appropriate to this level of engaged attentiveness would, should, look like. Without a more concrete model for such reflection, casuistry can quickly seem like a scholastic game, hair-splitting that loses contact with the human dimensions of the issue under interrogation. Cinematic reflection on how moral distinctions "play out" in ambiguous and complicated settings can be thought of as one form of such concrete thinking. In these two chapters, I want to show first how Pedro Almodóvar's 2002 film, *Talk to Her*, subtly raises the issue of the difference between morality and moral judgment, on the one hand, and moralism, on the other, where the latter is something like the view that moral judgments are always rightly connected with attitudes of blame and the lived-out implications of having blamed, and that such judgments have a kind of absolute, all-trumping importance in assessing one another's deeds. If this distinction is to be made in an interesting way, care must be taken that it be done without too easily "excusing" or patronizingly pitying or treating another as less than a full agent. And if the film itself is to be understood as reflectively attentive to such issues, it must be discussed in a way in which its aesthetic reflective modality is done justice to.

The Almodóvar film also raises a question that will recur. A somewhat abstract and certainly inadequate characterization of that question would be that many of the films discussed deal with the relation between self-knowledge and our attempt to understand others. It is "deal with" and "relation" that are immediately inadequate, and this because that dimension in human life is presented in the films in painful depictions of the catastrophic failure of both, often a violent failure; a rape in the cases of *Talk to Her* and *Chinatown* (an incestuous rape in that film), a murderous hatred between women in *Johnny*

Guitar, potentially murderous violence by a man against a woman in *In a Lonely Place*. And the issue is also present in the picture of the suffering of women in bourgeois, suburban relationships and marriages, in *Shadow of a Doubt* and *All That Heaven Allows*, and by attention to a neurotic male anxiety about women and marriage in *Rear Window*. And, of course, *Shadow of a Doubt* concerns a man's murderous, insane hatred of women. The violence is gendered in other words, and the attempts by men and women to know and trust each other in romantic relationships reliably fail in so many fine Hollywood and European films. There is an obvious reason why this is so: the social worlds depicted in the movie worlds are deeply poisoned by patriarchy, and the films would be far less credible if that were not acknowledged. But that in itself tells us very little, even though it would require launching into another different book to go any further beneath that particular surface. The aspiration here is to suggest a philosophical framework for such a deeper interrogation. That framework would consist in a refusal to regard the kind of attention we are called on to devote to the characters as psychological subjects as anything but deeply misleading if that attention is focused narrowly on the "interior" experiences of such subjects and their life histories, what philosophers mean by attending to "philosophical psychology" or "moral psychology." These are taken to be about the concepts involved in or attempts to understand the meaning and dynamics of our psychological lives, the concepts always presupposed in such investigations, and which can often direct avenues of inquiry in misleading and distorted ways, in particular with respect to the concepts we use to understand human motivation in moral contexts. But if these concepts of interior states and attitudes are fully intelligible only by understanding their imbrication in a particular historical, social world, especially relations of power and assumptions about gender, and if this imbrication affects not just beliefs but the emotional lives of characters, as, we are shown, it does, then we need some sort of stereoscopic attentiveness, privileging neither the one nor the other, neither an individualist psychology nor a potentially reductionist "ideology critique." And that will obviously concern the acting out of gender roles and the potential illusions of thinking of what are experienced as a character's "ownmost feelings," especially romantic feelings, as unproblematically and directly accessible as such. That stereoscopic attentiveness is, I think, much more difficult than it can initially appear, and the suggestion is that the imaginative richness of these films is an invaluable means of access to the issues. The aspiration is the same as Henry James's from his preface to *The Princess Casamassima*,

... the value I wished most to render and the effect I wished most to produce were precisely those of our not knowing, of society's not knowing, but
only guessing and suspecting and trying to ignore, what "goes on" irrecon-
cilably, subversively, beneath the vast, smug surface[,][10]

with the emphasis falling where James put it, however paradoxical and strange
it can seem: on *society's* not knowing, as if a collective subject with its own psychology, an ignorance that shows up particularly in attempts at the greatest
and riskiest intimacy we seek: in romantic relationships, relationships so often
poisoned by what "goes on" beneath that "vast, smug surface."

In Hitchcock's 1943 *Shadow of a Doubt*, the distinction in question, what
is not fully known in James's sense, is between innocence and goodness, mere
ignorant naïveté and genuine virtuousness. If there is to be such a distinction,
it has to have much to do with the way in which the latter trait of some person is "informed" by a realization about the existence of evil, and that should
mean an awareness of what is at stake in the unavoidable struggle with evil,
both in others and, in Hitchcock's treatment in so many of his films, in oneself. But when is such a realization genuine, truly informed? How should we
understand what happens in the experience of the transition from innocence
to experience? What does that do to someone? Might they not have to realize
that in such a struggle with evil, the simple insistence on the good, the insistence on maintaining one's own moral purity, might insure the triumph of evil
(an important theme in both the Western and the film noir genre)? And again,
obviously, a cinematic portrayal of such issues is not a documentary-like case
history for study. The depiction engages us aesthetically, and does so with a
highly selective, artificial, carefully composed, and edited "treatment" of fictional characters invented by the screenwriter and the director, accompanied
by music, carefully controlled lighting, selection of point of view, decisions
about pacing, and so forth. The question of what difference it makes that this
form of reflection on issues posed with such generality is a form of *aesthetic*
reflection in general, and cinematic reflection in particular, is one Hitchcock
was well aware of and will be a constant one throughout all the chapters.

In the third section, "Social Pathologies," the relation between social and
political form and individual psychology, especially between social and individual "pathologies," is what is at issue in the two films discussed, Roman

10. James 1984: 1102.

Polanski's neo-noir *Chinatown* (1974) and Douglas Sirk's great melodrama *All That Heaven Allows* (1955).

In the former, moral attention is shifted from notions of individual guilt and responsibility (although these are certainly not minimized) to the question of whether an entire form of life can itself be "wrong." The possibility derives in this chapter from Adorno's famous claim in his *Minima Moralia* that it *can* be wrong, or as he literally says "false," and is otherwise expressed by his claims that a basic way of living can be essentially "damaged" at its core; even that "life" itself "does not live."[11] What seems to be a distinctively human way of living, what is directly experienced as the struggles, pains, and joys of daily life, is no more human, no more a *human* life, a *richtiges Leben*, than elephants performing in a circus live an "elephant life." The film, in other words, is about such a collective form, signaled by its title, *Chinatown*; not "Jake Gittes"; not "Noah Cross." The attempts to isolate such wrongness "there," Chinatown, not "here," or in an individual agent, are utter failures in the film, which is actually, finally, about Los Angeles and American life, not an isolatable mysterious place or a demonic villain. But such a conception of "wrongness" attributable to something so basic, so deeply taken for granted that it is not even noticed in a quotidian existence focused so misleadingly on individual agents and the singular responsibility they bear as individuals, is elusive. Both the nature of the wrongness and the way of living alluded to so elliptically by "Chinatown" are elusive. It can't simply be identified by attention to the owners of capital, the organization of production, the importance of consumption, the distorting influence of money and power, although all of these factors have a clear bearing on the issue. In the film, the issue can be said to be raised and addressed by a distinctive cinematic means, or so I argue here: its "tonality," something like the "mood" of the narration as much as what is narrated. The very mysteriousness of what is behind the appearances, not rightly or at least fully identified as simply "corruption," emerges as a kind of pervasive and finally deeply credible foulness that builds as a powerful, inescapable presence, more than it is ever determinately identified. Cross is largely right, and the film shows us how right he is, when he tells Jake that he (and we) may think we know what we are dealing with, even as we condemn and blame, but we don't, and the film leaves us with the likelihood that we never will.

Aside from ways that movies might create some sort of hesitation about

11. Adorno 2016: 39.

moral judgments, or even their suspension, and aside from the implications of cinematic tonality and atmosphere, another cinematic technique discussed in chapter 6 and in the next section is cinematic irony. In the case of Douglas Sirk's *All That Heaven Allows*, this means a way of showing aspects of a lived world that intimates how much is not shown, where what is merely intimated but not shown is a dimension of social reality that is at odds with, even the polar opposite of, what is taken for granted as real in that world. To accomplish this distinctive way of showing, Sirk conceived ways of narrating his films as if from the points of view of the characters in it, what I call in the chapter the cinematic equivalent of "free indirect discourse" in literature; in this case, in watching the film, we actually see how the upper-middle-class world of Stoningham sees itself, complete with their fantasies, self-deceit, superficiality, and cruelty, all as a way of showing that constantly reveals what those persons try very hard to avoid seeing. This irony in Sirk (once it was seen and appreciated, something that took a while) is sometimes taken to be sarcastic, even contemptuous of that world, but I argue here that the irony has a different implication. To see that, one has to understand something about how the genre, melodrama, works in Sirk's hands, and the two issues specific to this film. One concerns the two forms of boundary policing enforced by Cary Scott's children and the townsfolk in her circle as they try to prevent her from marrying outside her class (to her gardener) and, even more anxiety-producing, the policing of age boundaries. She is an older woman intending to marry a younger man, and that sends everyone into a frenzy of warning and finger-wagging. The question posed is the interrelation of these boundaries and their policing, and their general relation to the effects of class stratification in the "internal" psychological lives, especially the internal romantic lives, of Cary Scott and Ron Kirby. The second question concerns a topic never adequately discussed in most of the philosophical tradition,[12] where it tends to produce clichéd, banal writing. This is the film's interrogation of the meaning of romantic love; or better said, what it has come to mean to people of a certain class, in a certain social world, at a certain historical time. Sirk's film treats it and the enormity of its significance in bourgeois life as a valuable, if rarely achieved, touchstone of genuineness, authenticity, and consolation, an escape from the ruthlessly conformist world that seems to require nothing but theatrical role-

12. Plato, Augustine, the French moralists, the early Hegel, Kierkegaard, and (I would count) Nietzsche are obvious exceptions.

playing. The irony with which such an aspiration is treated is clear enough, but again it is not dismissive or simply critical. Sirk is trying to explore just what sort of investment we have in romantic love, why we have invested so much, how much of that is an understandable but dangerous fantasy, and what we should conclude from what is treated as a failure in the film, even though, remarkably, given the subtlety of the irony, it is not acknowledged as, rarely even noticed to be, a failure by most audiences and critics.

In section 4, both the theme of love and the status of cinematic irony are discussed by considering two films by Nicholas Ray, his highly stylized, almost-camp Western, *Johnny Guitar* (1954), and one of his best films (and perhaps the best performance ever by Humphrey Bogart), *In a Lonely Place* (1950). *Johnny Guitar* is presented to us with all the elements of a traditional Western, especially since at its core, it concerns the common mythic fable in Westerns, the psychological implications of modernization (again, typically, the coming of the railroad), but the presentation is so stylized and operatic that we are immediately aware that the self-consciously exaggerated elements of the genre raise as an issue the question of the audience's expectations about Westerns, and the relevance of those expectations to contemporary life. These expectations are usually invoked automatically. But here the standard conventions are self-consciously quoted rather than directly invoked, or they are mentioned rather than used, and so their usual effect is suspended. They are seen in an almost anti-illusionistic exaggeration. This shows us that those expectations can effectively screen us off from noticing deeper psychological issues that escape the conventional plots. The main psychological implications at issue are dual: the out-of-control anxiety of the townspeople about Joan Crawford's character, Vienna, a saloon owner and ex-madam, and their jealousy about her cleverness in buying up the land the railroad will need, and, on the other hand, her smoldering but still alive love affair with the title character, Johnny Guitar, played by Sterling Hayden. Again, the two greatest aspirations of bourgeois society, for financial success and security (in what is often a zero-sum game, the source of great enmity and mistrust) and for stable romantic love (usually connected with the pleasures and intimacy of family life), and the tension between these, how the latter is possible in the former world, are on full display, although again treated ironically. Here the irony involves a contrast between a knowing irony, as when one, in a wise-cracking mode, says the opposite of what one says, and an unknowing form, where one unknowingly reveals that one believes the opposite of what one says, sometimes something clearly unknown to oneself. (Mercedes McCambridge's hysterical Emma is constantly inadvertently revealing her real motives for her moralistic condemnation of Vienna, and these have both to do with her own sexuality, her bitter envy of Vienna, and her wild anxiety about the future soon to arrive with the railroad.) This is once again an aspect of the theme introduced in chapter 6: a politics of American emotional life.

The complexities of the romantic theme, what the aspiration to love would mean in a certain form of social life, are on view again in Ray's *In a Lonely Place*. The social world in question here is not the Los Angeles of the noir era, upper-middle-class Eisenhower America, or the western frontier, but Hollywood itself. A script writer and veteran, Dix Steele (Humphrey Bogart) is a moody, disgruntled, potentially violent loner, who wants everyone to know that Hollywood films are false, dishonest, pandering, and in that sense "insincere." And he rightly thinks that the commercial corruption of Hollywood, its concern for profit and fame, infects all aspects of that world around him. The question he then faces when he meets Laurel, an actress with a shady and obscure past, that they both face, is how it would be possible to know someone well enough to trust him or her, to trust not just that they are honest but that their own (sincere) "presentation of themselves" is not itself a self-deceived and "Hollywood" fantasy, is reliable—an issue connected with the concern about what it is for a film (or a work of art) to be "genuine" too, to prove Dix's skepticism about the movies wrong. I treat the romantic theme in a way Cavell often does, as a problem of skepticism, a confrontation with the risks of trust given the deep uncertainty about others we have to live with, can never escape. I especially make use of what Cavell calls active and passive skepticism about other minds. The former focuses on how can I know another, the true nature of that other's (supposedly) inner life. The latter though is a concern, or an anxiety about whether I am ever truly known ("as I really am") by an other. And the two modalities are interconnected. The point of close attention to the film is to understand how they are interconnected, and whether there is any hope for some satisfying way to deal with the unsettledness of the situation. A major issue, a major difficulty, in any sort of satisfaction is the influence Hollywood movies have on our understanding of romantic love, the roles of men and women, the conditions of trust, and what we expect from romantic love. This sort of influence is not a good one.

Section 5, "Agency and Meaning," concerns two films that, in the stories they tell, make inevitable some engagement with very large-scale metaphysical questions, although, again, the way the questions are raised is distinctively cinematic, not discursive; that is, they strive for a certain compelling credibility rather than a firm conclusion.

In chapter 9, I consider Terrence Malick's *The Thin Red Line* (1998). The film invokes all the genre conventions of Hollywood war films, but again we see that such conventions not only function as commercial classifications, but also allow variations, sometimes extreme and, in the sense introduced above, ironic variations on the exemplarity treated here as the chief form of cinematic generality and so philosophical relevance. The meaning that organized mass killing could have, what sense it could make (if any) to those who participate, is one of the chief issues. As in many of the films discussed here, this question, too, is given a specific social and historical inflection: How is it possible for citizen soldiers of at least putatively pacific commercial, democratic, egalitarian republics to come to suffer the trauma of and engage in the killing required by modern warfare, especially in foreign lands, far away from their own homes and families? But Malick also approaches the topic with two highly unusual technical means: what I characterize as a constant concentration on the visual beauty, magisterial indifference, and sublimity of the natural world, and the unusual meditative interior monologue voice-overs by individual characters.

What we come to appreciate as we watch the film and see that question about meaning often raised is that the war comes to mean nothing at all, or something so venal as to be obscene (like career advancement). The usual convention of war films suggests the creation of solidarity between men, a solidarity of such profundity that nothing in ordinary life (certainly not politics) comes close, and that is usually offered as an explanation for the acts of selfless heroism that we see. There is no such solidarity here, and there is instead a great deal of emphasis on isolation, alienation from others, and loneliness. I argue that the basic attempt of the film is to invite our expectation of such conventions and then to refuse them. Malick has deemphasized what is traditionally understood to be the usual psychological issues and concentrated on something else. Malick has not allowed the narrative line or even character conflict to carry the primary meaning or the primary significance of what we are seeing, and while he realizes that an associative connection with the conventions of war movies is inevitable for the viewer, he also takes a number of steps to invert those expectations, frustrate them, and ironize them. This implies that we cannot any longer understand war as we have; the expectation that we can leads us to expect the genre conventions and then leads to our being lost when they fail us. This can be said to be about both the way movies have rendered human practices intelligible, the way they no longer can, and the problem of the intelligibility of the events themselves. This is connected to the way the film carries us from a kind of Rousseauean or romantic view of the natural state of things to a much more Hobbesian one. Showing this involves the most ambitious dimension of the film, one that gives the chapter its reference to "vernacular metaphysics." We see not the mere beings of nature, including us, but view them in light of the question of what it is for them to be at all, especially to be alive, a presence that cannot be rightly captured as a discursive theme but only in a kind of intimation or disclosure available to a visual art.

The last film discussed is the subject of chapter 10, *The Son* (2002), by the Belgian brother team, Luc and Jean-Pierre Dardenne. But I deal as well with the common formal and substantive treatment unique to all the eight feature films for which they are willing to accept authorship. These films always concern a basic moral question, one usually having to do with responsibility; they often involve some sort of recovery from a wrong committed by the wrongdoer against the one wronged; and they all manifest a heightened sense of the complexity of how we might come to understand the characters dealing with such a question. In several films, a theme common to many of the essays in this collection — especially in the chapters on Polanski, Sirk, Ray, and Hitchcock — continually arises: the connections between a character's psychological turmoil, stress, and confusion, on the one hand, and the quite distinctive characteristics of the social world in which they live, on the other. In the case of the Dardenne brothers' films, various cinematic properties involve ways of rethinking and challenging basic issues in our conventional understanding of the relation between agent and deed in ordinary action and in explanation of action and attribution of responsibility, and so they imply an unusual picture of human subjectivity. This bears on another issue especially prominent in the Sirk and Ray discussions: what we need to understand in understanding another and how we might come to understand another in a new way. This of course involves a question that has been at issue throughout: What is it to call these aesthetic objects "ways of rethinking"?

The film I concentrate on is the one I consider the Dardenne brothers' masterpiece, *The Son*. It concerns a man, Olivier, whose teenage son had been murdered in a botched robbery, whose marriage fell apart because of it, who quit his job working with his brother at their lumberyard and began working at a kind of halfway house, a retraining carpentry school for released teen ex-offenders transitioning back into society. The young boy who murdered his son is released to that school, and after much hesitation—and, most remarkably, without any clear reason for doing so, none he can formulate to himself, none he can give his flabbergasted ex-wife—Olivier accepts him as a student. This is the beginning of the challenge to our conventional views. The film makes very credible that Olivier really does have *no* reason to accept the boy (not one he is somehow unaware of); the decision is treated as mysterious, although we fear an eventual attempt at revenge. And the film, in its own way, continues to interrogate questions beyond how an action could count as such if not motivated by an intention of some sort, questions like: When can an action properly be said to begin and end? What is a part of the action, what not, and why? And these are all explored simply by the editing and camera work. Having been "raised," how the questions are pursued cinematically, in *The Son* and in other films by the Dardenne brothers, is the main issue for the chapter.

TWO

Cinematic Self-Consciousness
in Alfred Hitchcock's *Rear Window*

I. SPECTATORSHIP: LIVED AND CINEMATIC

Tell me everything you saw, and what you think it means.
LISA FREMONT, *Rear Window*

Filmed fictional narratives seem to most viewers to create some minimal transparency illusion, the illusion that the viewer is somehow magically present at various events, an unobserved observer in the scenes. But, of course, we also know that this cannot be literally true. We are not *in* the action, cannot be affected by what happens, cannot intervene. We occupy far too many points of view, including those of several characters, that no one present could. We are in some sense aware that what we are seeing is being narrated, has been photographed, and is being told to us in a visual way, and when this feature is unavoidably obvious, as when we are whisked back in time, or transported suddenly in one cut to another country, or are flying through the air, we easily accept a widespread convention. That is, we have learned to ignore for the most part that someone is purposefully showing us what we are seeing, has decided what we will not see, that the events are not simply magically present in front of us.[1]

---

1. A good deal of philosophical reflection on the entire photographic medium stresses that that medium is not representational but directly presentational, and this because of the automa-

Further, some directors do not want us to ignore their active involvement, even while the medium-specific character, the automatism feature, is preserved. They are able also to draw our attention to the director's narrational control, and so to the presence of the camera, not just to what the camera is photographing. When we do notice, the visible narrational element is what gives the film its reflective form. Such a narrative form cannot but suggest a purposiveness, its point, and so manifests that the aesthetic object bears a conception of itself, a source of unity and ultimately interpretive meaning. It seems odd to say that filmed fictional narratives are in this sense "self-conscious," embody an awareness of themselves, but this is just an elliptical way of saying that the director is self-conscious of the point of the determinate narrative form.[2] That point may simply be "to create funny situations" or "to scare the audience in a way they will enjoy," but it can clearly be more aesthetically ambitious; for example, to help us understand something better. This all corresponds to our own implicit awareness in experiencing an aesthetic object

---

tism of the camera. Photography is not made, at least not made like a painting; reality, we are tempted to say, as such, impresses itself on the film or is digitally recorded "as it is." This means that the world is present to us, but we are not present to the world; we remain unseen. The world is just there. These are Cavell's formulations. See Cavell 1979 and Shuster 2017: 1–84. However, this world is not *just* there to be inspected, merely attended to, as if from a perch on high, looking in, perhaps aided by equipment, binoculars, telephoto lenses. The film to be discussed in this chapter sets up the problematic of film this way, but it shows us that there are various ways of responding to this situation; essentially two ways in the film: Jeff's and Lisa's. When Cavell 1979 tells us that the film screen is a "barrier" even as it makes the world present to us, he explains that this screen "screens *me* from the world it holds—that is, it makes *me* invisible" (24; my emphasis). In one sense, yes; *I* am invisible. In another sense, this does not mean that all I must do to understand the world presented is watch, like a voyeur, a "peeping Tom," in the language of the film. In this case, here is something insufficient, deformed, about the way Jeff "watches" his little films, and that has something to do with the deformation in his relations with others, paradigmatically with Lisa.

2. I don't mean that the director necessarily has a determinate "message" or "theme" explicitly in mind, and always constructs everything to make such a point, or that the film must have such a message. (Louis B. Mayer was right: if you want a message, call Western Union.) The "sense" embodied in the narrative and so the form's determinacy can be intuitively at work; for example, simply in seeing that such and such a narrational move would "make sense" in the context of the overall film, or that it wouldn't; that such and such an action on the part of a character should be experienced as troubling; that a kind of self-blindness should be portrayed as destructive, not merely naive, and so forth. The idea that a work must be formally self-conscious about itself, bear a conception of itself, is worth a separate study in itself. For more on the issue, see Pippin 2014.

that that is what we are doing. "Implicitly aware" also requires a lot of philosophical unpacking, but there is a natural sense of something like such potential attentiveness becoming explicit when we find ourselves asking why we are first shown a character by a camera seeming to swoop in through a window (*Psycho*) or why there are so many close-ups of backs and backs of heads in the Dardenne brothers' films. But such aesthetic attending already embodies a norm. It can be done well, or it can be done lazily, sloppily, indifferently, in a biased way, or self-righteously. That issue will ultimately be the topic of the following.

There is no clearer example of this set of issues than Alfred Hitchcock's 1954 film *Rear Window*, and this has occasioned a good deal of discussion about the purpose of Hitchcock's triply thematizing all at once (i) the voyeurism in the plot, (ii) the striking similarity between the main character's immobile position watching the "framed" dramas he sees in the windows of the apartments opposite his and the viewer's position in cinema, unquestionably the most commented-on feature of the film,[3] and (iii) Hitchcock's calling attention to his control of what we see and when and how we see it, his insistent breaks from what is established as the main point of view, Jeff's.[4] Further, when, in the last twenty minutes of the film, Jeff Jefferies, the photographer, begins intervening and "directing" the actions that occur (Jeff, afraid a suspected murderer is leaving town, finally sends him a note and then calls him, sends his friends on a mission), we have a final allegorical connection made, (iv) between Jeff's (the photographer's) position and Hitchcock's. (This is a photographer, though, who, looking for evidence of a murder, *takes no pictures of Thorwald's apartment or his comings and goings*; never loads his camera although he is always looking through it. We shall have to return to that. This must be some sort of sign that Jeff is and is not playing a director-

3. This has been suggested by several commentators. See especially Douchet 1960–61: 7–15; Fawell 2001: chaps. 8, 9; Belton 1991; Stam and Pearson 1986. From a Cavellian point of view, what solidifies the reference is the fact that Jeff sees while (mostly) unseen; he is screened off, invisible to the people he watches. See Cavell 1979: 24.

4. For the most part, such a cinematic narrator is, in George Wilson's phrase, "minimal," effaced; certainly not usually present in the film, as if a character. And nothing about the biographical details of the actual makers of the film is needed to infer the intentions of the narrator. The intentions are what can be seen in the film. See Wilson 2011: 129. There are other versions of what has been called "an intentionalist" approach. See, for one example, Livingston 2009.

like role. Something is missing.) This last allegorical connection also reminds us that it was Jeff's vivid narration, with its intensity, passion, and unwavering conviction, to Stella McGaffery, his nurse, and Lisa Fremont, his girlfriend, and his friend the detective Tom Doyle, that initially brought into being the possibility of murder, creating an event out of several disconnected nighttime events. He creates out of what he views, what it meant. Put another way, he edits together the various scenes he has seen to make his own imagined film narrative, a murder thriller. He puts together in a kind of coherent sequence a tense marital situation, angry arguments, long-distance phone calls, three nighttime trips by the neighbor Lars Thorwald (Raymond Burr) with his metal sample case, no sign the next day of the wife. (This is all he has at first, but he thinks it enough.) Then he spies a large box, tied with thick ropes and carted away, sees some knives and a saw, a dog digging in the dirt and then turning up dead, Thorwald washing down the walls of his bathroom, and finally the wife's jewelry still at home when she has supposedly gone upstate.[5] Jeff's deep investment in what he wants to be true is also signaled by the strange fact that Jeff is, from the very earliest stages, absolutely and passionately certain that a murder has been committed, and immediately, dogmatically rejects any alternate explanation. When he is informed that he had been asleep when a crucial event occurred that refutes his entire theory—Thorwald had been seen by the superintendent leaving with his wife the next morning[6]—he is unfazed. This persists even after he hears more disconfirming information from the detective friend. (Mrs. Thorwald was seen being escorted to the train that morning; seen picking up the trunk, which turned out just to contain her clothes. All of this emphasizes, to the point of obsession, Jeff's investment in the narrative he

5. This all of course mirrors what we see and largely what we also do when watching a film; we are always implicitly asking what it means that one sequence follows another, and we form our hypotheses the same way as Jeff, usually with more tentativeness. The film itself is, as usual with Hitchcock, quite cinematic in this sense; 35 percent of it is without dialogue, as noted by Scharff 1997: 2, 179. It is often as if we were watching a silent film, and one long scene is even a pantomime. See Naremore 1988: 241. Scharff's book has a useful shot-by-shot summary of the film's 796 shots and is a valuable resource for its subject, Hitchcock's "symmetries and sub-symmetries, contrapuntal arrangements, trigger releases, slow disclosures, familiar images and those ominous transitions by way of fades; each scene is woven out of these elements, and their presence is detectable in different combinations—they are the poetics of his cinema" (180).
6. This must have been his confederate/lover, and it takes Lisa, not the detective and not Jeff, to surmise that the woman could have been anyone. (Mrs. Thorwald is an invalid and rarely seen.) The confederate likely got into the building when both Jeff and the super were sleeping.

has constructed.) When it is explained to him that when one observes people unaware they are being observed, not presenting themselves to others as they want to be seen, one does not at all necessarily see some truth about them—they could be presenting themselves to themselves in a way that is just as theatrical and a kind of self-pretense—he is indifferent to such cautions as well.[7]

This manner of Jeff's constructing his suspicion is obviously also linked to what we do when we try to understand what is happening in a film. We are guided by the director and the editor, but we have to do some work, remembering past scenes, deciding which should be remembered, interpreting how one past scene might or might not bear on a recent one, anticipating possibilities.[8] Usually this is no problem in commercial films because we are given very clear visual "advice" about how to do this. Even more to the eventual point here, it is also often what we do when we try to understand someone or some event in ordinary life. If we need to work at the understanding, if something does not make initial sense to us, one of the main ways we go about that work is to create this sort of narrational sense. We try to put what a character said or did into some sort of coherent pattern of remarks or actions in the past, requiring us to decide which might be relevant or not, bringing to bear what we have heard other people say about the person, what we know about remarks and deeds we might not have experienced, in the hope that all of this might reveal what was intended and so what the words or the action meant. This is usually much more revealing than isolating the words or deed in that moment and trying to "plumb the depths" by some deeper insight into their inner life, as if in search of some isolated truth-maker, fact of the matter. But there are ways of doing this sort of "editing" that are better or worse, and even though Jeff turns out to be right in this case, his way of going about this is quite problematic, and that fact touches on both ethical and aesthetic issues. This is because, inevitably, as noted, we are also often invested in some way in the clarification, and that investment can be self-interested, self-deceived, biased, subject to wishful thinking, and so forth. One of the ways this can become impossible for us to avoid acknowledging is when our views intersect with the lives of others, and

7. This is my suggestion about why one should be cautious. All Doyle says is, "That's a secret, private world you're looking into out there. People do a lot of things in private they couldn't possibly explain in public."
8. Cf. Cavell's remark that with images on a screen, "you are given bits of the world, and you must put them together into those lives one way or another, as you have yours" (1979: 156).

they respond, intervene in some way to challenge us. And, of course, one of the ways this can be *avoided* is by preventing such challenges, keeping our distance, staying inside our dollhouses or cages, psychological as well as spatial.

The Hitchcockian cinematic self-consciousness that we are interested in happens at the very beginning of the film and is dramatically signaled. Jeff, a photographer immobilized by a broken leg, is asleep (we soon learn) in the early morning heat. He is alone. But the bamboo blinds in his modest apartment rise like theater curtains on the courtyard scene and apartment windows visible from his "rear window," as the credits roll. (Staged drama, which the curtain and the open windows suggest, effaces even more any indication of a narrator.[9] The fourth wall has simply disappeared, and we take ourselves to be simply watching what the characters do and say.[10] Hitchcock seems to be introducing this "theater convention" into a movie in order to subtly contrast this transparency illusion we indulge more easily in theater with the contrasting but often unnoticed control of narration by a director.[11] There is another indirect allusion to the theatrical experience. In a departure from Hitchcock's brilliant use of music in his other films, there is no nondiegetic music in the film.[12]) I think Hitchcock is alluding to this difference again when he makes his cameo appearance. He is in the apartment of the composer and appears to be repairing or setting his clock. In the theater, the author "winds everything up" and it plays out without intervention. But a movie director can control the pace and timing of everything we see, intervening frequently, has control of "the clock" throughout. As if to emphasize his control even more, Hitchcock turns directly in our direction, something I believe he does in only one other

9. See again Wilson 2011 on this point and my discussion of his book in a review article, Pippin 2012.
10. The scenes are also separated in the film by a black screen, not dissolves, again suggesting the separation of acts in a theater, with the curtains closing.
11. There is an illuminating discussion by Belton 1991 of the way Hitchcock makes use of the techniques of both "showing" (as in theater) and "narrating" or "telling" (as in the novel), or mimetic versus diegetic narration, and especially how he mixes the two in his use of the spatial arrangement of the outside apartments and in the inside world of Jeff's. See also Rohmer and Chabrol 1992: 124, where they call the film "a reflexive, critical work in the Kantian sense," and that the "theory of spectacle" implied in the work requires a "theory of space" which implies a "moral idea" that "derives from it." (Their sense of the "moral idea" at work is "Christian dogma" [126]. See their all too pat summary of their whole approach to Hitchcock [128]. That can be contrasted with the approach taken here.)
12. There is, though, plenty of music coming from the apartments, and it has several functions at various points in the plot. See Fawell 2001: 120–22.

cameo, in *Marnie*. Moreover, it is almost as if we are to believe he is giving instructions to the composer about what is the theme music of the film, the piece he is composing that we hear throughout and that eventually is finished as—what else?—"Lisa."[13] Here, the blinds rising makes no diegetic sense; there is no one who could have raised them (except the director). Then the camera emphasizes its presence and control even more by taking the viewer on a little tour of the outside scene, all until we finally settle on a perspiring James Stewart, L. B. "Jeff" Jefferies, asleep in his wheelchair. (If we are to come later to have some doubts about the propriety of Jeff's voyeurism, we by and large do not at first notice our own compromised position, that our first look at Jeff is rather invasive, a man in a most vulnerable state, unable to look back, to project himself as he wants; asleep.[14] The film is "rounded by a sleep" again at the end, when Jeff is asleep once more, even more immobilized and unable to assert or project himself, and Lisa is awake, now even more able to manipulate her own appearance.[15] This is the beginning of what Lisa will call "rear window ethics," and, as is emphasized here, it will have something to do with the ethical dimensions implicit in cinema itself.) As if all that weren't emphasis enough, the camera shows us, calling attention to what will be important later in the plot and to the cinematic theme, Jeff's broken eight-by-ten view camera (no doubt a souvenir of his injury, caused when he stood in the middle of an automobile racetrack to snap the photo we are also shown) and, mysteriously, a framed negative of a woman's face, the positive magazine image of which we are also shown on the cover of a stack of the magazines in which it appeared. (Every positive image starts as a negative, and for some reason never explained Jeff keeps the negative of the photo framed and displayed. Is he able to connect the negative with the positive sides of human existence, or is he stuck in "negative viewing," especially, as we shall see, a negative view of marriage, domestic life, perhaps of women?)[16]

---

13. Lisa suggests that it is their song, and she is right: he is having a lot of trouble "completing" it. (She says of the music that it's "as if it's written expressly for us." It was.)

14. This is certainly not the only time Hitchcock reminds the viewer that he or she may be complicit with the actions of a character the viewer may also be tempted to judge morally. The most humorous treatment of the theme is our invitation to laugh at Joe and Herb in *Shadow of a Doubt* for their fascination with gruesome murder plots; this in a film that we have paid to see about a serial killer.

15. The 360-degree pan is repeated as well.

16. For an especially good treatment of Jeff's obsession with "the negative," sees Toles 2001, especially this remark: "No space for reflection is created in which the mesmerizing labor of the negative reveals its potential for infecting the knowledge and claims of social justice

And what we are shown involves the narration of a triple plot, a feature that always raises the issue of the meaning of the interrelation of the three plots. There is first the minimal plot, Jeff's growing obsession with voyeurism. He is recovering, immobilized by a broken leg, and he spends his days and many of his nights looking out his window and into the apartments of his neighbors. (There is a heat wave, and everyone has windows open and blinds up.) He follows the little dramas of people he gives names to: Miss Lonelyhearts, apparently a spinster looking forlornly for love; Miss Torso, an acrobatic dancer usually in various stages of undress, and apparently naively (but not credibly) uninterested in who sees her twirling, stretching, or wiggling her backside as she bends over; a childless couple who dote on their dog; a family with children (normal and apparently happy; they do not catch Jeff's attention and we see very little of them); a newlywed couple; a middle-aged woman who lives alone and sculpts; a composer who also lives alone. Aside from a neighbor who Jeff comes to suspect has murdered his wife, Jeff, his girlfriend, Lisa, and his nurse, Stella, initially pay most attention to the sad plight of the older, unmarried woman, watching her pantomime having a dinner guest, struggling with and rejecting a young, aggressive would-be lover, and contemplating suicide. They are all clearly embarrassed by what they see, but they do not turn away, and watch eagerly. In the second plot, they spy on a couple across the way, the wife, an invalid, and her caregiver, her husband, a costume jewelry salesman who seems the object of much criticism by the wife and apparently with good reason. Our early suspicion is that he is having an affair. (There are phone conversations, which she overhears and becomes enraged at.) Jeff will come to suspect that the man, Lars Thorwald, finally murdered, cut into pieces, and disposed of his wife, and that becomes the central plot. Almost as

---

or truth-seeking that are its putative higher ends. In other words, Jefferies's (or anyone's) capacity to envision the ideal, to act credibly in the name of a truth better than the radically imperfect 'givens' of the present can be subtly deformed by a consistent reliance on a terminology obsessed with negation and hidden tyranny" (169). The photography issue appears to have something to do with the argument between Jeff and Lisa about the future. Jeff wants to photograph spectacles, events that require no deep interrogation of or involvement by the photographer. She wants him to become a fashion and portrait photographer, a job where, presumably, much more psychological investment in understanding the subject is required. That that dialectic between mere spectatorship and involvement will be crucial in the film is an early indication of Jeff's skepticism that there is much more to know in any such depths than "the negative," and it is not worth the bother. On the other hand, the fashion photograph is an indication that he *can* do and has done what Lisa is asking.

important as the murder plot is the third, what appears to be a long-standing resistance by Jeff to marrying Lisa, played by Grace Kelly. Kelly, obviously in the running as the most glamorous and beautiful movie star in the history of cinema, and always gorgeously dressed in couture in the film, is nevertheless unable to get Jeff over his deep resistance to marriage. She even seems unable to arouse much sexual desire in the cold fish. He is visibly much more aroused "spectatorially," at a scopophilic distance, by Miss Torso than he ever is by Lisa, no matter her explicit request for a bed for the night, no matter her negligée.[17] Lisa wants Jeff to quit traveling the world photographing disasters and settle down in New York, where he can become a fashion and portrait photographer. He refuses and also won't allow her to travel with him, which she claims she is willing to do. Their relationship appears headed for a breakup.

What appears to connect all three plots is the issue of domestic married life, and especially Jeff's view of its horrors. Eventually what connects the narratives to the allegorical dimensions of film watching and filmmaking will be the problem of spectatorship in human relations, how things look, like romance, gender relations, and marriage, from the "outside," not the "inside." When his nurse Stella (Thelma Ritter), the voice of common sense, says at the beginning that "we've become a race of Peeping Toms," she cannot mean that we literally spend so much time spying on our neighbors through their windows. We have, though, become a nation of moviegoers and, beginning at around the time of the film, 1954, of television viewers, in a way suggested by the tiny framed windows. I don't think this just means to suggest that filmed drama and comedy interest us because we like to be voyeurs, unobserved observers, but that we watch these screens *like Peeping Toms*. That is the *uninvolved spectatorial way* we watch them, as if what we see asks nothing of us, is simply there "for us"; and therein lie both the aesthetic and ethical issues that will be discussed in the next section. Moreover, in a way that will link up to the spectatorship theme, the broader issues of gender politics, male power, and the limited options for women's resistance are all emphasized quite explicitly at the beginning and throughout the film. In a conversation with his editor,

---

17. When she is in his lap and they are kissing at the 45:27 mark in the film, things do seem to be getting romantic, but she actually has to plead with him to pay attention to her, that she wants all of his attention, and when he says, smiling, that he has a problem, which seems to be a reference to an erection, everything changes when he explains his problem. "Why would a man leave his apartment . . . etc." Lisa is crestfallen.

who has forgotten when Jeff gets his cast off, Jeff asks him how he ever got to be a big editor with such a small memory, and he responds, "Thrift, industry, and hard work . . . and catching the publisher with his secretary." (This occurs as a helicopter hovers over two women who are sunbathing on a roof and as Jeff watches the scantily clad dancer practicing her routines in front of the window.) Jeff is asked why he doesn't marry, and Jeff paints a picture of boredom, routine, and a "nagging wife." In fact, what little we see of the suspect's, Thorwald's, domestic life seems to reflect Jeff's view of the typical entanglements of marriage. From Jeff's point of view, we see a man prepare a meal for his wife and carry it to her, and kiss her lovingly, only to have her contemptuously toss it aside with some remark about the flower with which he decorated her tray. He makes a phone call and is then berated by the wife he must attend to constantly. (Tellingly, Jeff is just as unappreciative and ungrateful for the elaborate meal Lisa has arranged for him from "21" as Thorwald's wife is for hers. Jeff is as much an ungrateful nag as any wife we see in the film.) There is thus ample justification for John Fawell's characterization: "*Rear Window* represents an unambiguous, sometimes even vicious broadside on the male psyche and male sexual insecurity."[18] (This is all clearly contrasted ironically with the fact that the cleverest, wittiest, and bravest character in the film is Lisa. She also has the most reliable moral compass.)

It is also possible that his initial passionate investment in the murder suspicion has something to do with a projected fantasy of liberation from what Jeff thinks marriage is, what he imagines he might be tempted to do if married to a "nagging wife." The fantasy even has two sides, and the less obvious is more complex. That is, aside from seeing in Thorwald's marriage his possible fate being tied to a wife and yearning to be free, he sees someone immobilized, like him, being served a meal by a loved one, like him, and he sees her reject it unfeelingly; again, like him. He is drawn to attend to a scene of what he likely feels is his own ingratitude and insensitivity in the "21" dinner scene just noted and in his general whiny attitude about Lisa. And more generally, as has been often noted, seeing things so much from Jeff's point of view lets us feel his own anxieties about involvement with women. Virtually every small drama he attends to reflects this concern about marriage and domesticity, as well as a mostly unacknowledged anxiety that, in its absence, one suffers a soul-crushing loneliness. His perception already embodies what it means to

18. Fawell 2001: 6.

him; it is intensely *projective* in a way reminiscent of Proust's observations in *À la recherche*. The distinction embodied in Lisa's remark quoted above—"Tell me everything you saw, and what you think it means"—is a distinction or separation of moments undermined by what we learn about Jeff in the film. "What it means" to Jeff *is* what he sees. It is also a convenient diversion from Lisa's persistent questions about their future.[19] Given the anecdote about the publisher and what Jeff thinks he sees around him, it would appear that Jeff much prefers his current position, at least as a mode of life: merely watching, external, photographing surfaces, spectacles, only to move on to another visual excitement. But to return to the epigraph, in our case as viewers, this is all just what we see, or what we think we see. We don't know enough to have much investment, yet, in what we see, so for us, what it all means is another question. And nothing in Hitchcock goes unqualified. Jeff's self-involved, projective voyeurism is also what draws him, probably for the first time, into the lives of the others, diverts him for a while from the spectacle and danger he prefers, and forces him to simply look at the human condition in middle-class urban New York. As noted, he at first sees, in effect, only himself in various possible domestic situations, but that will change dramatically.

Finally, the fact that Hitchcock parallels our initial look at the Thorwalds at dinner with Jeff's dinner with Lisa has a number of psychological dimensions. The invalid parallel with Jeff is a figure of his own anxiety about being "feminized" by domesticity (one of the things he oddly complains about to the editor is the whir of electric appliances on returning home to a married life every day), and that is no doubt a reflection of his anxiety about his own masculinity; in Freudian terms, his fear of his own desire for such feminization, and that, finally, seems connected with his own need to demonstrate his masculinity by wild and reckless bravery, another exaggerated sign that he fears not being as masculine as he should be, and so needs constantly to prove it.

"What it means" for us has something to do with the context of Hitchcock's work, and what we have been discussing thus far is not an isolated theme in Hitchcock. In what are often regarded as his three greatest films, *Rear Window* (1954), *Vertigo* (1958), and *North by Northwest* (1959), the central character is a man north of forty (Stewart was forty-six and fifty in the first two; Cary Grant was fifty-five), unmarried (a bachelor in the first two; many times divorced in the third), no doubt anxious about entering middle age and the future of their

19. Douchet 1960–61: 8.

romantic lives, and each of the three is quite skeptical of and so deeply resistant to marriage. They are all attracted to and attractive to beautiful younger blond women, but despite happy-enough endings in *Rear Window* and *North by Northwest*, there is little hope that a stable marriage with any of these men will result. *Vertigo*'s ending is of course unqualifiedly tragic.[20] And in each, some feature of moviemaking and even what might call the ontological presuppositions of cinematic experience and their relation to ordinary life are present in some way, again suggesting a link between the romantic theme and the cinematic one. In *Rear Window*, it is the "externality" of the viewer's (or most viewers' assumed) position and the manipulative power of the director. In *Vertigo*, it is the fantasy creation of a fictional character, largely by means of "external" aids — clothes, makeup, gait, style. Both Elster and Scottie play the figurative role of director and character-creator. And in *North by Northwest*, the emphasis is on acting and pretense, Roger Thornhill pretending to be a nonexistent character, George Kaplan, because some rather incompetent spies believe the fictional character is real and is the advertising executive Cary Grant, advertising itself being some sort of figure for the creation of cinematic illusion.[21]

II. "REAR WINDOW ETHICS"

We've become a race of Peeping Toms. What people ought to do
is get outside their own house and look in for a change.
STELLA, *Rear Window*

The ethical question Lisa raises when she says "I'm not much on rear window ethics" appears to be the straightforward and obvious one that Jeff had just mentioned: is it right, "ethical," to spy on people just because one can ("even if one proves that someone did not commit a murder")? But the film is rais-

20. There are a number of deliberate echoes of *Rear Window* in *Vertigo*, starting with the fact that the same actor plays the marriage-resistant male. Both men begin the film injured and immobile to some degree (by a back "corset" and a leg cast), both voice satisfaction with their bachelor life, and Hitchcock even echoes the opening of *Vertigo* at the end of *Rear Window*: the aloof bachelor played by Stewart dangling from a ledge. See Pippin 2017 on Scottie's resistance.
21. The "reluctant, skeptical male" and the modern marriage theme is certainly not limited to these three films. There is the wife's poignant speech about her marriage in *Shadow of a Doubt* (1943) ("You sort of forget you're you" in a marriage); Cary Grant's suspicions and skepticism about Ingrid Bergman's character in *Notorious* (1946); and, in a class completely by itself, the strange brutality of the marriage in *Marnie* (1964).

ing a deeper and more complicated ethical question, already suggested by Stella's remark just noted, that one needs to go outside and look in, not just stay inside and look out.[22] Philosophically, this is the point of the clear link between the two plots, the Lisa-Jeff tension, and the uncertainty that initially surrounds just what, if anything, Jeff has seen: a murder or a dreary domestic spat. Both turn on Stella's inside-outside dialectic; on the one hand, Jeff's projective subjectivity, "looking" from inside his subjectivity out at everything else, never himself seen (least of all by himself), figured by his current position inside his apartment, but also evoked by the stasis, the immobility he suffers (so locked inside that everything outside is like a result of his projection), the effect of which keeps Lisa also "locked" into her position as fashion model, to be looked at from outside, not let in, treated as surface; and on the other hand, Jeff's almost immediate suspicion of a neighborly murder, the result of a similar spectatorial position, likewise unable to see himself from the outside, in this case, to appreciate his own eagerness to figure a domestic life as nothing but whirring appliances, banal routine, and nagging wives. Stanley Cavell is not writing about *Rear Window* when he wrote the following diagnosis, but he might well have been, and it is a fine summary of Jeff's and by extension our problem: "Our condition has become one in which our natural mode of perception is to view, feeling unseen. We do not so much look at the world as look *out at* it, from behind the self."[23] The suggestion implied by the developments in the film is that it is no easy thing to do what Stella enigmatically recommends, to stand outside and look in at oneself, and that such a task unavoidably requires a relation to an other that allows one to see oneself from just that distinct other point of view. It is especially difficult because the final point would be that these are not alternating stances but two sides of the same attitude. Moreover, as we shall see in other films under discussion, achieving such a successful dialectical relation is not to be thought of as the accomplishment of resolute, open-minded individuals. A form of life as a whole, from gender and power relations, to inherited fantasies about intimacy and loyalty and betrayal, are always already in place and inextricably involved in the possibility for such interrelation.

22. The dialectic of looking and being looked at is referred to in a number of ways. At one point, when Jeff tells Stella to step back from the window, that they can be seen, Stella says that she doesn't mind, she's been looked at before. "Being looked at," which Jeff in an existential sense avoids, is no problem for her, is part of the reciprocity and mutuality that constitute intersubjectivity.

23. Cavell 1979: 102.

Dramatically the issue is introduced subtly, in the famous scene when Grace Kelly first appears in the film. Jeff awakens to see her luminous, gorgeous face, as if conjured up in his dream state (a movie star from the "dream factory," but also a faint suggestion of her fantasy status, perhaps her merely fantasy status, for Jeff) (fig. 2.1), and he asks what appears to be a humorous, ironic question after some romantic banter and a slow-motion kiss (actually a so-called step-print technique was used): "Who are you?" Lisa answers by turning on, one by one, the lights in the room, as if in answer, "illuminating" who she is, and saying, "Lisa . . . Carol . . . Fremont," until she stands, posed to be looked at, fashion model that she is, in a lovely thousand-dollar gown (fig. 2.2). And that *is* the answer, for Jeff, at this point anyway. She is a model, a to-be-looked-at woman. He does not, in other words, immediately or in most of the film, acknowledge in any serious way her view of him, allow himself, in any serious sense, to be seen by her, imagine him from her point of view, see himself from the outside, as in Stella's recommendation. And she is not just a model for him, but a mere type, a Park Avenue, rich, spoiled girl, he says. That deeper ethical question concerns the appropriateness of this sort of spectatorial relation to others in general, not just in spying situations, not necessarily reifying or objectifying. It is more a matter of blindness and resistance, and it is a blindness toward others that cripples Jeff's own self-knowledge (it insulates him from others' view of him, a much more valuable potential source of self-knowledge than introspection), leaves him a bit smug and already tending toward being that "old bitter" unmarried man his editor warned him against. Of course, to a large degree (at this point), Lisa has accepted that role and function, as have the dancer and Miss Lonelyhearts. But she is already chafing under Jeff's thoughtless presuppositions about her and what she can and cannot do. She'll show him soon how wrong he is.

And all this, too, is connected to the cinematic allegory, with Jeff's position as viewer of those several mini-films, as that aesthetic theme becomes entwined with this issue of spectatorship. That doubling is not just meant as a remark on the rather banal explanation of what attracts us to cinema, the possibility of seeing while unseen. And this is not, at least not wholly, a cautionary critique of what cinema can do or what a mistake it would be to ignore the limits of cinema.[24] It is rather, I want to suggest, a critique of a common

---

24. It is true, as Toles 2001 notes, that the cinema is limited to what can be made visible, but what is made visible can also "show us" what might be invisible, although that requires work on our part. This is the issue of cinematic irony. See chapters 6 and 7.

and not at all necessary or unavoidable form of *cinematic viewership*, of the *way* Hitchcock clearly thinks that people watch movies, especially his movies, what they expect from them, and most importantly what they imagine (overwhelmingly what they do not imagine) that an intelligent film expects *from them*. In this respect, a question is being raised that is larger than one specific to cinema and includes all the arts, embodying a relation to the viewer that also bears on interpersonal relations. But it will take a closer look at some elements in the film before that claim can be defended. We will need to prepare for what I want to suggest is the most important "ethical" question in the film, the one asked by Thorwald when he first enters Jeff's apartment: "What do you want from me?"

This stage of the film is marked by a break in the enthusiasm and excitement that Jeff, Lisa, and Stella have felt in figuring out how Thorwald murdered and disposed of his wife. The detective Doyle (Wendell Corey), a smug, indifferent presence throughout the film who cannot hide his weary contempt for these amateurs, informs them that the mysterious trunk was retrieved by Mrs. Thorwald after all. She is very much alive. Jeff and Lisa are severely disappointed. The murder possibility had obviously drawn them together, given them a bond, in a way that the next scene in the Miss Lonelyhearts drama does not. In their dejection, they watch her bring home a man she has picked up. She lowers her Venetian blinds, but before she can close them, he assaults her and she has to fight him off. They watch, do not look away, do not even look alarmed or surprised, but they are clearly embarrassed, and even ashamed of themselves (fig. 2.3). (Later, Jeff and Stella see her prepare to attempt what they think is suicide, and they are ready, finally, to intervene in Miss Lonelyhearts' life, but by then the plot developments—the police arriving in Thorwald's apartment—distract them. She might have died if not for a mere accident: she hears what appears to be the finished tune the composer had been working on, and that music seems to turn her from suicide.)[25] Lisa is also appropriately embarrassed that they are sad that a woman is *not* dead. They are, she claims, a couple of "ghouls." They had spent so much of their time together looking out the window, and Jeff had spent so much time avoiding Lisa's serious attention to their future, that this is their first serious engagement face-to-face, and about a weighty topic. They have begun to deal with each other, rather than

---

25. This is in keeping with Hitchcock's own obvious enormous faith in music, I suppose one would have to call it, in both its powerful role in narrative and its closeness to what he strove for, "pure cinema," audiovisual images packed with content, with as little dialogue as possible.

co-viewing these little films. So a phase of the film does seem over. They finally confront the fact that the expectation of privacy is a human entitlement, and we sense some closure as, after this conversation, Lisa ceremonially closes all three blinds and announces that "the show is over," and prepares for the "preview of coming attractions," her negligée. (She still uses the language of spectatorial cinema to describe their relationship.) Jeff even resolves, starting tomorrow, to take seriously the imperative "Love thy neighbor." But then a neighbor screams.

The third-floor couple with the little dog has discovered him dead, and Miss Lonelyhearts announces that he has been killed, his neck had been broken. It will turn out that Thorwald had buried part of his wife (probably her head) in the garden, and the dog had gotten too curious, was sniffing and digging in the wrong spot. The wife of the couple then makes a speech decrying the lack of humanity in the apartment complex, their indifference to each other, the fact that they are not at all neighbors, they do not watch out for each other, care at all for each other. Hitchcock clearly stages this as a voice from an older generation, decrying (rightly we are given to believe) what has happened in more recent urban culture: that the younger generation has become alienated from each other, even indifferent to each other. The couple sleep outside on the fire escape during the heat, figuring that they are the only tenants not so isolated, always inside what James Naremore calls their "doll's houses,"[26] and what Chabrol called "a kind of human rabbit hutch, a variety of cages in which humans live in close proximity to one another but in isolation nevertheless."[27] The speech is obviously a reflection on Jeff's isolated, spectatorial position as well, although he is being drawn out of this isolation by the murder; eventually, literally *tossed* out of his window. However, what connects all this with the cinema theme emerges when the dog's owner, in her justifiable rant about her so-called neighbors, asks an extremely odd question: "Did you kill him because he liked you, just because he liked you?"

This is an extraordinary suggestion about a killing motive. One can (I suppose) imagine killing a pesky dog who is destroying one's garden, or yapping all day, or biting one's children, or even a dog so friendly that he bothers one

---

26. Naremore 1988: 374.
27. Chabrol 1985: 139. The sculptress also sits outside, and even speaks to Thorwald, but only to criticize him for the way he is gardening. We also see her sleeping with a newspaper over her face. At the end of the film, she is asleep again.

constantly and so forth, but none of that is relevant here. Who would kill a dog "just because" the dog was affectionate? It suggests immediately by contrast a great resistance to being loved.[28] That, of course, brings Jeff and his resistance to Lisa to mind. Which, in turn, raises again his spectatorial position, looking out but "letting no one in," enjoying his god-like perch above it all, just as he had enjoyed the kind of action photography that made up his professional life. And all of that, in turn, returns us not only to Jeff's position as a figure for cinema viewing, but to the question of *how* he watches. I noted previously that, at the interpersonal level, our interpretive attempt to understand each other, involving as it often does an attempt at some narrational sense requiring our own editorial skill, can be done well, or poorly, lazily, or simply stupidly, informed by insufficient experience, little sense of how it might be done. And we can find all sorts of ways of preventing any external interference with the narrational pattern we have established in the little dramas we have narrated for ourselves. In this case, we have seen Jeff's over-investment in the very idea of "Thorwald murdering his nagging ball and chain" (we can imagine him saying if he were ever honest with himself), as well as over-invested in the sense he thinks he has made of the isolated dramas in each of the apartments he has selected for attention. It turns out that he will be wrong about Miss Torso. She was not playing the field but was no doubt dealing with professional contacts ("juggling wolves," as Lisa puts it sympathetically) while awaiting a boyfriend's return from the army, a short, nerdy-looking man whom Jeff would never have anticipated in his clichéd attitude toward her.[29] He cannot come up with any view of the composer, invokes a romance magazine stereotype for Miss Lonelyhearts, and clearly (and it turns out wrongly) thinks of Thorwald as simply a sociopathic killer. The fact that he was "right" about the murder is not a result of any interpretive finesse. He has *the plot* right, just as many viewers of Hitchcock watch and follow the plot successfully and take great pleasure in the technical brilliance of the editing, pacing, intersecting threads, and so forth. But they see nothing else, or they casually adopt some cliché about Hitchcock as their interpretive result, the meaning of the narrative: he is a perverse voyeur, a sadist, a cold, manipulative technician, a champion of the male gaze, a Catholic director convinced of universal and profound sin-

28. This of course also brings the project of Cavell 2002a to mind, and his treatment throughout his work of the problem of skepticism as a form of resistance.
29. No doubt, this is Hitchcock's comment on the viewer's expectations too.

fulness, a cynic, or even the much more accurate cliché, but still a cliché, that he is a "humanist" at heart, and so forth. Many of his films, but especially *Rear Window* and *Vertigo* (above all, *Vertigo*), seem to me great protests against this. The final turn of this screw occurs when the windows, the screens, of both apartments, Jeff's and Thorwald's, are breached.

III. INVOLVEMENT: LIVED AND CINEMATIC

After the dog's death, Jeff and Lisa notice that the only light that did not come on was Thorwald's, as if, they think, he already knew what happened and who did it. As they try to figure out why he would kill the dog, Jeff remembers that he had taken several slides of the courtyard in the weeks of his confinement. As he unpacks the slides, he mutters, "I hope I didn't take *all* leg art." This is a reference to a shot we had just seen a few minutes before of Miss Torso's apartment. All the viewer can see are her two legs exercising. So we know Jeff had been taking photographs and that he has an overdeveloped interest in Miss Torso's body (not, apparently, in her), but we don't know why he took no photos recently with his huge telephoto lens; none of any of the potentially incriminating scenes he has seen, and none just now of Thorwald washing down his bathroom walls or, soon, him packing to leave, the presence of his wife's jewelry and so forth. (Jeff surely must have high-speed film and know how to take photos in low light.) It is as if he wants to keep his involvement *purely* observational, as if even the imprint on his film is too much of an intrusion from the outside. At any rate, it is an odd omission by a professional photographer, especially since we now learn that he *has* bothered to take photos even *of the garden* and the row of flowers that were the cause of the little dog's death. The two yellow zinnias in the flower bed are shorter, and, as he realizes, "Since when do flowers grow shorter in two weeks?" This realization and the sudden sight of Thorwald packing begin the first intervention in the outside world.

Jeff writes a note. Hitchcock shifts to an overhead shot and dramatically zooms in as Jeff writes, "WHAT HAVE YOU DONE WITH HER?" and puts the note in an envelope with Thorwald's name on it. There could be a score of explanations for why the zinnias are shorter, aside from Thorwald having dug up what he had buried there (which no one has seen him do), but this "discovery" and the dog's death, and now the sight of Thorwald packing up, have moved Jeff to this staged intervention. The first stage is this note, still a pretty non-involved involvement, although it is Lisa, clearly enjoying the role, as she has called it, of the private eye's "girl Friday," who must deliver the note and is almost caught. When she returns, Jeff obviously looks at her with new respect and desire. (All of his is going on while Miss Lonelyhearts—noticed by Stella—is preparing for her suicide.)[30]

Then another stage of involvement, a bit closer. They need Thorwald out of his apartment so Stella and Lisa can dig up the flower bed; Jeff, to lure Thorwald out, calls Thorwald on the phone, pretends to be a blackmailer, and arranges to meet him. Still no risk to Jeff, as he notices when he stumbles on the word "we" and admits the two women are taking all the chances. Meanwhile Miss Lonelyhearts' suicide preparations go on apace, unnoticed by our thrilled amateur detectives. The phone call works, Thorwald leaves, and the coast is clear.[31]

The final act begins. Jeff keeps watch as they dig. They find nothing, but Lisa, in an extraordinarily risky and brave move, climbs up and into Thorwald's second-story flat, and, given all the associations built up, it is just as if she is leaving one world, the world of the audience, and literally entering the fictional world of the "Thorwald movie," as dramatic a moment as any that has occurred so far (fig. 2.4). I don't know of any way to prove the point, but given the detective theme and this moment, Lisa climbing into the Thorwald world must be a reference to Buster Keaton's great 1924 film, *Sherlock, Jr.*, where essentially the same conflation of worlds occurs and a character climbs into a movie screen (fig. 2.5). In this case, we keep our attention divided between the dangerous "merged" world Lisa has created and Jeff, the viewer, helpless, reacting like a terrified movie audience, squirming, grimacing, no longer just a distant spectator, but, unable to help, still in the audience world, connected to his beloved, now in mortal danger.

The large issue involved here involves an implicit (deeply implicit but visually arresting, nonetheless) reflection on the limitations of viewing our relation to our world as observational, empirical, or here spectatorial, *a relation of*

30. Hitchcock seems concerned that we understand just how maladroit Jeff is at interpreting what he sees, saying what it means. At one point, he sees Miss Lonelyhearts get out a sheet of paper and start to write, and he mutters that Stella was wrong; she is not preparing a suicide. But she certainly is; she is obviously writing a suicide note. The only thing that stops her is the sound of the composer's music.

31. Thorwald puts on a ridiculous white hat as he leaves, and that immediately makes him look far less threatening, much more ordinary than in Jeff's obvious fantasy. This prepares us for the pathos created when he appears soon in Jeff's apartment.

knowing;[32] attempting to test whether our representations are true. Framing the whole problem that way is misleading from the start and insures futility; that is, unresolvable skepticism, here figured by Jeff's frustration and anxiety. There is never any "proof." Anything can be discounted. The truth of our world, in a sense that would need much specification, is a result of, disclosed by, an active, engaged involvement—allowing our presence to it, not just its presence to us—and it is brilliant that Hitchcock has conceived this point as involving great danger.[33]

The involvement/non-involvement dynamic reaches a crisis level when Thorwald discovers Lisa in the apartment and begins to struggle with her. She calls out to Jeff, but, in an astonishing last sign of Jeff's immobility, distance, reticence, and all that entails, even though for all they know she could be being murdered, neither he nor Stella call out *to him*! They don't yell at him to leave her alone, that they see him, that they have called the police. Perhaps Jeff is still in full "cinematic mode," assuming that doing so would make as little difference as the person who yells out "Don't open that door!" at a horror film. Perhaps he is simply afraid of giving away his position. But this is of a piece with his not putting any film in his camera, not willing even to take that step of involvement. The police do arrive, and Lisa indicates to Jeff that she has somehow managed to keep Mrs. Thorwald's wedding ring, but in signaling him, she also alerts Thorwald to Jeff's observing presence, and the most tense part of the film begins. That other "outside" world invades Jeff's. The phone rings. It is obviously Thorwald but he says nothing, was clearly only checking that he had the right apartment, and we soon hear Thorwald's slow, heavy, and, for Jeff and for us, terrifyingly ever-closer footsteps climbing the stairs to Jeff's apartment, and he enters. Lisa has penetrated that outside cinematic world, and now, in a stunning move, the counterpart involvement occurs, as if a character steps out of the screen and into the viewer's world. (We are shown that Jeff, with his heavy full-leg cast, can't get out of his chair to lock his door; he is defenseless against this intrusion.)

32. This is of course Heidegger's theme, one that greatly influenced Cavell 1979.
33. While what Lisa does convinces Jeff that she is far more courageous and adventurous than he had supposed, he does not seem to appreciate that she is involving herself in a way he never would, a reticence that is metaphorically figured by his immobility but that, we are coming to understand, is a function of his permanent "spectatorial" position, his photographing, knowing, from the outside.

"What do you want from me?" Thorwald asks, and then, "Your friend, the girl, she could have turned me in. Why didn't she? What is it you want? A lot of money? I don't have any money. Say something! Say something! Tell me what you want! Can you get me that ring back?" Jeff tells him the police have it by now, and Thorwald advances toward Jeff. As many commentators have pointed out, Raymond Burr's pained, suffering, and pathetic tone instantly humanizes what Jeff and we had considered a stereotypical monster murderer; the voice virtually creates another character, the real Thorwald, not the character in Jeff's film, albeit still a murderer. Then in a cinematic staging of astonishing brilliance, Hitchcock enacts visually the culmination of the themes of cinematic viewing and the lived-out dimensions of the spectatorship/involvement relation in a single scene.

Jeff's protective strategy is to use what would normally be his "illuminating" flashbulbs to *blind* Thorwald momentarily, to keep him from seeing where to advance. This of course figures into Jeff's general resistance to "being seen," to anyone "looking in," to allowing even Lisa to see him honestly; all this, even though he is of course also trying to save his own life. But for this to work, he *must also "blind" himself*, shield his eyes from the flash so he can see how to work the next flash efficiently. The extraordinary, even somewhat childish image of Jeff with his hands over his eyes, flashing his blinding bulbs in blinded self-protection, makes a complex point in a densely compressed way, all in a single image: that his "Peeping Tom," external, spectatorial relation to the world has resulted in his own infirmity, a kind of willed self-blindness about others but especially to himself (fig. 2.6).[34]

And this bears directly on the cinematic theme. It is as if the "Thorwald film" has come alive, invaded a world Jeff had thought of as ontologically separate, sealed off, and has challenged the way he has watched his "films." "What do you want from me?" is a question I think of as one Hitchcock poses to his audience, and it implies another: What do you think I, my films, want *from you*? "To assault you, toss you out of your insulated, sealed-off world; to involve you" might be a general answer, but more specifically, here and throughout

---

34. Toles 2001 has argued that this image of self-protective blinding is meant to suggest "the drastic limits of the camera's power to image truth" (179). I have been suggesting throughout that the limit at stake for Hitchcock arises from deficient or lazy modes of attending more than from the limits of cinema, but the two positions are not incompatible.

the film, Hitchcock appears to be signaling a demand for a kind of cinematic involvement, an interpretive one.[35] Throughout, we have seen all sorts of cinematic signs of the limitations and distortions in Jeff's mode of viewing, that it is self-involved, anxious, negative, but mostly everywhere based on an assumption of a strict walled-off separation between the world of the viewer and the movie world, an inside-Jeff world and an outside-to-be-viewed world. We saw aspects of that assumption in his relation to his work and to Lisa and certainly to any romantic entanglement. But the assumption has also been revealed to be a distortion of virtually every scene he watches, and in the terms introduced at the beginning of this chapter, this is a result of the simplicity and laziness of his mode of narration, how he attends to what he sees. He can be said to have an impoverished notion of cinematic form, like a reader who reads "only for plot." Hitchcock was always so careful in his films to include visual details that repay multiple viewings[36] that he is clearly demanding something from his audiences, a mode of attending he must feel (on the evidence of *Rear Window*) that he is not getting, that the formal devices alone, all of which quickly become Hitchcock stereotypes, do not for most viewers (at least until the French discovered him) inspire any depth of interpretive involvement, raise any question about the point of the stories he tells. The cinematic object is just treated as there to be viewed, an occasion for the viewer's experience, of significance only for that.[37] And of course, if we start off assuming that that is what commercial film is exclusively for, objects made for consuming subjects, designed to cause experiences that will entertain in various ways, will cause who cares what sort of experiences so long as they encourage consumption, then, given that Hitchcock was certainly deeply interested in the financial success of his films, and so actively encouraged audiences to think of his films as mere scary entertainment, it might appear that the assumption is justified.

---

35. Is it a coincidence that he chose for the actor who plays Thorwald an overweight Raymond Burr, or that Burr, thirty-seven at the time, was made up to seem older, perhaps about Hitchcock's age at the time, fifty-five?

36. For some evidence, see Miller 2016, especially his chapter on *Strangers on a Train* ("Hidden Pictures"), and my account of the difference that multiple viewings of *Vertigo* makes in Pippin 2017.

37. This touches on a very complicated problematic prominent in reflection on modern art from the time of Diderot until the advent of minimalism, postmodernism, the rejection of all appeal to authorial intention, and beyond. It is the problematic that Michael Fried has called "theatricality," and it touches on all sorts of ethical and political issues as well as aesthetic ones. For an account of how, see Pippin 2005 and 2014: chap. 3.

But this film itself suggests otherwise; it highlights an implicit demand on the part of Hitchcock's films to be "let in" to the viewer's world, so that "what we see" and "what it means" can be worked at beyond figuring out how the plot events fit together, and beyond the self-involved meanings the events seen had for Jeff and audiences like him. And just as in *Vertigo*, where Hitchcock links the creation of fantasy characters by Elster and Scottie with the creation of fantasies by the Hollywood "dream factory" in order to show the limitations and dangers of such an attitude to others as well as to cinema, the dynamic of spectatorship and involvement plays out at both levels, cinematic and social, in the film's conclusion.

We are shown that the temperature is twenty degrees lower now, perhaps a sign that there will be a less feverishly projective attitude by Jeff toward others as well as to what he sees across the way in the new seven-week period he will be laid up with his second broken leg. Or at least that this would be possible. The composer's song has been finished, and we are reminded that for some artists, the only consideration is the one he expresses: "I hope it's gonna be a hit." That is *not* "what it means" to Miss Lonelyhearts, as she tells him, "I can't tell you what this music has meant to me." (The contrast drawn above continues to be made.) Thorwald's apartment is being repainted. The older couple has a new dog. Miss Torso's boyfriend, Stanley, comes home and, after a long time away from his gorgeous girlfriend, is only interested in what she has in her refrigerator. (This is yet another sign that Jeff has not understood what he has seen. He—and through him, probably we—mistook Miss Torso as a party girl, interested in the most prosperous men. But she has been faithful to her nerdy Stanley all along.) In line with that little Jeff-like joke, the very last dialogue we hear is from the newlyweds, whose initial romantic flame had been shown to cool to a boring, routine duty, at least for the husband. The wife says, "If you had told me you had lost your job, we would have never gotten married." (Another of Jeff's stereotypes subverted.) Much of the Jeff world of boring domesticity and futility seems still available, if the mode of attending remains the same. And then we are shown a complicated future for our couple. Again, as at the beginning, we see Jeff asleep, this time smiling, but now with two broken legs, even more immobile, emphasizing his continued mere spectator, non-involved position. As we hear the composer's recording ironically intone its last phrase, "Lisa," we see her in jeans, pretending to be reading a book called *Beyond the High Himalayas*, as if ready to travel the world with Jeff. But when she notices Jeff is asleep, she pulls out a *Harper's Bazaar* and smiles (fig. 2.7). On the surface it would seem that nothing has changed much. But the tone of the ending is upbeat, not ironic. Lisa seems confident that she can now somehow negotiate her relationship with Jeff from a position of something closer to equality; that she will not only be seen but understood. It is clear enough that managing the attempt at a new form of mutuality will still be quite difficult, but Lisa seems confident that there will at least now be some measure of mutual respect and, better, mutual comprehension, that there will now be a new way for them to connect what they see and what it means.[38]

38. Wood 1989 argues that overall the film is "therapeutic" for both Jeff and for the viewer, but it is hard to see how, since in his concluding paragraph Wood emphasizes quite rightly the deliberate almost mocking superficiality of the "loose ends tied up" summaries of the various plots, that the "semi-live puppets enclosed in little boxes" are still subject to the "frustrations and desperations" that "can drive them to murder and suicide," and that "we are left with the feeling that the sweetness-and-light merely covers up that chaos world that underlies the superficial order" (107).

Moral Variations

THREE

Devils & Angels
in Pedro Almodóvar's *Talk to Her*

Stanley Cavell has written that the "dramatic mode of the film is the mythological" and that this mythical dimension is actually "the typical."[1] There would seem to be little typical about a world of comatose women (fig. 3.1), a barely sane, largely delusional male nurse, a female bullfighter, and a rape that leads to a "rebirth" in a number of senses. But comatose women, the central figures in Pedro Almodóvar's *Talk to Her*, are, oddly, very familiar in the mythological genre closest to that film: fairy tales. Both Snow White and Sleeping Beauty are comatose women who endure — "non-consensually," we must say — a male kiss, male sexual attention. (Siegfried's awakening kiss of Brünnhilde in the extraordinary third act of *Siegfried* should also be mentioned.)[2] Someone apparently must manifest some act of faith, must believe that these corpse-like women are not dead, and believe it strongly enough to kiss them. Then there is a kind of inversion of these fairy tales in Heinrich von Kleist's story and Éric Rohmer's film, *Die Marquise von O*. Here the kiss is actually a rape, but the rapist again emerges as some sort of Prince Charming after all (he had originally saved the Marquise from rape by a group of Russian soldiers),

---

1. Cavell 1979: 213.
2. Perhaps the Smiths' song "Girlfriend in a Coma" from the 1980s also deserves a mention. I am indebted to Jessica Burnstein for this reference.

and there are echoes of that disturbing notion of reconciliation as well in the Almodóvar film. (Alicia, after all, does awaken.) In the Kleist story, a woman must place an ad in a newspaper asking her unknown rapist (she was drugged and asleep) and the father of her unborn child to come forward. He does eventually, and the story ends with their marriage and with one of the most enigmatic lines in all of literature, as enigmatic, I think, as our complex reactions to Benigno's act: the Marquise says that she would not have thought her new husband a devil if he had not first appeared as an angel, as if one person *can* be both devil and angel, that, to the extent that one can be an angel, to *that* extent he also can be a devil.

We do not seem to recoil morally in the fairy tale cases, as if the sleeping beauties were victims of unwanted male attention, as if yet more examples of male fantasies of passive, wholly dependent women whose very waking lives depend utterly on bold sexual attention by men, regardless of considerations of equity or consent. This is probably because the narrative frame of the fairy tales suggests that such a moment is fated; it *must* happen, these princes are for these women and them alone, and vice versa. The kiss is (at least seems intended to be understood as) also more like medical attention to accident victims; the princes can't just leave the beauties sleeping there, and we presumably are meant to think that Prince Charmings are universal types; that they would, by definition, be the object choice of any woman once awakened; and, given the fate theme, especially be the object choice of these princesses.

We *do* recoil, however, at Benigno (Javier Cámara); it is simply horrific imagining him on top of the nearly lifeless, unmoving body of Alicia (Leonor Watling). We also have a very different reaction on a second viewing. Once we know what Benigno will do, what we had first taken to be his tender medical ministrations now look suspicious. He is occasionally all too casual about Alicia's nudity; his complimentary remarks about Alicia's breasts might have rushed past us on first viewing. They don't on a subsequent viewing, once we know where his attention is leading. But still, all in all, I think it is fair to say that we also hesitate to place this rape in exactly the same category as the brutal attempted rape of Uma Thurman's comatose character at the beginning of *Kill Bill: Volume 1*, or Terence Stamp's imprisonment of Samantha Eggar in William Wyler's *The Collector* (or I think we should, at the very least, hesitate to *some* degree). That very hesitation, or what appears to be something like a sympathetic treatment of Benigno by Almodóvar, is just what can understandably generate a certain unease in many viewers.

There are several obvious elements to this hesitation, to the indeterminacy and unsettledness of our moral response to the character and the act (something ultimately essential to this being an aesthetic treatment, not an example of, or illustrative of, a moral theory). Part of it (hesitating about equating as instances of a similar kind both Benigno and Uma Thurman's attacker) has to do with the fact that the fairy tale context just suggested is close to the fantasy world occupied *by* Benigno. His act of faith (as he sees it), of keeping faith with Alicia as still a responsive, communicative subject, is for most of the film more delusional than heroic and often simply pathetic. For one thing, Benigno is presented as a figure of desperate loneliness (as is Marco [Dario Grandinetti], in a different way), a man who for twenty years lived in a situation crazy enough to drive him slightly mad himself, living only for his mother, attending her, we come to learn, with virtually the same intimacy and diligence required for Alicia, although, bizarrely, the mother was not an invalid but just, according to Benigno, "lazy."[3] And Benigno clearly imagines that he and Alicia have a deep bond because of this, that she is not so much in a "persistent vegetative state," as she is simply someone as alone as he is, that the world he lives in is almost as dark and impenetrable as hers.

Benigno's own view of the rape (figured for us by a very strange silent film he is recounting to Alicia on the night of the rape and which portrays what he is about to do as a return to the womb) is in keeping with this presentation of his mental state as delusional, something that would obviously qualify any moral condemnation. But Benigno's psychopathology only explains part of our hesitation, a hesitation I would describe not as an unwillingness to apply the category of rape, nor as a wish to excuse what Benigno did. It rather seems a hesitation simply to leave the matter there, a hesitation about the adequacy of a moral response *tout court*, and so a way of raising the question of *this* sort of "qualification" of a moral response; that is, *what* sort of qualification is it? Or what would it mean to concede the authority of the moral point of view, but deny it the sort of absolute trumping power that, for many, comes with such authority? The most interesting dimension raised by the film is just this: *How* does a moral judgment lie alongside of, become imbricated in (or not),

---

3. We only hear the story about the mother from Benigno in the office of Alicia's father, a psychiatrist. He certainly could be lying or exaggerating; by telling the doctor that he washed his mother "front and back," he could already be trying to create his "cover" for stalking Alicia: that he is harmless because gay or has somehow been rendered asexual.

color or shadow, all the other reactions, projections, and anxieties involved in living a life and responding to another? (This is, of course, the most interesting theme of many film noirs: something that Almodóvar is quite aware of. At the end of *Bad Education*—a much more noirish film than *Talk to Her*—Juan and Berenguer go to a film noir festival while the deadly heroin they have given Ignacio does its work. As they emerge, Berenguer [the pederast priest] says, "Those movies all seemed to be about us.")

Moral philosophers sometimes distinguish between so-called first-order moral judgments (in this case, the judgment that what Benigno did was rape and was wrong) and second-order judgments (whether or to what degree to blame Benigno, to hold him to account), and they argue that the former judgment can be made without requiring the latter. They also sometimes distinguish between the act itself and its consequences, and in this case that might lead one to say that whatever Benigno had intended by having sex with Alicia (and it is very difficult to infer what exactly he thought he was trying to do or bring about), her recovery cannot be *credited* to him.[4] In both cases, especially the former, Benigno's delusory state seems somehow to be both exculpatory and to block an attribution of Alicia's recovery to his actions.

I don't wish to dispute any of this, but I don't think our "hesitation," as I have called it, is based on an appreciation of Benigno's psychopathology. As noted, there is a mythic dimension to the film as well, and in that dimension Benigno's actions are in a certain way affirmed more directly, rather than excused, even though the act is morally heinous. The way this all works in the film is by constant and explicit contrast with the very "secular," fantasy-less Marco-Lydia (Rosario Flores) parallel plot, and by its (the film's) indubitable affirmation of Benigno's point of view with regard to the "talk to her" advice that gives the movie its title. This highly paradoxical attitude embodied in the film gives it its power and much of its mystery. The rather conflicted state one is in at the end of the movie recalls Nietzsche's claim in his *Genealogy of Morals* that it is a sign of a "higher nature" or a more "spiritual nature," to be able to endure great "divisions" in the soul, to be a "battleground" of incompatible commitments (I: 16).

We might also note here that Almodóvar's films very often anticipate, solicit, direct, and then up-end or undermine expected audience reactions— including, but not exclusively limited to, moral reactions—as a matter of

---

4. See Strawson 1974. See also Bennett's (1995: 46–61) clear exposition.

course. In almost everything he has done, Almodóvar clearly tries to present such issues in ways that will effect a kind of "double shock." The first shock is the oddness of the variation on the typical itself: nuns who take heroin and psychedelic drugs (*Dark Habits*); a mother who sells a child to a pederast (*What Have I Done to Deserve This?*); kidnap victims who fall for their kidnappers (*Tie Me Up! Tie Me Down!*); a pregnant, AIDS-infected nun, and a search for a father and husband who turns out to have become a woman (*All about My Mother*). In *Women on the Verge of a Nervous Breakdown*, a soap powder commercial presents the mother of a serial killer bragging that she can get her son's clothes so white, so free of bloodstains, that it even confounds the forensic police. There are pederast priests (*Bad Education*), and of course the rape of a comatose woman in *Talk to Her*. But the second additional turn of the screw is as interesting and as unusual, for all such cases are not presented as if an invitation to a kind of prurient realism, but clearly with an eye toward some redemptive humanism, some deflection of the discomfort we feel, for example, at obsessive, often nearly insane love (as in the French *l'amour fou* tradition, or the love affair in *Live Flesh*), so that a moment of affirmation is also, quite unexpectedly, possible. In all such cases, while we seem first invited to respond within the conventions of comedy, as if slightly superior to the drag queen camp characters with whom Almodóvar populates his films, there is always also some reversal in which something like the inner strength or reserves of moral courage or great loyalty or generosity is manifested, the dedication and sacrifice of characters we might be tempted to mock or treat simply as "exhibitions."

In fact, there is also a great emphasis on the complexities of exhibition, on gesture, dress, costume, and display, and we are invited to read these signs and gestures conventionally at first, in order to demonstrate subsequently that they are elements of a much more complex drama in which the interpretive work is much more difficult, the results much less determinate. The difficulty of knowing who anybody actually is or what part they are playing, in whose narration, from what point of view, reaches a kind of apotheosis in *Bad Education*, which features a plot in which a character has written a story about a person who was abused by a priest, became a transvestite, and wrote a story about the abuse, with which he is trying to blackmail the priest, and the author in the story is supposed to be author of the story, the character we see on-screen originally. Except *that* character is *not* the character of the story and within the story. It is actually his brother, who has murdered his transgendered brother (the real author) and is pretending to be the real character. This "point-of-view uncertainty" is often invoked in Almodóvar's films as a way of reminding us how little we know about the characters whom we are tempted to judge conventionally and often morally. So in *Talk to Her*, everyone, especially Alicia's father, thinks they know that an effeminate male nurse just *has* to be gay, and everyone is obsessed with the heterosexual affairs of a female bullfighter, as if her femaleness itself were hard to believe.

Another qualification or reason to hesitate in our judgment is purely aesthetic. The Pina Bausch dance, *Café Müller*, that begins the movie is clearly a kind of allegory of the film, a way of letting us know that the narrative frame of the story is certainly not "realistic" in the conventional or theatrical sense, that the action we are about to see has much more the logic of a dream (or a myth) than a standard plot.[5] The silent movie at the center of things, *The Shrinking Lover*, makes this "irrealizing" point again, and I will return to both the silent dance and the silent movie later. That is, Benigno's fantasy is as strange and crazy as the silent movie, and the film we are watching is more like an expressivist silent film or an avant-garde dance than a straightforward melodrama.[6] But for now we can appreciate that such an unusual way of framing what we are about to see also makes a straightforward moral reaction as incomplete and inadequate as would be the judgment that the Lisa Berndle character in Max Ophüls's *Letter from an Unknown Woman* is simply a deluded crackpot who foolishly throws her life away and those of her son and husband and even her great beloved; or as inadequate, say, as the final end-of-discussion judgment that Medea was simply a "bad person" for having killed her children.

The judgment about Benigno also appears qualified "inside" the film by the fact that the far more realistic and sober "scientific" assessments of Lydia's comatose condition by Marco and Lydia's former boyfriend (Niño de Valencia, "the Valencia Kid") seem somehow connected with Lydia's death; and it is all even more qualified by Alicia's rebirth: her return to consciousness and eventual mobility and possible life. Marco quite properly points out at one point that what Benigno is doing is indistinguishable from "talking to

5. There are of course other fantastic elements in the film drama itself; not the least of which is the way Alicia looks—her muscle tone, weight, complexion, and so on—after four years in a coma.

6. Cf. Almodóvar's remarks: "Benigno is insane, but he has a good heart," and "he's a gentle psychopath." Of most obvious relevance for this discussion: "His moral sense is different to ours, he's an innocent who, in his parallel world, has yet to reach adulthood" (2006: 213).

plants," but within the narrative frame created by the movie, Alicia clearly seems brought back to life by what Benigno does, even though what he does clearly calls for moral recoil. There is also an echo of the Bausch dance that is relevant to this issue in the horrific scene of Lydia being gored by the bull, and not just because Rosario Flores is so extraordinarily balletic. On the one hand, what Lydia is doing is very foolhardy. She opens with a kind of pass, a *porta gayola*, that is usually only attempted at the very end of a *corrida* when the bull is very tired and weak.[7] (She is on her knees, with the cape in front of her, and expects to make a pass just by shifting her body, not her feet.) But this pose dramatizes something we can already sense from the implied comparison with the dance choreography: she has no help, as Alicia does (nor does Lydia in her coma), no one to "clear the chairs away," and that is the way she wants it; she is facing this huge animal, this agent of death, on her own, as if supremely self-sufficient.[8] In fact, in this magnificent scene, the expression on Lydia's face suggests such defiance and hubris, such a "silent" but eloquent challenge to what seems to be the embodiment of male power, perhaps even male sexuality, in this huge bull, that we fear some line has been crossed, that she is infinitely admirable for this expression of will, but, we know, doomed (see fig. 3.2). There is also something mythologically significant in the fact that both these utterly passive, inaccessible women are *rendered* comatose violently, forced into a state that is sometimes intimated as a figure for the "forced" role of the feminine itself, at least by Benigno, in that chilling scene where he treats talking to Alicia as an instance of the general advice one ought to follow with regard to all women—talk to them, take them seriously—as if this might not occur to us without a reminder; as if the default position of most men is to act as if women were comatose. But that is an independent topic.

Of course, all these sorts of questions can only arise if we assume that we can attribute intentional states, even moral attitudes, to the work itself, and that prompts some very familiar issues in aesthetics, some of which are noted in the first chapter above. But for purposes of this discussion, I think we should just agree at the outset that Benigno and his act *are* partly treated sympathetically by Almodóvar. For one thing, Benigno is allowed to present most of the movie's details to us, and this point of view is only directly challenged by

---

7. All this is according to Almodóvar's commentary on the DVD version of the film.
8. There is also an amazing shot, a kind of close-up of the bull after the goring, that says something like: "I know I am supposed to lose, but you shouldn't have tried to show me up like that."

Marco, who is clearly sympathetic, and this only occasionally. The last thing Benigno has done (within, let us say, the frame of relevance, salience, and moral import created by Almodóvar and Benigno) is to treat Alicia merely as an object, a thing to be used for his pleasure. Indeed, Almodóvar spends a great deal of camera time detailing the quite involved ministrations of Benigno and his fellow nurses (Rosa and Matilde) for Alicia, clearly treating the ablutions and dressing as ritualistic in a religious sense, all in a way parallel with the long beautiful scene of Lydia (whose name means "bullfighting")[9] being dressed for the bullfight. (Compare with the undressing of Father Manolo's vestments in *Bad Education*.) Benigno's care for Alicia is clearly meant to be enveloping and tender (although for the most part only from his point of view, and even though we slowly begin to see that there is something dangerously obsessive and possessive in his treatment). Even (and again here our unease) the sexual assault cannot fully be understood except within such a context. And everything he does also seems continuous with the insistent humanism (the insistent refusal to *allow* her to slip into the status of mere objecthood) embodied in his "talk to her" advice to Marco, the journalist with whom he forms a deep bond of friendship. (Personhood, the film almost suggests, depends on this kind of affirmation and faith exhibited by Benigno; it is a status achieved only by virtue of such reciprocal affirmations and is not a matter-of-fact property of some animals. Or at least it cannot be effectively sustained as a status without this expressed and continual commitment.) It is this sympathy (essentially *Marco's* sympathy, a reaction not unconnected with his own failings) and the hesitation it provokes that we must understand.

Indeed, in many ways the movie is mostly about this growing, awkward friendship between the two men, not so much about the two women and their fate.[10] It is Alicia's comatose body that initially connects them, and this link is the pivot on which our ultimate reaction to the film will turn. Marco walks by Alicia's room once when she is naked and being attended to. Benigno invites him in, and Marco is clearly extremely uncomfortable in the room with Alicia's body (which, incredibly, remains a beautiful body in its comatose state) so visible. We are not really sure if he is uncomfortable because he feels sexu-

9. Again according to Almodóvar's commentary on the DVD soundtrack.
10. In fact, the relationship of the two men is more like a love affair than a friendship, romantically charged, if not physical. It is by talking to Alicia that Benigno finds something he has clearly never had—a deep friendship, but with Marco.

ally excited by the sight and is confused and embarrassed by this response, or because he is quite understandably puzzled that Benigno could treat Alicia's need for privacy so cavalierly, exposing her so calmly to strangers. Likewise, it allows a measure of doubt about Benigno to enter the viewer's mind; we are not sure if this exposure is just part of the infamous depersonalization and lack of privacy endemic to hospital culture, or if this is a sign that Benigno's proprietary sense of his control of Alicia is already way out of hand. (This dialectical relation between respectful subservience and nursing as a form of control will emerge again later [see fig. 3.3].)

Later, in the crucial "talk to her" scene at the heart of the film, this same uncertainty about Alicia's nakedness happens again, but the viewer now seems to be led away from some of these doubts and toward Benigno's point of view. Marco remarks to Benigno that he could never touch and move Lydia in the way Benigno ministers to Alicia, that he is somewhat repelled by her barely alive physical form. Right before this conversation, he had learned that his position as principal lover and chief mourner had all been an illusion, that Lydia had turned back to Niño even before the bullfighting accident, and so, with all the best will in the world, he had "read" everything wrong; that there was something almost as comical in his position as the *rejected* lover, dutifully attending a woman in love with someone else, as there is in Benigno thinking he will marry Alicia. Even with both women in comas, the various love triangles continue to be upset and to re-form. After Marco's remark about his distaste for Lydia's body and Benigno's advice—"talk to her, tell her that," as if he is encouraging something like couple's counseling—we also see from this moment on that Marco accepts at least some aspects of Benigno's point of view (perhaps because he realizes that an important aspect of his own reasonable, prudent view had itself been a great illusion); accepts that however deluded and morally inappropriate, there is something in Benigno's relation to Alicia (his keeping faith, his refusal to allow her any object status) that moral and even scientific categories alone will not capture.

This is so to such an extent that by the end of the film, Marco comes more and more to reoccupy Benigno's life, his place in the world, and that is yet another factor in our hesitation (as instructed by the logic of the film) to condemn Benigno—this fact that we begin to see him through Marco's eyes. He lives in Benigno's apartment after the latter's suicide, reoccupies Benigno's "view" of the dance studio, and begins even to live out Benigno's deepest fantasy by beginning what we are clearly meant to think is the start of a relationship with the now-recovering Alicia. And most of all, despite his early insistence that talking to the comatose Alicia was like talking to plants, Marco himself begins to talk to the corpse of Benigno in Benigno's grave. This all suggests that Marco has learned something from Benigno's craziness, so much so that the characters even seem to merge.[11]

This happens visually. There is a Bergmanesque, or *Persona*-like, scene at the end when Benigno is in prison that makes this point extremely well. Almodóvar has set up the shot so that the reflections of each man superimpose on each other in the glass partitions; they merge with each other (see fig. 3.4). The scene also establishes that Benigno's environment now perfectly mirrors the profound isolation of his life: in a glass cage, able to see others but almost as cut off from them as from his beloved Alicia. The contrast with the central "talk to her" scene will also establish what an extraordinary acting job is done by Javier Cámara as Benigno. His character changes very dramatically after the exposure of what he has done (or, one could say, after he knows he will get caught). The sweetness and gentleness of the nurse are replaced by a kind of grim determination; the effeminate features, the graceful, confident gestures, are all gone; and an almost violent, barely suppressed rage can be detected, all as if trying to suggest again that these two opposed elements can coexist, even as the monstrosity of Benigno's violation can at the same time be an act of faith and affirmation, that it being the former does not exclude it being the latter. The echo of Kleist's devil-angel dyad and the familiar moral complexities of film noir are again relevant. (One should note also that the transformation is disturbing too. It faintly suggests that Benigno might have been originally acting out a part, playing himself as an idealized type—"caring and innocent nurse"—and that what we see now is not a new role, but the unadorned Benigno. Whether this changes what I have been calling our "moral hesitation" is quite a complicated issue, as complicated as the question of difference between being who one is and "playing at being who one is," an issue that will become central in the discussion of Sirk in chapter 6.)[12]

---

11. The role of friendship is stressed in another related way in Almodóvar's comments: "I treat the character of Benigno as I would treat a friend," and "It's like when a friend has done something terrible and you decide to turn a blind eye, just so as to keep them as a friend." And finally: "Deep down I like Benigno's moral ambiguity. I think he's one of my best male characters; and Javier Cámara, one of my best actors" (2006: 219).

12. The simultaneous existence of these contradictory moments opens on to a far more serious philosophical issue. From antiquity on, a central assumption of moral reasoning was, had

At any rate, Marco's reaction to the new Benigno, beginning when Benigno tells him that he wants to marry Alicia, indicates that Marco realizes he had been treating Benigno's obsession in too mediated, symbolic, or expressivist a way, that he had not realized how deadly serious Benigno was about Alicia. And since both Marco and Benigno's coworker Rosa express what Almodóvar clearly takes to be the standard, reasonable, initially sympathetic audience reaction (Rosa says on the phone to Marco: "He [Benigno] has done a monstrous thing, but that doesn't mean he shouldn't be helped"), we also feel somewhat shocked, perhaps guilty in having believed in Benigno's harmlessness; perhaps engaged too much with the literary and figurative and fantastical dimensions of the actual plot, we might say. We also clearly feel what Marco and Rosa feel: the pull of loyalty to a character in the way in which we might feel such a pull for a brother or sister or child who had done something horrible, where such an act, while a reason to condemn, is not a reason to abandon.

But still, in many ways *Talk to Her*, by making use of rape, takes the greatest risks with viewer reaction, and an obvious question is whether this can be said to work. (There is a much more complicated dimension to this question than the aesthetic success: the fact that for all the pathos and melodrama and even horror, the movie also works as a comedy: a much longer issue.) In *Talk to Her*, we might say, whether it all "works" or not comes down to an interpretation both of how to characterize the rape—as a straightforward abuse of intimacy and power by a self-absorbed neurotic, or as (at least from Benigno's point of view) a genuine act of love, even sacrifice (as it turns out); or a mere case history, the pathological acts of a deluded ill man; or as a quasi-mythic reenactment of a male fantasy about female dependence or male power. The question of what it means that Benigno's rape is somehow—and it is not at all clear how—tied to Alicia's recovery requires some decision about these alternatives, or about how to think of all of them together, if they are in some

---

to be, the unity of the virtues. In any striving for the good, if one dimension of that striving, one virtue, can coexist with what is also a violation of any possible striving for the good, then moral life is fundamentally incoherent, makes no sense. Much of tragedy raises this issue, and philosophers have always tried to find a way to deny such appearance or, like Hegel, to claim that the ethical contradiction is only temporary, a historical incompleteness. But melodrama can also raise the problem and does so here. Kant, for example, would have no trouble condemning Benigno, full stop. There is no discursive case made in the film, no implied argument, that could "refute" Kant, but we are *shown* something of the limitations of the moral point of view. In some sense, it is inhuman.

sense all true, as they probably are. Put another way, the movie will sound the right tone, will end up, let us say, credible, if the clear link between Benigno's monomaniacal, even psychopathological dedication to Alicia could *also* seem a version of love, even redemptive love (as if truly powerful or genuine love is only possible just this side of such obsession, perhaps even sometimes indistinguishable from it; or that the idea of romantic love *without* possessiveness, jealously, idealization, and even some moral blindness is all as great a fantasy as Benigno's. This is another similarity to Ophüls's *Letter from an Unknown Woman*.) These are, in sum, the many factors behind what I would suggest is our *hesitation* to characterize Benigno as finally belonging to the same category as the *Kill Bill* rapist.

Almodóvar is clearly aware that he is taking such risks, and he marks the fact by opening the movie with Pina Bausch's avant-garde dance *Café Müller*. The part of that dance that we see is a mime of two women who are apparently blind, dashing about helplessly and eventually into walls, always threatening to stumble over the chairs in the café, aided by a man who frantically tries to move the chairs out of the way before the dancers stumble. But that particular Bausch dance as a whole is often much more violent, depicting romantic relationships as inherently aggressive, abusive, and catastrophic, and choreographing men and women frequently hurling each other into walls. Feminist critics have accused her of irresponsibility in presenting such dances without taking a strong position against such violence, and the dance critic Arlene Croce once wrote of Bausch's use of the "pornography of pain" (see fig. 3.5).

The silent language of dance also introduces the main abstract theme in the film: the relation between speech and silence; the main thematic terrain where the question of the film's credibility plays out. Speech and silence, both in themselves and as figures (often ironic ones) for agency and passivity or objecthood, must be considered within the many other such images associated with that theme—Alicia's comatose silence; the struggle against (silent) animals, brute "dumb" beasts (snakes and bulls); Lydia's silence with Marco about the resumption of her relationship with her former lover; the meaning of Marco's "expressive" tears (at both the beginning and end, and when he first meets Lydia and is reminded of his former girlfriend, Ángela, a particularly angelic-looking actress); the silent movie, *The Shrinking Lover*, that images in some way the rape itself for Benigno; and then a final Bausch dance (*Masurca Fogo*), this time with a woman rising up from and floating up above a line of reclining men, as if a soul set free from the body.

In such a context, it is clear that part of the point of the parallel plot with Marco and Lydia seems to be to emphasize the necessarily incomplete and even deceptive character of spoken conversation, how little gets communicated despite the conversations, especially in comparison with how much can be communicated by silent means. All of this emphasis tends to reduce our confidence that there is such a clear contrast between silence and speech, even "consensual" speech. In the central conversation between Lydia and Marco after the marriage of Marco's ex, Ángela, at an extraordinary Andalusian baroque church in Córdoba, Marco is desperately trying to tell Lydia, finally, everything he had held back about Ángela. But they are not really listening to each other. Lydia is herself trying to find a way to confess about her resumption with Niño, and Marco realizes that he has prevented something and covered something over by, ironically, for once trying to be so honest, by hogging the conversation and so forth. And there are several other examples that are meant to demystify the unquestioned value of speech itself as a vehicle of communication or sign of consent. This contrasting plot suggests that while it is mostly, it is not *entirely*, ironic when Benigno says that his relationship with Alicia has got a lot more going for it than most marriages.

The bizarre silent movie, *The Shrinking Lover*, is worth a bit of a digression here too. Originally Almodóvar had included more of the plot, which tells the story of the man's mother as a great villain. She had murdered the boy's father and kept her son a virtual prisoner, until he was shrunk and liberated by the female scientist. This indicates even more clearly that Benigno views himself as liberated from his own mother by Alicia, even though she has caused him to diminish in stature, and that the scientist asleep figures in his imagination for Alicia in her coma, and that when he enters her vagina in a kind of reverse birth, he means to be there permanently, to die and merge somehow with the scientist (see fig. 3.6).

Almodóvar, as he frequently does, cannot resist presenting some of this story as also an allegory of film and the relation of film to fantasy. There is a shot of a sleeping woman's face in close-up and of the little man in front of it that echoes almost exactly the scale of a thirty-feet-high movie screen to a normal person, suggesting at once that Benigno's fantasy is an idealization and mythic exaggeration in a filmic sense, and that Almodóvar wants his *own* film to be viewed like that (expressionistic) silent film: somewhat surreal, more expressive than directly communicative, not a case study, as much at the very edge of moral intelligibility as the attempt to judge the acts of the shrunken lover.[13] We have to be careful here, because it is easy to misstate the importance of this invocation of the inevitable role of fantasy in love, which all clearly has to do with the contrasting subplot. That is, Benigno is indulging a fantasy, projecting a movie in which the real Alicia can play no real part, contribute nothing. But—and this is the difficult point to state properly—in a more ordinary, less fantastical sense, so is Marco. Lydia is merely a character in Marco's drama, replaying the role of Ángela, and in which Lydia's continuing love for Niño is not noticed, is ignored, even by her. She is in that sense almost as "mute" as Alicia. None of this, of course, means that what Benigno does is the same as what Marco does, but this theme—Marco's repetition of Ángela, Benigno's repetition of his relation to his mother, Lydia's repetition of the role of Benigno—is worth an independent discussion.

That Benigno thinks of his rape of Alicia in terms of the silent movie also helps us understand more of the pre-rape scene before Almodóvar cuts away. On Benigno's reading, Alfredo, the tiny lover, is entering his beloved's body forever, in some way merging with her. And we sense some unease as Benigno begins to form the intention to consummate his love of Alicia, something that clearly happens as he is massaging her thighs and recounting the movie. We don't sense any moral qualms on his part; just that he realizes that he is crossing an absolutely decisive line—after four years when it must have occurred to him often—and that there will be no going back. We don't exactly know why he thinks things have come to this, why just now they cannot go on as before, but he clearly realizes that now nothing will ever be the same. Given how meticulously he and the other nurses chart Alicia's periods, he might even know that she is likely to be ovulating and be intending to impregnate her, something that will clearly be discovered. If that is so, then he sees himself in some fantasy as sacrificing himself for her, as if he knows, as he says later when he is in prison, "how it will come out," that she will have the child and reawaken (but his life will be destroyed).

To return to the choice of the Bausch dance: it is in the face of this particular silent drama that the action of the movie begins. Marco weeps at this spectacle of the futile attempts of men to save women from their blindness and apparently great sorrow; perhaps by this point in the dance, he is also weeping

---

13. The same scale is shown in *Bad Education*, as the two boys and their first sexual intimacy is shown from the back of the movie house, with the huge melodrama dwarfing the real characters.

at the futility of any hint of a successful romantic duet. But his tears appear to be an aesthetic response, evoked by admiration of the beauty of the attempt, not prompted by a sadness at the tragedy of failure. This intrigues Benigno, who happens to be sitting next to him, and who looks on in wonder as the tears stream down Marco's face. And all of this is a preview of sorts, since the dance is clearly meant as a foreboding account both of the suspended state of the two women in the story, Alicia and Lydia, dreamy, blind, as if floating in a void; as well as of the futile but passionate attempt of the male dancer, Benigno, to steer them away from harm, to continue attending to them. That Marco finds all of this so moving is an immediate attraction for Benigno, who has spent the last four years of his life spending all day and many nights ministering to Alicia's every need and, of course, talking to her.

The next day, he eagerly tells the story of this encounter to Alicia, clearly as moved by the tears as by the performance. And the film is off and running, creating the viewer's odd but undeniably strong bond with Benigno, and so the hesitation I have been discussing.

I conclude two things from these brief remarks. First, while Benigno's world is a pathological and ultimately destructive fantasy, aspects of his care for Alicia highlight, in a "mythical" way we might say, dimensions of the status of subjectivity itself. The premise of his actions seems to be that such person-hood (and often gender itself) is a normative status, actively conferred rather than merely found, based on real capacities but capacities that have a potential status realized only in the conferring, and that no "scientific" fact settles who is and who is not worthy of such status, just as no mere performance can succeed in establishing such a role. As such, it is a status that can be denied or conferred, within social practices and in contexts too complex to allow for easy rules for guidance. Benigno's act always seems mostly altruistic, dedicated to Alicia, but as we all know, the fantasy that a vegetating person is still a subject, that she merits such status, can also be a destructive and self-serving, self-indulgent fantasy, and of course there are times when we end up not so sure about Benigno in this respect. (It seems to me an open question whether one should characterize the film, for all of Almodóvar's anti-clericalism, as still profoundly "religious.") We normally expect that such conferrals must be *mutually* recognitive to be successful, but the film, again in what amounts to a very risky and easily misinterpreted move, works both to undermine our natural confidence that the verbal and explicit signs of mutuality, consent, and reciprocity are altogether trustworthy, and at least to suggest that such

conferrals and sustained commitments are often required without the availability of such signs and that these acts of faith are dangerously extreme; they
can easily tip over into the kind of unintended but real brutality of Benigno's
rape. Love itself is sometimes treated as a species of this type, a "commitment"
to another not driven by reflection or reason, something that can have a grip
on one even if not reciprocated, never certain or securely established *even*
when the commitment is mutual and "spoken." This is why the coma image
also functions mythically: it raises the similar question of keeping faith with
a beloved who has "gone away" in some way, has "become someone else," but
who might return, go right again. (References to theater, movies, and performing run throughout most of Almodóvar's movies and have a lot to say
about this theme. Such theatrical exhibitions are not treated as egocentric
displays, manipulative forms of emotional control or phoniness, just by being
theatrical; but rather as provisional forms of a kind of social address, vaguely
interrogative, as if the characters are asking for a response that will confirm the
role they want very badly to play. As in "if you treat me as a woman, or a man,
or a parent, I will be, can be, one," and the clothes and feminized behavior are
therewith more interrogative, more aspects of a striving, than declamations;
are requests to be so treated, sometimes requests offered plaintively, with a
kind of pathos, sometimes self-deceptively and self-destructively. Sometimes
of course the external display is a mere disguise, quite unreliable as an interpretive guide, as with police badges in *Live Flesh* or nun's habits in *Dark Habits*.)

The question of how socially instituted roles, even personhood itself as an
instance of such roles, could be said to function successfully (or not) introduces an unwieldy number of large issues. But, in the same uncomfortable
way in which Almodóvar is trying to render credible the idea of both condemnation of and solidarity with Benigno, he is deliberately trying to confound a
number of the distinctions on which many such roles are founded. The most
confounding involves his treatment of the dense, mutually implicative relation
between subservience to (obsessive dedication to) another, and such subservience as also a form of mastery or domination. This comes out especially in the
gender issue, as those roles are traditionally understood: that is, "womanly"
men who function very much as males ("male" nurses) and masculine women
who are also very much beloveds, fought over by men ("female" bullfighters).
Or, of course, men with breasts, as in *Bad Education*.

Second, I have been suggesting that Almodóvar's treatment does not
undermine a moral judgment of Benigno but qualifies its ultimacy. This is a
difficult point to make. First, we tend to mean a great many things by "moral-

ity," but I mean the modern residue of Christian humanism (systematized by Kant), where moral injury to another amounts to treating another as a means or object, making oneself an exception, and where moral agency requires a could-have-done-otherwise power of initiating action "because one decided to," and so where guilt or remorse at having failed to so treat others is the most typical or appropriate reaction. We tend to think of such considerations as *so* decisively trumping all other sorts of evaluation of acts or persons that any raising of such considerations can sound like a claim for diminished responsibility or a plea for excuses.

But the question is not excusing or forgiving Benigno, certainly not by appealing to any diminished capacity on his part or just by calling him beautiful or aesthetically successful. But what does anyone uncomfortable with what I have called our "moral hesitation" about Benigno really want? That Benigno be punished *more*? That Alicia remain comatose? That Marco abandon his friend in disgust? Would that make our response more acceptable? The question has more to do with decoupling a moral judgment from the reaction with which it is deeply linked—blame, itself a kind of sanction that in most contexts seems inevitable, but here seems finally beside the point.

The movie works, I think, by concentrating a good deal of our attention on Marco's point of view and his reasons for neither abandoning Benigno nor, it is crucial to add yet again, excusing him at all, but for expressing some sort of solidarity with, even partly merging with, Benigno; and those reasons do not rest simply on pity for Benigno's deluded fantasy world. He seems to have learned that there is something redeemable at the core of Benigno's fantasy, that his care for Alicia and especially his desperate attempts to "talk to her" were acts of faith that he was not capable of, much to his detriment, and that the rape, horrible as it is, still cannot be fully understood except within his pattern of daily, intimate four-year care (see fig. 3.7).

But perhaps the crucial point is much more simple: that Marco has become Benigno's friend, indeed his only friend ever.[14] And friendships, like erotic love, are not subject to some sort of moral filtering, cannot simply be trumped by moral judgments about the "worthiness" of friends or lovers. (What would

14. This raises another issue worthy of an independent discussion: why Marco agrees, at Benigno's lawyer's request, to lie, not to tell Benigno that Alicia has awakened. I don't think we are meant to believe that keeping this news from Benigno provokes his suicide (it might have been much worse for Benigno to know that Alicia was alive and that he was locked up and could not be with her). But it does raise as a question why, from Marco's point of view, he does not "talk" to Benigno about this.

the world be like if they were?) What we are to make of this complication is not easy to see. As Marco, in the last scene, senses a future relationship with Alicia, he knows he must eventually tell her the whole story of Benigno and is naively convinced that it will all be, as he says to Katarina, the ballet teacher, "simpler" than one imagines. Almodóvar admits his own perplexity about all of this when he has Katarina, his filmic alter ego in effect, respond, "I am a ballet teacher, nothing is simple," as we hear yet again an echo of those Kleistian angels who can also be devils (see fig. 3.8).[15]

15. Cf. Almodóvar 2006: 213, in which Almodóvar says about *Talk to Her*, quite rightly I think, "But he [Benigno] falls in love with Alicia and that changes him, literally. As it would a child unprepared to live an adult love. In *Talk to Her*, Benigno is a kind of angel."

FOUR

Confounding Morality in
Alfred Hitchcock's *Shadow of a Doubt*

Alfred Hitchcock's 1943 film, *Shadow of a Doubt*, concerns a serial murderer, Charles Oakley (Joseph Cotten), who marries and then kills wealthy, lonely widows, making off with as much of their jewelry and cash as he can. Charles senses that the police are on to him so he decides to hide out by staying with his sister, Emma Newton (Patricia Collinge), and her family in Santa Rosa, California. He has a particularly close bond with the niece named after him, Charlotte "Charlie" Newton (Teresa Wright). As the film develops, Charlie comes to experience "shadows of doubt" about Uncle Charles. She finally realizes he is "the Merry Widow Murderer," but she does not turn him in to the FBI agents hanging around, waiting for certain evidence that Charles is their man (evidence Charlie has but withholds). At one point, when the FBI agents think the case has been solved by the death of a second suspect, Charlie knows this is false, that the real murderer is her uncle, but she lets the agents leave town without enlightening them. She does this because Charlie knows that her mother will be devastated, will probably never recover from such news, and she bargains with Charles that she will keep his secret if he agrees to leave town, where the FBI can presumably eventually capture him. (It is not clear how this will ultimately protect her mother, because we assume that if Charles is captured, his sister will eventually hear about it. It is apparently the prospect of Charles's being arrested in front of her mother and the neighbors that Charlie wants to avoid.) A series of tense, suspenseful events occur in the film's dénouement, until Charles is finally killed while trying to murder Charlie on the train leaving town. The film then ends with a bizarre, laudatory funeral for Charles, the entire town still believing he is the very model of civic virtue. The irony of the scene is as thick as any in Hitchcock. We would normally assume that soon they will all have to be disabused of this fantasy, even Charlie's mother, but the film ends with this damning irony, and no hint of any future revelation. So much for a very brief plot summary.

As indicated in chapter 1, I mean to consider film as a form of moral reflection itself (perhaps less controversially: a form of moral exploration), but one that still preserves a strong distinction between such reflection and discursive philosophical reasoning. This film raises a particularly interesting dimension of this approach. Filmed fictional narratives depict actors pretending to be fictional characters saying and doing various things; very particular, even unique, odd characters doing and saying very particular things. If there is to be some philosophical resonance, the question is how do such cinematic representations intimate anything of the kind of generality required for a philosophical purchase on our attention? Such a level of generality would have to go beyond what the characters themselves think about things; beyond even what the director may believe about things, and such that an implied claim is present: that this or that is "how things are." One obvious way this implied claim can be accomplished: the director can control so much of what we are shown, can signal what we should attend to, that he can make use of that power to focus our attention on issues other than particular events in the plot or the unique features of character alone. (And we can also gain such insight by placing the film in the director's body of work and noticing repeated large-scale concerns.) There are features of *Shadow of a Doubt* like this, features that seem to address a general issue. Here are some of those features:

1. The great ease with which Charles, the serial murderer, fools the entire town except his niece Charlie and the suspicious out-of-towners, the FBI agents. This invisibility of a serial killer, despite many manifestations of his insanity, is astonishing, and even occasionally amusing in the film, and bears on the question of what to think of "ordinary" life, a question explicitly raised several times in the film. The townsfolk's general difficulty of distinguishing real from apparent seems to be deeply connected by a general idea embodied in the film about what kind of place Santa Rosa is, and that

itself is not localized; it is meant to bear on the question of who Americans are. (It is widely thought that this was the film where Hitchcock finally found his footing in his new country, understood how to make films for an American audience. That turns out not necessarily to be a compliment to those audiences.)

2. As noted, the theme of ordinariness is stressed throughout and very often, by, for example, Charlie and by the FBI agent who becomes close to her. It arises in the film as a specific kind of question, as if we are being asked: What does it mean to be ordinary? Is it all right? Acceptable? A good thing? Or is it boring and banal, conformist and stultifying?

3. There is a mysterious *bond* between a character manifestly good, virtuous, and a character manifestly evil, nihilistic, and vicious; between Charlie and Charles. How in the world could there be such a bond? Is the status of the good-evil distinction itself at issue?

4. The transition from innocence to experience as a mythological genre is clearly invoked by our watching Charlie, who has just graduated from high school, learn in a rather brutal way an essential truth about the adult world—not only that things and people are not often what they seem, but they may be radically other than that, the exact opposite of what they seem. This mythological framework raises the broad question of how genre distinctions and repetitions work in narratives like this; that is, in the way that mythic repetitions do.[1]

5. The intimation of the theme of incest is just barely below the surface in the film. It obviously concerns the Charles and Charlie attraction, but above all the relationship between Emma and Charles, sister and brother. And this introduces what we might call a psychoanalytically inflected generality. At least a question is raised *about* American family dynamics.[2]

To begin to understand such issues, I should turn in a very general way to Hitchcock as the maker of a genre unto itself, the ironic suspense thriller. In a recent book, I called the theme that runs through almost all Hitchcock's films "unknowingness,"[3] and I mean primarily our unknowingness with respect to

1. Pippin 2010.
2. This is the focus of a valuable article by Perez 2014 and is called the "double incest" theme by Wood 1989: 300.
3. Pippin 2017.

ourselves and to each other. (This is not skepticism. To modify the famous Pascal maxim, we know too much to be skeptics, but much too little to be complacent.) Now unknowingness in various forms in general (from ignorance to being deceived, to fantasy thinking, to self-deceit) is something like a necessary condition of the possibility of Hitchcock's cinematic world. There is no other director as adept and insightful in exploring cinematically what it is to live in, to endure, such a state of profound unknowingness (which is something that, as Shakespeare showed us, can also be the subject of great comedy), as well as depicting what great risks lie in store for anyone who challenges everyday complacency, the easy confidence that things are largely what they seem. (As just noted, that danger is on view in the film we are to discuss, an "innocence to experience" fable that intimates something of some generality about such a transition, and, perhaps, that the transition, if honestly confronted, is deeply traumatic.) That easy confidence itself, not acknowledging or appreciating the depth of this unknowingness, is also full of risks, chief of which is a moralism narrow enough to count as a kind of blindness and a smug self-satisfaction. (The family is treated this way, if also gently.) As noted in my discussion of *Vertigo*,[4] the list of Hitchcock's films in which the wrong person is blamed for or suspected of something, often confidently, smugly blamed, is very long, and the primary technique, *suspense*, used by Hitchcock to draw viewers into the film, to "co-experience" it rather than merely observe it, is one built around either what we or characters know that others don't, or what we and other characters don't know but need badly to know in a dangerous situation. There are "shadows of doubt" everywhere in his films, doubts that have all sorts of implications for what the characters decide to do, how they presume to judge each other morally, and it is a kind of doubt that is not easy to eliminate.

There is, in other words, a kind of constant struggle for mutual interpretability, to avoid, on the one hand, complacency (like believing that how people present themselves to you is the way they are) and, on the other, cynicism (everybody's self-presentation is false and self-interested; no one can be trusted; intimacy is far too risky).

In this film, we begin with the assumption that we understand well the difference between innocence and experience, what it is to be a child, and so not to understand what the adult world is, and what it is to come to understand it. We think we understand what the difference is between a good person and a bad

4. Pippin 2017.

person. We are reasonably confident that we are adept at making such distinctions. We also think we know what the implications are of making such a distinction; what difference in our conduct toward such a person this ought to make. In this sense, it is enough of a philosophical achievement simply to say that many Hitchcock films compellingly, credibly, greatly complicate *any* such self-confidence. I hope this is all enough to get us started with the details of the film.

As noted, the title refers, it would seem, to niece Charlie's mind. The shadow is the one that falls over her uncle for her when she first sees him getting off the train, clearly pretending to be sick then suddenly recovering. Charles, stooped over, comes dramatically erect when the train leaves and strides toward Charlie. The phallic imagery is complete with cane. (He had used the excuse of illness to explain why he never left his sleeping berth, in case the FBI might be on the train. Charlie is, she often says, in tune with him and therefore knows something is wrong with his self-presentation. In several other early scenes, too, one could say that she knows something is "off," but she doesn't know clearly that she knows.)

The movie focuses our attention self-consciously on this small town, Santa Rosa, California, almost all of whose citizens are completely incapable of dealing with, of understanding, really seeing (or seeing through) a visiting, charming relative of the Newton family, whom *we* suspect from the opening scene of being a criminal, and whom we soon learn is the Merry Widow Murderer, a serial killer. His niece Charlie begins to suspect something right away and eventually learns the awful truth. A major question thus arises, the central one: What could be the meaning of this *bond* between an innocent, smart, ambitious, well-meaning, and very good girl (fig. 4.1) and a serial killer, the personification of nihilistic, narcissistic evil, Uncle Charles (fig. 4.2); especially since they seem so happy with each other, genuinely "in tune" (fig. 4.3).

But the first visual image we see in the film is immediately baffling. As the credits roll, we see what appears to be a nineteenth-century ballroom dancing scene, several couples in old-fashioned dress waltzing to what we soon learn is the "Merry Widow Waltz" (fig. 4.4). Where are we? If we did not know something about the film's time period, we would think we were in a past time. But if this is fantasy or a dream, whose is it? From whose point of view? What does it mean or suggest that Charles, who appears to be the origin of the images, would be daydreaming such things? Something of its meaning unfolds relatively soon in the film, but we remain unsure of the opening's meaning for the film as a whole.

FIGURE 4.1

FIGURE 4.2

FIGURE 4.3

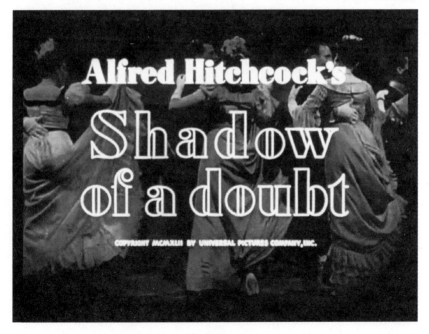

FIGURE 4.4

The opening image becomes a bit clearer when Charles, after giving presents to the family, including an old photo portrait of his and Emma's parents, remarks about the past that "everybody was sweet and pretty then, Charlie, the whole world. A wonderful world, not like the world today, not like the world now." So his daydream (when we first see him awake on his hotel bed) of waltzing couples must have been this nostalgia fantasy, a golden age somehow lost and not at all like the "foul sty" he will later call the contemporary world. His young nephew Roger expresses the current view of such an age; that it was a long, long time ago: "1888; whew."

That fantasy world would be Charles's view simply of the world *before*, perhaps before an accident changed him ultimately into a serial killer (his head injury is analogous to the trauma Charlie will soon undergo when she learns the truth), or perhaps before the world changed into the urban landscape of Newark, New Jersey, shown in the film's first scenes. Or perhaps it refers simply to a fantasy world imagined before it had monsters like Charles in it. We will soon learn that Charles is a psychotic killer of women (whom he calls "fat wheezing animals") out of some extreme (but never fully explained) misogyny. But he is mostly a nihilist. Killing is no different than talking or eating; the universe is devoid of any moral structure.

There is a connection with Charlie again at the first family dinner, as she begins humming that very tune, the "Merry Widow Waltz," played in Charles's daydream. And she tells us the answer—that tunes can jump from one head to another—in this case from Charles's head to hers. (So we have further evidence that the first scene was a fantasy of Charles and his rather ironic meditation on the nickname given him, the Merry Widow Murderer.) And he *fears* the song she is humming, perhaps because he fears Charlie's access to his mind, as their strange bond is stressed again. Before she can say aloud the name of the music, he deliberately spills his water and stops the conversation. All this descends from the waltz in the opening, but the waltz will reappear throughout, when Charles is under stress, and will be played at various other moments in the film.

But the actual opening of the film narrative is also dense with intimations of meaning below the surface. There is a camera entrance through a window, opening with someone in bed, our first shot of Charles (fig. 4.5). And right away the theme of *this* world now versus the past emerges. The contrast is obvious; a somewhat pastoral (Santa Rosa as if from an earlier time, the time of the dancers, pre- or non-urban) versus urban life today. We see a desolate

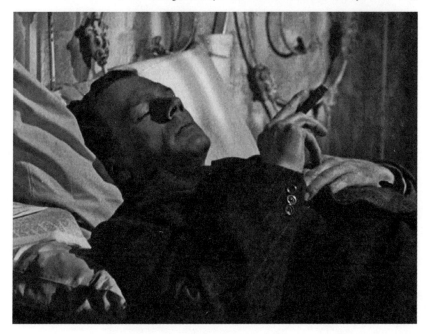

FIGURE 4.5

scene, material dumped in front of a "No Dumping Allowed" sign, as if there is no, or only very weak, real allegiance to law; as if staying on the right side of the law is a matter of just what you can get away with. The suggestion is of unjust wealth, maldistributed, a film noir world; something suggested, too, by the odd off-center camera angles (fig. 4.6).

The city kids we see outside Charles's building are playing in the street instead of fields, and we see an ominous first shot of a brooding, daydreaming, smoking Charles. His apparent indifference to money is emphasized (it's on the floor, scattered on a bedside table), as if to signal right away that this is not why he kills, for money; as if he kills in chilling indifference to human life or his own gain. (He keeps the jewelry, of course.) The landlady comes into a room of shadows and closes the blinds. (We are reminded of the superstition that with a dead person in a room, you close the blinds; and this introduces the strong role of superstition in the film. We hear many examples: Never throw your hat onto a bed; sing at table and you will marry a crazy husband; step on a crack and break your mother's back. Superstition of course is one way of dealing with unknowingness.) Charles's other niece Ann has another way—read two books a week. That might protect you. Her brother and the youngest,

FIGURE 4.6

Roger, puts his faith in science. Charlie places a lot of faith in telepathy. Their father and his friend Herb escape, are lost in fantasies of murder and getting away with it. And all of this is contrasted with the easy confidence, charm, and charismatic power of Charles.

But on the arriving train, he must pretend to be sick to avoid being seen, perhaps recognized. The police are after him, following him, so our first encounter with Charles emphasizes what is a constant recurring theme in Hitchcock, *pretense*; the theatrical roles we adopt, often unknowingly and sincerely, in daily life. The distinction not only runs through this film, but throughout all his films. Who really is the murderous neighbor in *Rear Window*? Is Alicia a bad character in *Notorious*? Is Eve trustworthy in *North by Northwest*? Or who really *is* Roger Thornhill? Is Norman Bates who he seems to be in *Psycho*? Who is he when he is his mother? Who is Madeleine, who is Judy in *Vertigo*? We constantly are dealing with the possible difference between a self-presentation in the public world and a supposed real self, or who one is for oneself. The theme is one of wariness of others and a constant interpretive struggle. There are shadows of doubt everywhere in Hitchcock. (It is on the train that we see our cameo of Hitchcock, playing bridge with a doctor and his wife. We note that he holds all spades, or the perfect bridge hand; one chance in 635,013,559,600 deals. There is a great deal of chance in life, but in a movie, Hitchcock holds all the cards, and we should attend carefully to the details [fig. 4.7].)

We then have our first look at Santa Rosa. We see it in a way as it sees itself, peaceful, contented, cheerful. The first noticeable aspect of town life is the kindly policeman keeping order. The force of order is friendly, grandfatherly. All is in tune, harmonious; but we already sense that the forces of law and order here are incapable of dealing with anything really serious; certainly not with Charles (fig. 4.8). We also note the little but significant things—the voice-over that tells you it is Santa Rosa is *Charles's* voice. Why? Is it a signal that his point of view, his perception of the amiable stupidity that characterizes the town, is the objective one?

Our first introduction to Charlie is of a very unhappy and morose young woman, someone who appears dissatisfied with the world as it is now, even if not with the murderous rage of her uncle. She complains to her father that nothing ever happens in the town, and that her mother works "like a dog" and is never acknowledged or appreciated properly. That dissatisfaction is the first

FIGURE 4.7

FIGURE 4.8

sign of the niece and uncle's bond. This is especially so since we note, too, the striking similarity to our first look at Charles in Charlie's pose on the bed, and her melancholic tone, dissatisfaction with ordinary life (a dissatisfaction that is soon supported by what we see) (fig. 4.9).

The two seem to be two sides of the same coin, but what coin?

Another link quickly emerges: Charlie sends Charles a telegram just as he sends her one. She gets the idea of a visit just as he gets the idea of hiding out with his sister's family. It almost seems as if Charlie is suggesting to him that he come and hide out with them; that they won't understand you, but I will, she appears to promise.

Charlie and Charles of course raise the famous themes of doubles in Hitchcock's films. Guy and Bruno in *Strangers on a Train*; Madeleine and Judy in *Vertigo*; Norman and his mother in *Psycho*; Roger Thornhill and his fake double, George Kaplan, in *North by Northwest*; the two characters Ingrid Bergman plays in *Notorious*; there are numerous examples. In many cases, one is like the other's secret let out, a fantasy version; just as the fantasy version wants to think it is really the other, good side. And Hitchcock clearly suggests that he and the viewer are another double, as if we are Charlie and he is the Uncle

Charles we are fascinated by; as if Hitchcock is warning us about himself; that these films are not at all what they seem to be.

Charles gets off the train feebly, assisted by the conductor and doctor, apparently very frail, almost too weak to stand. But as he sees Charlie, he straightens up; comes erect would be a better way to put it, throws off his coat, and starts strutting confidently with his cane, yet another phallic symbol (and the train itself is photographed with the usual suggestion of powerful sexual potency). Is some aspect of the bond sexual, incestuous? Charlie notices the radical change in his bearing and for a while does not let go of the issue, saying three times, "You're not sick" and "That was the strangest thing." There is of course heavy irony in Charlie's "You're not sick." Yes, he is, actually, *very*; but not in the sense she now means. But right away, she suspects him; perhaps is beginning to suspect that the ordinary world is not what it seems, and we see one illusion transformed in front of us, sick Uncle Charles turns into amiable old Uncle Charles, as the notion of the self as a theatrical accomplishment appears again. Charles must note this suspicion and must see how quick and sharp Charlie is; she almost does not let his faked frailty go by, almost starts pressing the point.

FIGURE 4.9

This is also a very common theme in Hitchcock, given fullest treatment in *Vertigo*: the adult world is adult by being a complex web of personae, the public roles one assigns oneself, how one wants to be perceived, and our confronting various desires by others, who have their own agendas for seeing us as they want to. And all of this occurs vice versa; their struggle to be seen a certain way and our attempt to see them as they are, complicated by our desire, sometimes our need, to see them a certain way.

This is most complicated in romantic relationships. Am I being loved for who I am; if he or she knew me as I really am, they would be disgusted, et cetera. Here this issue is at its most elemental: an amiable, gift-giving public persona and a murderous, nihilistic, sadistic psychopath, the real person. As we shall see, the greatest irony in the film is that this real self is brightly shining through the cracks of the theatrical, normal persona almost *all the time*. It is hidden in plain sight. And only Charlie sees any indications of that reality.

In another mark of their closeness, Charles will sleep in Charlie's bed, and as he looks over the room, unable to conceal a smile at the gullibility of these townsfolk and, having been warned about the bad luck of throwing his hat on the bed, does so anyway, with a flourish. These people are not going to be a problem at all. They will be good cover.

In yet another ceremonial demonstration both of their closeness and the hint of incestuous desire, Charles gives Charlie his present for her privately, a ring, and the movie now begins to be downright creepy. Everything that Charlie says about their bond is fraught with this metaphorical reference to innocence and experience, virtue and vice, Santa Rosa and Newark, the orderly ordinary world and the world of unreason and madness often underneath it. She thinks of the sophisticated, beautifully dressed Charles as her redemption from ordinariness, and she emphasizes again that they are not the normal uncle and niece, that she is deeply in tune with him. They are "sort of like twins." (We will hear a speech later by the FBI agent Jack Graham, a speech about how good the ordinary is, how wrong it is to want to be other than ordinary; he is a cop; he knows where that leads. The FBI agents have followed Charles to Santa Rosa and get into the Newton house by pretending to have selected Charlie's family as the "most perfectly ordinary" family in America, as if they are working for a magazine. This is something that greatly upsets Charlie, is a badge of shame for her, not an honor. Throughout, this will be a recurring question: What, if anything, *is* wrong with being ordinary?)

FIGURE 4.10

In the scene where Charles gives her the ring, the ring of a woman he killed with his bare hands, we can see how threatened Charles feels by her persistent insistence that she knows some secret about him. But he is still quite confident and insists she take the ring, putting it on her finger as if in a mock marriage, standing too close to her, looking too intently at her. We note, too, how old-fashioned, even how old maidish, we might say, Charlie's clothes are. (We learn later that the out-of-date outfit had been a previous present from Charles.) Sexual innocence and emerging sexual desire tinge, color, almost every scene between them, and so there is obviously heavy irony everywhere in the scene. At the end of the scene, we see that Charles has slipped up; Charlie notices the ring is already engraved with someone else's initials, and this is what finally gives him away (fig. 4.10).

We have seen enough of this theme to ask: What sort of bond, between goodness/innocence and sadistic narcissism/evil, could this be? There are some obvious answers—that goodness, even if motivated by good motives, always *also* involves motives that are not purely good, but egoistic. (These are Nietzschean themes: e.g., humility is fueled by great vanity; pity is a way of expressing one's superiority, of putting the other into a position of subservience; and so forth.) And that evil always finds a way to treat what it is doing as good. (Charles's bizarre speeches about women imply that he thinks he is doing these "fat wheezing animals" a service by killing them. Somehow or other, in his own mind, he acts "under the guise of the good.") Or sometimes one has to do something that would be considered evil in order to accomplish a greater good. (This will come up in Charlie's decision at end, in the most important scene.) And there is the Platonic point in the *Republic*: a band of thieves must observe some rule of justice in order to achieve evil ends. Perhaps most broadly, we can say that good and evil are "bound together" in that no triumph of one side over the other is ever complete or lasting, and a morally good motive or judgment must face, take in, its own limitation and the limits of any expected result. Evil is all too often successful in the world; the bad thrive, and the good often fail. Somehow this must all be borne; a life must be sustained in the light of this dreary fact. (Graham, the FBI agent, tries to minimize all this, saying that the ordinary world, ordinarily good, just goes a little crazy sometimes and requires a little watching. But that scene is framed ironically, as we shall see.) However, the most important issue the film is raising is not the objectivity of moral distinctions (Charles is clearly evil, and Charlie is clearly good) or these dimensions of their bond, but the confidence with which we *apply* the distinctions. For there to be such confidence, we must be relatively certain that we understand another's motives, have described the action properly, and that we understand ourselves well enough not to doubt our personal stake in some moral condemnation. Hitchcock is constantly disabusing his viewers of such confidence, and in this film, Charlie trusts her "bond" with her "twin," trusts her self-knowledge and knowledge of others so much, is so reluctant to judge him, that she keeps faith in Charles for a long while; almost catastrophically long, if Charles's two attempts to murder Charlie had succeeded.

We could also say that good and evil are comprehensible only by contrast, but there appears to be a stronger sense of their understanding each other. Perhaps it is that good would not be good without an active struggle with evil, something that Charlie has not yet had to do. Her goodness is innocence more than goodness. And evil is only evil in the awareness that what is done is a violation of the good, and done anyway, something Charles's nihilism suggests. These elements also play into Nietzsche's sense of the complexity of moral standards: the two moral postures are not strict contrasts, oppositions. For example, Charlie's dawning distaste for bourgeois domestic life *is* on a continuum with Charles's nihilistic rage at it. And this link is true of Charles too: that rage of his is also attracted to something like peace, the end of such violent rage; even death. So perhaps the religious terms used at the beginning are not accidental but ironic: Charles "can save us"; "it's a miracle." "He heard me." All of these turn out to be true in a way that is the opposite of what Charlie means. She is "saved" from the innocence and naïveté so obvious in the rest of her family, and saved by Charles, by having had to struggle with him. And this seems to be Hitchcock religion: there is a hell but no heaven. (We recall Charles enveloped in all that cigar smoke, satanic.)

Let us return to the family with all this in mind. In our first viewing, the treatment of the family can appear to be affectionate. We trust the appearances. But, perhaps on second viewing, we notice that no one really pays attention to the young son, Roger; Ann has also created her own world, has contempt for what her father reads; Charlie is bored to death; there is no real affection from their father, Joe; their mother doesn't know who she is; there is actually only a thin veneer of familial warmth. Emma is so excited by Charles's visit, we realize by contrast how dissatisfying her life had become, and we sense that she doesn't really know this, cannot acknowledge it. Each is lost in their own world; Emma in the past; Ann in books; Joe in crime magazines and fantasies of murder—Joe and Herb are both rather impotent men who harbor a love of violence that seems some kind of mirror for Charles's very real violence. (This is another uncomfortable link or bond with us, the viewers. We laugh at Joe and Herb, but we are watching a film about a serial killer, to be entertained.)

It is little wonder that the family, apart from Charlie, cannot even hear the speeches that give Charles away. He says almost the same murderous things in both. The second occurs later in the bar. But the first one is right out in the open. As he speaks, the continuum of dissatisfaction between him and Charlie (although Charlie is already entertaining obvious doubts about him and their bond) is again on view. And in the first, the dinner table speech, we note the significance of the moment when Hitchcock breaks the first and most important rule of all film acting: Don't look at the camera.

Charles tries to compliment "women in these small towns," saying they "keep busy." But the cities are full of women, "middle-aged, widowed, husbands dead, husbands who spent their lives working, making fortunes.... Then they die and leave their money to their wives, their silly wives. And what do the wives do, these useless women? You see them in the hotels, the best hotels, every day by the thousands, drinking their money, eating their money, losing

FIGURE 4.11

their money at bridge, playing all day and all night, smelling of money, proud of their jewelry but of nothing else; horrible; faded, fat, greedy women." Charlie interrupts to say, "They're alive, they're human beings," and Charles turns to us as well as to her (fig. 4.11) and says, "Are they? Are they, Charlie? Are they human or are they fat wheezing animals? And what happens to animals when they get too fat and too old?"

All Emma can say in response is "For heaven's sake, don't talk about women like that in front of my club." And she unknowingly proposes the next victim for Charles, another widow, "that nice Mrs. Potter."

This first, glaringly obvious incident of the mind of a psychopath shining through the cracks of a public persona, the dinner table speech, is something only Charlie is upset by! Innocence of that magnitude can be culpable too, as can ignorance. Herb and Joe think they know all about murder, but they are right in front of a serial killer, talking this way to them. (And, knowing we will feel superior to these clowns, Hitchcock is again pointing out that we, too, have come to the theater to indulge our imaginations about murder plots. And so what differentiates us from Joe and Herb? Perhaps that is the point of the glare at the camera.)

It is probably fair to say that Charlie suspects something without being able to admit to herself that she suspects it; she tells herself it is curiosity fed by the secret bond they have. But when she had seen Charles destroy part of the evening paper, and then she sees it hidden in his coat, she cannot resist, in her own conscious mind playfully, investigating further. (It was a story about the Merry Widow Murderer and the manhunt for the two possible suspects.) We note that when Charlie pulls out the newspaper story, Charles comes right at us again, striding aggressively toward her and grabbing her hands violently, and we note the sudden shift from violence to an unmistakable suggestion of attempted sexual intimacy (figs. 4.12 and 4.13).

And she investigates further, rushing to the library to check that day's paper. The library scene is the decisive moment when she leaves the teenage world and enters the adult world, quite a dramatic moment and staged as such. She will now have not just the suspicion that Charles is someone else, but that the adult world is full of people, perhaps everyone, who must be carefully assessed and interpreted, cannot be taken at face value, that the view of themselves they act out in the public world is liable to be built on fantasy, need, vanity, and self-deceit.

FIGURE 4.12

FIGURE 4.13

We should note here, too, how Hitchcock has, in cinematic terms, elevated this scene to a kind of mythic dimension, a moment of general significance, not just an aspect of a story about a particular young woman. In a way she is discovering that Charles is at least partly right: the world *is* a foul sty—it has people like Charles in it. We note the powerful effect of the shift in music, from a pleasant and everyday version of the "Merry Widow Waltz" to something dark, ominous, and foreboding. And that dark version of the "Merry Widow Waltz" is very effective: it confirms that she was in tune with Charles—she knew and somehow did not know that she knew that something was off. (It was in his head in the beginning, and now it is in her head, visions, nightmares, as he will say, of more victims of his murders.) The camera pulls back and up, and we sense another consequence of full entry into the adult world—a sense of aloneness, being finally, fundamentally, on one's own (fig. 4.14). The expression on her face in profile tells the story of this awakening (fig. 4.15). (It is this revelation that confounds our security in moral distinctions, in our ability to ascribe motives to others, and so to be able to describe properly what they are doing. It is not an occasion for a complete skepticism, but there is not a

FIGURE 4.14

FIGURE 4.15

recognized philosophical literature on such a state of confusion and unknowingness, or on the virtues appropriate to such states.) This is true about us
too, true about Charlie's motives, as we shall see. The decisive moment occurs
when Charlie reads the name of the last victim and knows that it is her initials
engraved on the ring Charles gave her.

This returns us again to the ordinariness theme. The family think of themselves as perfectly ordinary, and we are about to learn that every moment of
the ordinary can be extraordinary, full of meaning, although it appears boring,
banal. We recall Graham, the FBI agent, raising the topic of the ordinary to
Charlie and defending it vigorously. But she resists and tells him flat out that
she will not help him capture Charles in town. We tend not to believe her, but
Hitchcock has managed to introduce quite a large theme under the surface of
a conventional thriller set in a small town. Ordinariness in the film means primarily the world of the family, and Charlie is in effect acting out something
like an Antigone role, saying here that she sides with the family, with her duties
to her family and mother, and not with the state, not with her duties as a citizen. This is so extraordinary that, as noted, we tend not to believe her, or even
notice the magnitude of her decision, but this is exactly what she *will* do. She
knows the FBI is wrong to think that the man who died while trying to escape
was the murderer, but she lets Graham ride off without telling him, hoping
she can get Charles out of town on her own. In fact, she tells Charles that if he
"touches" her mother (a strange and intimate phrase to use, raising the incest
theme again, a much stronger element of the brother-sister relationship than
with Charlie), she will kill him herself. In fact, we, the viewers, tend to think
of Charlie as such a good girl, that I would wager that for most viewers, the
dense moral complications of Charlie's attitude, threatening to kill him, not
helping the FBI, goes, if not unnoticed, not judged. This is a remarkable effect.

So there is a discovery here of the profound, massive depth of the illu-
soriness of the adult ordinary. Not only can Uncle Charles be other than he
seems; he can be the moral *opposite* of how he presents himself to be seen, a
dimension of himself he will reveal in the upcoming speech in the bar (with
its central image of tearing the fronts, the facades, off houses). It is also the
moment when Charlie must learn that Santa Rosa has bars, girls not like herself, but like her high school classmate Louise. It has an underworld. It will
now be impossible for her to treat as harmless her father's and Herb's fascination with brutal, bloody murders, and eventually she will be allowed to see

what kind of despair, every day, her mother feels about her role in life, what lies behind her appearance.

Charles knows that Charlie is now deeply suspicious, takes her to a bar and both demands to know what she knows and actually tries to justify the murders to her. In this defense, we descend even deeper in Charles's nihilistic loathing. As he talks with her, he violently twists, as if strangling it, a napkin, and the more he talks, the more he confesses in a strange way, as if he could persuade Charlie of his view of the world. In the speech he again mentions, with contempt, her ordinary little life and how much it conceals from her about the truth of the world. "How do you know what the world is like? Do you know that the world is a foul sty? Do you know that if you rip the fronts off houses, you'd find swine? The world is a hell, what does it matter what happens in it? Wake up, Charlie. Use your wits, learn something."

They are occasionally interrupted by Louise, the barmaid, and we hear about another aspect of what has become the ordinary world—the materialism of a consumer society. She professes an almost religious awe about the emerald ring, and when she says, and then says again, that *this* in modern society is what is worth dying for, we believe her, believe that she believes it, is not exaggerating.

But Charles thinks he is off the hook. The other suspect has been killed in a way that makes identification impossible, so they assume he must have been the murderer. (He had walked into an airplane propeller. Hitchcock never cared much for the plausibility of his plot details.) But the bond between Charles and Charlie, unfortunately for Charlie, goes both ways. He sees immediately that she is not convinced (the shadow of her doubt is visible for the rest of the film) and that she deeply suspects him. There is even a clear moment when he decides he has to murder her. (In the first attempt, he loosens a stair tread so she will fall to her death, and in the second, he manages to lock her in a garage with the car motor running and no way for her to turn it off.) Charlie is framed in the doorway when he decides, when in effect a death sentence is pronounced, all without a hint of sadness or regret. "What does it matter what happens in it" is, indeed, his credo. It doesn't even matter if Charlie is killed (fig. 4.16).

The second murder attempt fails, ironically, because of Herb, the "murder expert," who happens on the garage where Charles had left the car running with Charlie locked inside.

FIGURE 4.16

And then the most intense and most significant scene in the film is about to occur, Charlie's descent down the staircase, having found the telltale ring, and Emma's speech about her brother—the latter the justification of what Charlie is willing to do, how far she is willing to go.

First, let us remember what we have noted before, that Charlie now knows that the dead second suspect is not the murderer, her uncle is. But she does not tell Graham and lets him drive off. She has kept her word. She has not helped him. And this is the good character in the film, the best, really. Second, she has become something far different from the innocent teenager we initially saw. At this point in the film, we do not doubt her insistence that if Charles does not leave, she will kill him herself. (We might be a bit bewildered by the change, though; by what she now says she is capable of.)

In the next scene, as we watch her go down the staircase, we see that Charlie has retrieved the ring, the piece of physical evidence that will doom Charles and is—again silently, visually—threatening to expose Charles if he does not leave. But she does not expose him. He accepts the implied deal Charlie is offering and announces he is leaving, and Charlie learns that Mrs. Potter is going along, placing her at great risk. Amazingly, Charlie seems willing to allow this, shows no interest in warning Mrs. Potter or prevailing on Charles to go alone. She seems willing to issue a death sentence for another merry widow.[5]

The issue at stake now is complicated at this point in the film. Here is a summary of the steps that seem to be involved. Charlie had had a deal with Graham not to say anything to Charles or anyone, especially her mother, and Graham agrees to arrest him out of town. Charlie discovers the ring evidence and tells Charles to get out of town or she'll kill him herself. Charlie does not tell Graham that their belief that the second man was the culprit is false; that Charles is in fact the Merry Widow Murderer. Charles tries to murder Charlie twice. At this point, Charlie seems to realize that it is useless to try to continue to protect her mother. Charles is capable of killing anyone, and, now terrified because she knows Charles has tried to kill her and that he may try again, she finally tries several times to call Graham, presumably to tell him the truth. Failing to reach him, she stages her visual threat to Charles. Since she had tried to call Graham, it is reasonable to assume that once Charles leaves (and Charlie herself does not have to worry about being murdered), she will tell Graham the truth and Mrs. Potter will be safe. But it is not entirely clear. Perhaps with Charles out of the way, not a threat to her or likely to be arrested in front of her mother, she will keep quiet to continue to protect her mother (especially after the intense emotional despair her mother will shortly reveal in a poignant speech about her life). The FBI will continue to think the real murderer has been killed. Most importantly, she does not know if she can get to Graham in time to save Mrs. Potter, but she *still* stays silent. We never know enough to resolve any of this, even though this indication that Charlie can deal with Charles inside the amoral world he inhabits, can accept the terms of that world and prevail, is the most disturbing dimension of their "bond" that we have yet seen (figs. 4.17 and 4.18). (In a beautiful small touch, once Charlie sees that Charles has accepted the deal, she discreetly covers the ring with her left hand, as if sealing the bargain.)

All of this underscores the difficulty of understanding a character's intentions in doing what she did, and it makes it very hard to know whether we should condemn Charlie for protecting her mother and putting Mrs. Potter at great risk. This all, that is, does not lead us to any moral or general philosophical

5. Both Wilson 2008 and Perez 2014 note how morally compromised Charlie's proffered "deal" with Charles is, with Perez again connecting the scene with the incest theme. See also Rothman's (1982: 232–33) take on the "romance" between them.

FIGURE 4.17

FIGURE 4.18

FIGURE 4.19

truth. It more often has the force of adding a kind of shading or qualification on what we think we understand about issues like jealousy or betrayal or
romantic love, or the relation between family and the law. We often get more
confused by complex aesthetic treatments like this, but this is a philosophical
consequence of some importance too.

Then the full force of what had worried Charlie about her mother at the
beginning—the dreariness and lack of significant purpose in her life that was
destroying her, robbing her of happiness—surfaces in bitter poignancy. By this
point, this all strikes the viewer as deeply credible, as the pathos of a housewife
stuck at home in small-town or suburban America is given beautiful expression
by Patricia Collinge, the actress who plays Emma (fig. 4.19). She is clearly in a
free-falling despair at going back to life without Charles.

She explains how close they were growing up. "Then Charles went away,
and I got married, and then you know how it is. You sort of forget you're
you." The screen goes dark and we hear her last words, "You're your husband's
wife . . ."

We have been watching Charlie while she speaks, and Charlie is obviously
deeply pained. Everything she had halfheartedly thought about her mother's

FIGURE 4.20

plight is far more true than she had ever imagined. The others are shown being uncomfortable hearing about this expression of intense affection for a brother. There is no reaction shot of Joe, the husband. (It is in this scene that the vague allusions to incest become more explicit, and the excessive reaction of Emma seems to be making everyone uncomfortable in just this sense. In more general terms—that is, Charlie's loyalty to her mother at the expense of her responsibilities as a citizen—Emma's reaction touches on the dangers of the "absolutization," we might call it, of the family as the exclusive source of authority and order and love. It falls in on itself in a way that does not grant each his or her own independence and autonomy.)

On the train leaving town, Charles prevents Charlie from leaving and tries to kill her by throwing her from the train, but Charlie manages to twist away and propel Charles to his death. The film closes with an elaborate funeral for Charles, a parade even, as if for a head of state. It is all way over the top and full of an irony about the town's ignorance and blind innocence that is almost bitter. But some elements of it are even stranger.

For, we should note that with respect to the issue of Charlie's choice between her family and her duty as a citizen, Hitchcock does not soften the choice by suggesting a love affair blossoming between Graham and Charlie, as if to bring the law inside the circle of family obligations and familial love. Earlier when the FBI agent professed his love for her in the garage before the second murder attempt, he hears what no one who has just professed love wants to hear: Charlie saying that they can be friends, that, in effect, "she doesn't feel that way about him." And as they stand outside the steps of the church, Hitchcock has them both facing outward, with Charlie only occasionally glancing at Graham (fig. 4.20).

But Charlie also says that she couldn't get through the funeral "without someone who knew," and we are startled. That means that Graham, the FBI agent, knows that Charles is the real murderer and has kept completely quiet about it, has not made that public, apparently has not informed his superiors (who would certainly have made it public, rendering this elaborate funeral and closing laudation impossible). He apparently believes that this representative American town could not well withstand the revelation, and he tries to console Charlie, tries to disabuse her of Charles's view that the world is a horrible place, insisting that it just needs watching and goes a little crazy every now and then. In other words, he tries to re-create the myth of the ordinary, of its fundamental goodness, even though as he does so, we realize that it is all built on a fiction, a lie as enormous as the grotesque laudation of Charles we hear coming from the church. The minister is talking about heroes like Charles, and the last words we hear are about him and his like, "the beauty of their souls, the sweetness of their characters, live on with us forever." This seems yet another doubling, here equating the tranquilizing narcotic about the ordinary that Graham is trying to give Charlie, and the ludicrous ignorance embodied in the last words we hear.

FIGURE 2.1

FIGURE 2.2

FIGURE 2.3

FIGURE 2.4

FIGURE 2.5

FIGURE 2.6

FIGURE 2.7

FIGURE 3.1

FIGURE 3.2

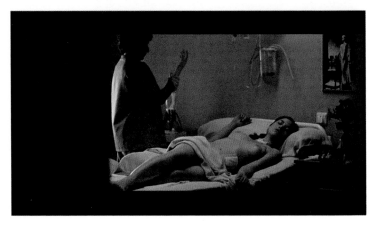

FIGURE 3.3

FIGURE 3.4

FIGURE 3.5

FIGURE 3.6

FIGURE 3.7

FIGURE 3.8

FIGURE 5.1

FIGURE 5.2

FIGURE 5.3

FIGURE 5.4

FIGURE 6.1

FIGURE 6.2

FIGURE 6.3

FIGURE 6.4

FIGURE 6.5

FIGURE 6.6

FIGURE 6.7

FIGURE 6.8

FIGURE 6.9

FIGURE 6.10

FIGURE 6.11

FIGURE 6.12

FIGURE 6.13

FIGURE 6.14

FIGURE 6.15

FIGURE 6.16

FIGURE 6.17

FIGURE 7.1

FIGURE 7.2

FIGURE 7.3

FIGURE 7.4

FIGURE 7.5

FIGURE 7.6

FIGURE 7.7

FIGURE 7.8

FIGURE 7.9

FIGURE 7.10

FIGURE 7.11

FIGURE 9.1

FIGURE 9.2

FIGURE 9.3

FIGURE 9.4

FIGURE 9.5

FIGURE 9.6

FIGURE 9.7

FIGURE 9.8

FIGURE 10.1

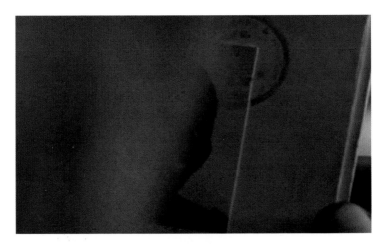

FIGURE 10.2

FIGURE 10.3

FIGURE 10.4

FIGURE 10.5

FIGURE 10.6

FIGURE 10.7

FIGURE 10.8

FIGURE 10.9

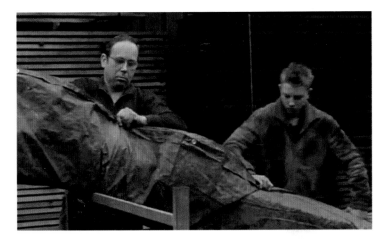

FIGURE 10.10

FIGURE 10.11

SECTION III
Social Pathologies

Cinematic Tone in
Roman Polanski's *Chinatown*:
Can "Life" Itself Be "False"?

Wrong life cannot be lived rightly.
(*Es gibt kein richtiges Leben im falschen.*)
THEODOR ADORNO, *Minima Moralia*

I. NOIR AND NEO-NOIR

Villainy—often extreme, horrific, satanic villainy—is as much a staple of American film noir as the entrance of the femme fatale, confusing double or triple plots, the weakness and fragility of the grip of moral norms, and ironic "unhappy" endings. In Roman Polanski's *Chinatown* (1974), often cited as the finest example of the "neo-noir" genre, as well as in many of the best noirs, what appears to be the ordinary world of rational expectations, planning, moral courage, and attempts at mutual understanding is in reality, we learn, a world where none of this really matters or is even possible, that events are actually manipulated by unseen and malevolent self-interested forces that frequently cannot even be identified. But very often the malevolence has a source, an arch-villain. Kaspar Gutman (Sydney Greenstreet) and Joel Cairo (Peter Lorre) in *The Maltese Falcon* (1941), Johnny Prince (Dan Duryea) in *Scarlet Street* (1945), Ballin Mundson (George Macready) in *Gilda* (1946), Whit Sterling (Kirk Douglas) in *Out of the Past* (1947), Arthur Bannister (Everett Sloane) in *The Lady from Shanghai* (1947), Mike Lagana (Alexander Scourby) and his brutal henchman Vince Stone (Lee Marvin) in *The Big Heat* (1953), Hank Quinlan (Orson Welles) in *Touch of Evil* (1958), and such female villains as Phyllis Dietrichson (Barbara Stanwyck) in *Double Indemnity* (1944) and Cora Smith (Lana Turner) in *The Postman Always Rings Twice* (1946) would only be the beginning of a long list.

Chinatown successfully re-creates many of these markers of the "noir world" (or at least as many as it can in a color, Panavision anamorphic format film, most of which occurs in daylight),[1] both by cinematic means (dialogue, the score, narrative pacing, and the characters' sense of futility and confusion) and by setting the film in the Los Angeles of 1937, near the beginning of the noir period, conventionally fixed at 1941 and *The Maltese Falcon*. (The aptness of such a setting and such a bleak moral atmosphere for indirectly representing the United States of the 1970s is also no doubt intentionally suggested.) This is the setting in which we meet Noah Cross (played with cunning and flair by John Huston), whose perfidy is mythic in scale, willing to build shoddy dams that burst and kill hundreds, willing to cheat farmers out of their water in a drought so that he could buy their land, to treat the public or common good as wholly his to profit from, to murder anyone in his way, and to impregnate his daughter and groom his granddaughter for the same fate. It is hard to imagine a noir villain remotely his equal.

Pointing to such similarities raises an obvious but very broad question, unmanageable in this limited context. Among the many characteristics of the role of genre in Hollywood production, one of the oddest is that some genres appear to have births and deaths; others, not so much. Romantic comedies, suspense thrillers, crime procedurals, bio-pics, historical epics, all extend back from the present into the heart of the "classic Hollywood" period, the 1930s, 1940s, and much of the 1950s. Musicals, Westerns, melodramas, and noirs all became extremely popular for a period of time, and then seemed to fade away in importance and frequency. Noirs are a bit of an exception since the bleakness, fatalism, and general style or atmosphere of noirs persist in crime pictures and in other genres too. There are noir Westerns, and if we count some of the work of Dennis Potter, even noir musicals. But, as noted above, the convention is by now pretty fixed that film noir should be dated from 1941 and *The Maltese Falcon* (interestingly, for our purposes, a John Huston film) to either 1955 and Robert Aldrich's *Kiss Me Deadly*, or 1958 and Orson Welles's *Touch of*

---

1. There are attempts. Many of the indoor scenes are latticed with bars of shadow from blinds, a sepia tone colors some daylight scenes, and the last scene set in *Chinatown* is classic noir. And some of the noir references are both clear and ironic, as if even the fatalism so prominent in noirs is not sufficient to express the degree of impotence of all the characters other than Noah Cross. Jake Gittes assumes that Evelyn Mulwray must be the murderess (as if Jake has seen too many noirs), whereas she is, multiply, a victim, guilty of nothing but love for her daughter, raped by her father, and shot dead by the police.

Evil. This flourishing period seems to have had something to do with postwar unease, paranoia, and anxiety, especially about the changing status of women that war production required. The reemergence of a complexly plotted, bleak, clearly noirish Hollywood feature film in 1974, one that inspired passionate pro and con reactions[2] (much like the reception of noirs themselves) is a social and historical question worthy of reflection in itself. As noted, the film even seems to have a classic noir villain, played by the man credited with making the first film noir, John Huston. But even more interestingly, that apparent similarity can be misleading.

For the film's theme is not individual moral evil itself and does not appear to attribute the source of the evil we see simply to Cross as an individual character (although the temptation to do so is overwhelming). The theme is, rather, as the title announces, "Chinatown," a marker for something unfathomable, inexplicable, an evil "unattributable" to a villain (no one knows who is responsible for what in "Chinatown"), but characteristic of a world itself, and not just the world of Chinese immigrants in Los Angeles. For example, the film's famous signature closing line, "Forget it, Jake; it's Chinatown," makes no literal sense. Cross's murder of his former partner, his swindle, his rape of his daughter, all of which culminate in the police shooting the fleeing Evelyn Mulwray and Cross getting his clutches on his granddaughter, have nothing to do with Chinatown. That place is simply where the final scene occurs. At least, it makes no sense unless the speaker means to refer to what we have just seen, that Evelyn and Noah Cross exemplify "Chinatown." In fact, the reference seems meant to do duty for the whole social and historical world set out by the film, and the most prominent characteristic of that world appears to be its *unintelligibility* (already an invocation, among many others, of a crude stereotype, Asian "inscrutability"), an unintelligibility that has a number of particular inflections and existential implications in Polanski's treatment.

II. "CHINATOWN"

This idea or image of Chinatown is like a spectral presence throughout the film, both to suggest that, no matter how confusing and dangerous Los Ange-

2. Most of the criticism was about the bleak ending, and the sense of hopelessness it left us with. The screenwriter Robert Towne called it "the tunnel at the end of the light." It was not the ending he scripted (Biskind 1994: 72).

les can seem, at least it is not Chinatown, and, much more ominously, and more and more prominently, that the distinction between Chinatown and Los Angeles is an illusion, that we (the bourgeois world and its rule of law) are *in* such an unfathomable world and can never escape. The references, that is, work to create a foreboding atmosphere of dread, anxiety, uncertainty, and confusion about our own situation that the characters displace or project onto this "other" place, until finally the last words spoken are truer than the speaker realizes. The world of Los Angeles itself is Chinatown, and the advice being offered Jake (forget it; do nothing because nothing can be done) is a chilling expression of a despairing cynicism in the face of this fact.

The screenwriter, Robert Towne, apparently originally conceived the title to refer to Jake's psychology. As the producer, Robert Evans, remembers an early conversation between them:

> "... what's it called?"
>
> "*Chinatown.*"
>
> "What's that got to do with it? You mean, it's set in Chinatown?"
>
> "No. 'Chinatown' is a state of mind—Jake Gittes's fucked up state
>   of mind."
>
> "I see," I said, not seeing at all.[3]

But once Polanski made the script into a film, the reference is hardly so limited (the only thing "fucking up" Jake Gittes's mind is his memory of a particular, and, we will find, typical, failure in Chinatown), and the ironic identification of Chinatown, as moral anarchy and unintelligibility, with Los Angeles (for Polanski, the Los Angeles of the Tate-LaBianca murders as well) gradually becomes inescapable, as the vastness of the corruption and the extent of the evil everywhere becomes ever clearer to our representative in the film, Jake (Jack Nicholson). (Except for one or two exceptions, the story is narrated from Jake's point of view, and that point of view is ours. We see and learn what he sees and learns as he does.)[4] None of this is explicit or is pointed out by anyone (except ironically in the last words), and it is more intimated by Polanski's creation of a general tonality or atmosphere. Chinatown, and what it comes to mean, hovers over *everything* that happens; it cannot be confined to a distinct place. Nothing anywhere is what it seems, Jake's naive confidence that

---

3. Evans 1994: 257.

4. See the helpful account by Eaton 1997: 32–35.

he can figure everything out seems less and less credible; the musical score, dominated by a plaintive, melancholic solo trumpet, constantly suggests that this will all not turn out well, no matter what anyone does, or thinks he has discovered, and the references to Chinatown keep reappearing throughout.

The allusions begin with a racist joke told to Jake by his barber to distract Jake from his anger at another customer who had disparaged Jake's profession. (Jake believes he has discovered a "love nest" where Hollis Mulwray meets his mistress, and the newspapers blast this scandal all over the front page of the paper the customer is reading. In reality, Mulwray is helping his wife protect the young girl from Noah Cross, the father of both Evelyn and her daughter, Katherine.) The customer, it turns out, is a mortgage banker, and Jake points out to him that at least he, Jake, does not foreclose and throw people out of their homes. Already, the moral taint unavoidable just by inhabiting the contemporary world is suggested: one can either be a snoop, making what should be private more or less public, or a banker who throws people into the street, or a barber who cannot afford to make moral judgments. Everyone is a customer. Everyone has to make a living and that means everyone has to participate in the ruthless profit machine. (As we are reminded later, even the police must "swim in the same water as the rest of us," a disturbing image since the big fish there in the water with us is Noah Cross.) Jake rushes back to the office to relay the barber's joke to his operatives, and we see the ironic inverse of the femme fatale entrance. Evelyn (Faye Dunaway) is not the object of a male gaze but stands behind Jake, unobserved, powerful, and rich (her lawyer is with her, armed with a lawsuit), and hears him repeat his tawdry Chinaman screwing joke.[5] In an instant, Jake's seeming coolness, his unflappable air, and so his apparent inheriting of the sangfroid superiority of Sam Spade and Philip Marlowe, are forever destroyed. He is little more than a braying adolescent male. So much for Evelyn's "first impressions"[6] (fig. 5.1). And this early diminution of Jake's status is reemphasized throughout the film, physically marked by his

5. Like many other femme fatales, Evelyn shares the fate of being bound to a man she cannot abide and cannot escape, in this case her father. She shares, that is, the same fate as the femme fatale in *The Killers, The Lady from Shanghai, Out of the Past, The Big Heat, Double Indemnity, The Postman Always Rings Twice,* and many others.

6. There are of course several noir heroes who do not fit the type portrayed by Humphrey Bogart, Dick Powell, or, in a near parody of the type, Ralph Meeker's Mike Hammer in *Kiss Me Deadly* (1955). Dana Andrews especially, say in *Laura*, or Robert Mitchum in *Out of the Past* (1947) play against this type. See the discussion of the significance of the difference in Pippin 2012.

cut nose, all a somewhat odd feature of the character, judged by standard hard-boiled detectives in other films. He is easily set up by the fake Mrs. Mulwray, Ida Sessions (Diane Ladd); ultimately understands very little of what is going on (does not finally even seem to understand what Evelyn tells him about the incest). And he is largely incidental to the action, which is generated by the attempt on Evelyn's part to keep her daughter/sister away from her father, Noah Cross, an attempt that is understandably hysterically ramped up when Evelyn loses her protector from Cross, her husband, Hollis Mulwray (Darrell Zwerling). Jake even manages to set up, and then to lead everyone of relevance to, the final scene, the scene of Evelyn's death. But any judgment about Jake depends on the role of the references to Chinatown in the film, and given that role, what it would be reasonable to expect anyone to know and to do.

At Mulwray's mansion, Jake finds an Asian butler, maid, chauffeur, and gardener, and again a stereotype is invoked. The gardener is trying to tell Jake what he is doing, that the salt water in the tide pool is very bad for the grass, but he says, and Jake repeats, that the water is "velly bad for the glass." If Jake had heard anything other than the mispronunciation, he would already have had the film's most important clue. The fact that the water is salt water is what reveals that Mulwray was murdered in the tide pool, and that will lead Jake, finally, to conclude that Noah Cross was the murderer. These stereotypes, and there are more to come, appear to function as defense mechanisms. Chinatown may be a dangerous and unfathomable place, but the crude stereotypes create the illusion that "we know" what "they" are like, and we are superior to them, can make them the butt of jokes. In "our" world, they are not dangerous but humorous, an obviously fatal piece of self-deceit.

When Jake discovers the place where Mulwray's body was discovered, he meets there an old police colleague from Jake's own Chinatown days, Lou Escobar (Perry Lopez). He asks Lou if he is still arresting Chinamen for spitting in the laundry, and Lou tells Jake that, in the first place, Jake is behind the times. They have steam irons now. (Jake's knowledge of Chinatown and its mores is out-of-date, a sign perhaps that his imagination is not up to what "Chinatown as LA" is now capable of.) And second, Escobar says that he has made lieutenant and made it out of Chinatown, creating the suggestion that Jake, whatever he may think, has not really made it out.

When Jake is summoned to meet Cross, he is warned by Cross that while Jake may think he knows what he is dealing with, he most certainly does not. Jake replies that that was what they used to tell him when he worked in China-town (fig. 5.2). Ironically, Jake gives plenty of signs that he believes that this *is* true of Chinatown, that no one, at least no one from the outside, knows what is really going on there, who is running what show, what the rules are. If Jake could have carried that lesson with him in his new PI job, he might have been more hesitant to trust what he thinks he has figured out, that Evelyn committed the murder. Then again that lesson might be better expressed by what Jake says when asked what he did in Chinatown. "As little as possible." This is also one of the closing pieces of dialogue in the film, a somewhat neglected line, said quietly by Jake (almost inaudibly) as he contemplates the mess that has been created; Evelyn dead, Cross with his daughter/granddaughter.

Jake and Evelyn finally sleep together in a scene marked both by tenderness and a notable lack of erotic charge. Neither of them seems much interested in sex,[7] and Polanski does not even hint that Jake is the kind of lady-killer associated with the private detective stereotype. Evelyn wants to know about Jake, in their postcoital, cigarette-afterward scene. He tells her that he was a policeman in Chinatown, occasionally wearing a uniform (perhaps intimating that he occasionally did what a police officer should do, but only occasionally) and that the experience was very painful, that he does not want to talk about it. She presses him and he says that he was trying to protect a woman, and in so trying, he ensured that she did end up "hurt."[8] This is exactly what he is about to do to/for Evelyn, reminding us again that the presumed difference between LA and Chinatown is an illusion, and that one of the most dangerous entanglements in such a world is love.[9] Chinatown (Los Angeles, the contemporary world) is a world where good intentions and commitment to others not only do not much matter, but they can even be dangerous. They assume what moral action always does: that one knows one's own motives, that one understands what is happening, and that one can predict safely what a course of action will bring about. Since none of these assumptions is true, doing "as little as possible" seems the safest choice. Assuming these conditions have been met is not only naive, but very dangerous.[10]

---

7. Evelyn, no doubt, because her avowed promiscuity is tied in various ways to the trauma of incest, and Jake because, we sense, the woman he tried to help in Chinatown was so important to him, that he isn't "over" it.

8. He is clearly so traumatized by the event, it is likely that he got her killed.

9. This can be a noir theme apart from any Chinatown-like problematic. One of the best examples is Nicholas Ray's *In a Lonely Place*. See chapter 8.

10. Of course, Chinatown *is* also a police district smack in the middle of LA, also a separate place. But the stake for the characters in so isolating it and mystifying it as another universe is defensive and self-deceived, and it is truly distinct only by being paradigmatic of corruption,

Finally, the polysemous "Chinatown" is invoked in other related ways. When Jake is being prodded by Evelyn to tell her more about Chinatown, he finally says, "You can't always tell what's going on . . ." but instead of saying "there," he turns more toward her and says, ". . . with you." *She* is now his China-town, dangerously opaque to him, even as he begins to trust her.[11] Here the dialogue makes Towne's original point with Evans, that "Chinatown" is also a state of mind, as in "you may think you know what you are dealing with, but, believe me, you don't," although in this case he at least knows what he doesn't know, that Evelyn, however attractive, is still hiding something and may be quite dangerous. For one thing, she, or her eye, is "flawed," there is a black mark in the green of her iris; a stain, it would seem; ultimately the ineradicable stain of incest, and the site also of her death, the mark of why "life" for her is impossible, as the policeman's bullet seems to pass through her and out that eye. The image is nicely echoed in Jake's pursuit of her after she receives the phone call that prompts her departure. He kicks out one of her taillights and follows the "one-eyed" vehicle and the "flawed" Evelyn to the house where he will learn the truth. This is the "flaw" that likely makes her so wary, closed off, mistrustful, and Jake's suspicions about what she is holding back, combined with that wariness, are what likely makes the romance between them so ten-tative and even somewhat formal. In fact, from her point of view, the stain is even harder to bear because she assumes some responsibility for it. When, after the famous (and much parodied) "she's my daughter, she's my sister" slapping scene, she begins to tell Jake what happened and starts, "My father and I . . ." Not "my father used to come into my room" or something similar to other incest revelations in films and television. And even more remarkably, when Jake offers, "He raped you," Evelyn, weeping, looks directly at Jake and shakes her head decisively.[12] Whatever it was, she is insisting, it was not rape. She par-ticipated. The unfathomability of "what's going on" with Evelyn, introduced in

---

especially the corruption of the police, a force actually and famously one of the most corrupt in the country. Perhaps Cross is allegorically indicating something of his understanding of the Chinatown-LA relation when he tells Jake later that if you can't bring the water to LA, bring LA to the water.

11. But he only begins to trust her. When he follows her and discovers Katherine, the daughter/sister, he is back to claiming to know that she is the murderess of her husband.

12. It goes without saying that victims of incest are simply and unqualifiedly victims, no matter how successful the perpetrator is in making them think the two of them were equally respon-sible. Creating such a feeling of guilt on the part of the victim helps protect the abuser, and adds another level of evil to what is already an unspeakable crime. This issue here is the bur-den Evelyn *thinks* she bears.

the scene in bed as another dimension of the unfathomability of Chinatown, has reached an even darker, more horrific region.

In sum, the film's repeated references to and warnings about "Chinatown" create an atmosphere or tonality so ominous and threatening that it raises the question of whether the unambiguous and profound evil present in the film might not be the product of one or a few bad individuals, but that a whole form of life can be said to have "gone wrong," become "false," not "truly" what a human life must be to count as such, so damaged (*beschädigt*) that no "right" life in such a world is conceivable. (The possibility that Evelyn's flaw or stain is not just hers, but the "*human* stain"—she calls it a sort of "birthmark"—or that the form of life we experience in the film is not a "damaged" form, but *the* form of human life, inherently and irremediably deeply corrupt, is a possibility we will consider later.)

A film, that is, can have a mood suffused through it, something not quite the same as a signature style, but an effect of a consistent, controlled style. Ford's Westerns, the great ones, create a mood of historical fundamentality, that matters of great political and social significance are at stake (the place of violence in a civilized life, for example); Hitchcock's films sustain a mood of brittle anxiety and eventually dread, given that we and the characters never know what they need to know; Sirk can create scenes of desperate emotional intensity, and can even string several such scenes together successively; David Lynch can create a sense of perversity in the way a character smiles or walks or eats. In this film at least, Polanski creates and sustains a constant, uneasy mood among all the unknowing characters, that *something is not at all right here*, and this is the reason people are so often reminded of Chinatown. They sense the situation is beyond them, either beyond their limited capacity to understand (ever), or, as in the case of Cross's relation with his daughter, beyond any being's capacity to understand; that there is nothing here that is understandable.

This is the clear implication of the epigraph cited above from Adorno's *Minima Moralia*, subtitled *Reflections on a Damaged Life*. (The moral corollary of the claim: "Today . . . it is part of morality not to be at home in one's home." At the most metaphysical: "life does not live.")[13] Adorno meant the life of late capitalism (a "profit economy"), mass-consumer societies, manipulated by the "culture industry" to such an extent that "right life" is not *possible*; objectively available coherent courses of action, even possible ways of

---

13. "Das Leben lebt nicht." Adorno 1951 is quoting Ferdinand Kürnberger.

living, are all compromised or "damaged." But the bearing of this mode of assessment, shifting our attention from individual moral agents (while not denying their individual culpability) to a different notion of "wrongness"— one borne by a form of life itself, as unjust, exploitative, dehumanizing in its very nature—should be clear. In any such world, one is morally complicit with such wrongness just by surviving, by existing at all. We might think this a radical and initially implausible notion. We immediately call to mind moral heroes under Nazism, or people of conscience in all sorts of horrific and objectively hopeless corrupt and depraved societies. But Adorno does not say that moments of right action are not possible, but rather that no *right life* is possible, and these moments of moral heroism are not instances of *living* rightly but, if only at least once, *acting* rightly. Even so, given what was said above about noir villains in general, and the singular villainy of Noah Cross in particular, such a sweeping indictment does not seem plausible. There seems a clear center of responsibility for what is so wrong about Los Angeles: Cross and those who serve him. But what does Cross have to do with "Chinatown"? That is the question that can be illuminated by what I've referred to as "tonality" or a cinematic representation of a mood or common "attunement" in the narration. Something like these terms are needed because the issue does not concern false beliefs, even collectively held false beliefs, or a society subject to delusions that need to be, and can be, corrected. *Life itself* has become "false," and this is not a feature representable discursively (by a set of propositions listing what is commonly felt, believed, hoped for, etc.), but in the way a life is, can be, cannot be, lived. Cinema is well positioned to give us some sense of what that might mean or at least "look" and "feel" like, and that is especially true of this movie. We need to discuss first one more prominent feature of the film's narrative.

III. THE DOUBLE PLOT

As other commentators on the film have pointed out, the structure of the film forces us to ask what the two plots, the water swindle plot and the incest plot, have to do with one another, if anything. Their relationship is not a standard plot and subplot relation, for one thing because it is not at all clear what is to be the major focus and which the minor. Psychoanalytically inclined critics obviously focus on the incest plot, and the sociohistorical critics on the water plot, but for many in each camp, the other plot is a digression, diversion, or distraction.[14] And it is certainly true that the film itself had an impact on water policy in California, that that plot, loosely based on the Owens Valley case, had a real-world effect. The details of the real event and the film's treatment of it are in some dispute, but Vernon Shetley sets out what appears to be the most reasonable and widely accepted view:

> ... no one disputes the fact that a group of the city's wealthiest men, privy to inside information about the plans of the Department of Water and Power, bought up land cheaply in the San Fernando Valley and realized enormous profits on their purchases when the Owens Valley Aqueduct, completed in 1913, made water available to irrigate that land. Though the dates have been shifted from the early part of the century to the 1930s, the film presents with a fair degree of accuracy the fundamental structure of the San Fernando conspiracy, a conspiracy in which wealthy and powerful interests manipulated public agencies for private profit.[15]

Robert Towne, at least, had a clear idea that the water plot was the most important. He said:

> A man violating his own child is not as serious as a man who is willing to violate everyone's children. . . . Maybe it's because America is a puritanical county. I felt the only way to drive home the outrage about water and power was to . . . cap it with incest.[16]

On this account, the incest plot is a kind of intensifier; it is there to intensify our outrage at what Cross is willing to do. That may be so; the revelation after the slapping scene certainly intensifies our disgust with Cross, but that can hardly be the end of the relationship between the plots.

For one thing, it remains unclear in the film just what Cross did and was willing to do and why. This confusion is not helped by the fact that the film ends with so little of the plot elements resolved, so few that each plot, as a

---

14. Far and away the best discussion of the double plot, and the relation of the themes in each, that I have found is Shetley 1999: 1092–109. Aside from his thoughtful interpretation itself, Shetley provides a concise and illuminating summary of these different approaches.
15. Shetley 1999: 1094.
16. Quoted in Eaton 1997: 64. No textual source is given.

narrative, does not seem to have the clear endpoint in standard beginning, middle, and end narratives. Evelyn dies but that "resolves" very little. We don't really find out just why Cross murdered his own business partner, and the fact that their last, photographed fiery conversation could have been about either Hollis's discovery of the plot to force farmers out of the valley by denying them water and blowing up buildings, poisoning reservoirs, which is what Jake thinks, or about what appear to be Hollis's attempts to hide Katherine from him, which is what Cross himself suggests when he answers Jake's question about the argument by saying it was about "the girl."[17] Nothing about his motives is all that clear either. He doesn't need the money he will gain by the success of the water swindle, as he admits to Jake, saying it is all about "the future," whatever that means. Towne's remarks are a bit hysterical here. Cross is not willing to "violate everyone's children." He wants the desert valley to become a garden, with plenty of children, just as long as he owns the land and profits from the great bounty that will result from the building of the dam. This is in itself already mysterious, or at least confusing. If he really doesn't care about the money, why not let the dam be built and the farmers already there on the land in the valley prosper? His tactics are illegal, and he certainly is willing to harm the families now on the land, but this is basically an insider-trading sort of offense, and as far as I can see, it completely pales in comparison with the incest plot. It would be a different matter indeed if, for example, he knew the water were contaminated, and that he was consigning many future generations to cancer and other diseases.

Moreover, are we to believe that the police will write off Hollis's murder to Evelyn, which is why they are pursuing her and forcing Jake to help them, because they believe she did it in a jealous rage? Will they even pursue the case? Are we to think that they will just not believe Jake, or figure there is too much danger to themselves in believing him? Are there to be no legal services involved in the determination of what should happen to Katherine? Cross just gets to "take" her, fold her physically into himself in an ugly parody of intimacy when he takes her out of the car, shielding her eyes with his hand.

17. Jake may be right, and Cross may be trying to create a diversion, but it is true that Hollis and his wife are clearly trying to hide the girl from Cross, that he is clearly hunting for her aggressively, that the attempt to hide her is ruined by Jake's photograph, and that Huston's line reading suggests a kind of pathos that seems genuine. At any rate, it is another instance where the two plots seem congruent in some way.

One thing we do know about the incomplete resolution of each plot is that no one attempting the "right thing," in the loosest sense—Jake's wanting the truth to come out, Evelyn's wanting to protect Katherine from Cross—succeeds, and this leads us closer to the question of "no possible right life" suggested above. For the plots do share a strong metaphorical link. The link is voiced in an utterance by Evelyn in the climactic scene, "He *owns* the police," and by Cross when he is trying to persuade Evelyn to back off, "She's *mine* too." The legitimacy of private property, which should begin in the right over my own body, the entitlement to non-interference by others, does not settle the question of rightful extent of ownership, or the question of what may be privately owned. The Romans may have treated children as property of the father, but no serious theorist of capitalist modernity has ever advanced such a claim. Katherine is not and cannot be "his," any more than Evelyn was. But it is also not enough to show that in both cases, the issue for Cross and men like him is simply power, the power especially never to be subject to the will of another, always to be able to subject others' will to one's own. Not that this is insignificant. As Shetley points out, both water and daughters represent the possibility of fertility and in that sense the power to control the future. As he compellingly puts it:

> Each [water and daughter] is a means of projecting oneself into the future, either through bloodlines, or the creation of wealth, for what is capital but wealth that has outlived its creation, even its creator? Noah Cross's incestuous acts and his land swindles turn on his desire to monopolize for himself the possibilities of life and fertility that water and daughters represent; in both cases, what ought to be exchanged is instead hoarded, what should circulate is instead entrapped and held back.[18]

---

18. Shetley 1999: 1098. Cf. "Its [Chinatown's] power arises from the way in which the institution of private property itself, the very foundation of the capitalist economic and social order, becomes identified with the horror of incest" (1100). This seems to me a rare overstatement. Nothing in the film that I can see (nothing in the point of view we are encouraged to adopt) justifies this as a claim about "private property itself." Although it is true that one might say that Cross's debased understanding of the entitlement that comes with property is a possible pathological implication of the institution, one that becomes hard to resist if great wealth is concentrated in a few hands. Shetley also makes illuminating use of Lévi-Strauss on the incest taboo as the basic dividing line between nature and culture, the basic affiliation not based on any biological imperative.

But this still leaves somewhat mysterious why Cross, mortal being like the rest of us, should expend such energy, take such risks in the service of such megalomaniacal control of a future he will not see. At one point he seems to suggest that he wants it simply because he can have it. In a crucial scene by the tide pool, he tells Jake that he doesn't blame himself for the incest, and he expresses what appears to be one of his founding principles, if not his lodestar, "You see, Mr. Gittes, most people never have to face the fact that at the right time in the right place, they're capable of *anything*" (fig. 5.3). This is not the film's finest moment. Such nihilism is simplistic, and although we are three years from the sexual assault on a minor charge that eventually led to Polanski's exile, the assertion sounds creepily like his own all-purpose excuse for his behavior. Our natural or immediate reaction is to think of the line as Cross's self-deceived and pathetic excuse for himself, but the more we note that the center of "wrongness" in the film is "Chinatown" (or LA, or the US, or capitalism, or even modernity), the line begins to emerge as the film's point of view. This need not be meant as some comment on human nature, as it is characteristic of this distinctive form of life, the one so mysteriously and elusively evoked in the film by the mere mention of "Chinatown."

The tide pool scene also resonates unintentionally with our theme. Cross tells Jake that Hollis Mulwray loved tide pools, because they were where life mysteriously began; they were the source. This tide pool, though, was the site of Mulwray's death. That life itself should now be the site of death sounds like Adorno's quotation from Kürnberger, that "life does not live." The source of life now—in Los Angeles and the industrialized West with its social organization based on acquisition and consumption—is the place of death; more generally of "death in life."

But in this case, the exercise of power made possible by unimaginable wealth has a central dimension crucial to the effectiveness of the film, and that "locates" to some extent the Chinatown social pathology (or locates Evelyn's flaw, Cross's limp, Jake's scar). For the idea of capitalism as a legal system, as rightful, requires a distinction between public and private that is both acknowledged in the regime's basic law and attended to and actively sustained by enforcement and official expression. The idea that there can be a collective allegiance to a common good is also the idea that the state's monopoly on the use of legitimate coercive violence cannot be understood as at the service of whatever private interests are predominant at the time. In such a case there would be no state, no genuinely public sphere, no politics, just some (putative) collective means to insure that the use of public power be consistent with some sort of like use for all, always subject to manipulation by anyone with wealth enough to manipulate without penalty. This returns us to the "false life" issue.

IV. "FALSE LIFE"?

Clearly, the somewhat vatic pronouncement that "life does not live" or that there is no "right" way to live in a false life means referring to a normative, not physical breakdown. Everyone who is alive obviously exists, is living, not dead. But life in some sociohistorical setting might not be lived "as life should," as a human life. Elephants performing their dreary routines in circuses are alive, but not living the life cycle of elephants. And we do not mean that some aspect of their lives is not as it should be, but rather they are simply *not at all* living as they should. Their whole way of life could be said to be false to what is "truly being" the creatures they are; just as there is no "right" way to be an elephant in a circus. As we have been seeing, the references to Chinatown all suggest a moral chaos at *this* level of generality. *Everything* there is inscrutable; and this is because *no one* seems to know what the rules are; *no one* seems to know who is running the show; the best thing one can do there is "as little as possible." There is no reliable public agent; law is only a means. The one thing we do seem to know is that, whatever is "really" going on there, it is corrupt and dangerous; only someone very wise in its ways could survive for very long, and imagining such a person is very difficult for those of us, most of us, who are not such persons.

Once the characters and the audience have come to realize the disturbing truth that there is very little if any difference between LA and its Chinatown, we also seem to be prompted to come to the disturbing conclusion that Jake may have reached: that there is nothing to be done. We will never understand enough of what we need to know to manage to live as life is meant to be lived. The suspicion that *this* is our fate is, I have suggested, indirectly created by the film's tonality, its sustaining a mood throughout of confusion, justifiable paranoia, and outcomes that do not at all match what was intended, and this keeps building an *atmosphere* of confusion and impotence among the principals; not something one can be said to "come to believe." There could be no determinate content to such a belief. The main feature of LA-Chinatown is that no one can figure out *what* is appropriate to believe about their situation.[19] It is heroic in a way, or anti-heroic, that Jake refuses Evelyn's offer to "drop the whole thing" after she drops the lawsuit, but it is his pressing forward on the matter that dooms all the principals to the final Chinatown scene. Evelyn does not understand why Jake has been hired to snoop around Hollis, but, veteran Cross that she is, she is willing to back off, do nothing, "forget it." This makes it unclear why she filed suit in the first place. That is certainly not going to help with the publicity problem. It is also not clear why she later hires Jake when he tells her that it is likely that someone murdered Hollis. If someone murdered Hollis, she must have a pretty good idea who it was. Jake's conclusion that Evelyn murdered her husband leads him to take several steps that finally reveal to Cross and to the police where Evelyn and Katherine are. The many close-ups of pained, confused, suspicious, and befuddled faces (especially Faye Dunaway's brilliant, intense, brittle, barely in-control performance) build this sense of futility and frustration among the participants and in the viewer. So it is appropriate that we too, the viewers of the film, are left so confused about such things as Cross's motives, the police's intentions, the fate of Katherine, or what it means to suggest that Jake should just "forget" about the fact that a vast water swindle is succeeding, and that a sexual predator has gotten his hands on a new young victim.

We have noted that the one thing one can say about Noah Cross and, we have to assume, the real world as he (and perhaps Polanski) sees it, the "dark world" meant in the same paranoid sense as "the dark state," is that the main feature prized in such a world is power, control, even over "the future." In general, this in itself is not surprising. Human beings cannot assure themselves and their kin of their own welfare if they are subject to the will of others who are primarily interested in *their* good. A degree of independence, or freedom from interference, is a feature of what makes a human life human. But so is the inescapable fact of our dependence on other persons. We are finite beings who depend on others for the achievement of our ends, and in a world of highly divided labor, this dependence is more and more unavoidable. The most sig-

---

19. Noah Cross can seem to know what is going on in "Chinatown" in all its dimensions, because he makes the rules. But he doesn't seem to understand his own motives, doesn't seem to understand anything about human attachments, and so ends up murdering his old partner, getting his daughter killed. In general, whatever *can* be made intelligible about Chinatown always comes "too late." We still don't understand what we need to understand when we need to.

nificant arena in which this tension must play out is the political world, and that means especially the state's assumption of a monopoly on the legitimate use of coercive violence. If it becomes more and more likely that there is no such thing as "the state," that it is an institution run for the benefit of an elite, that the police can be owned, that we cannot be assured there is a genuinely public sphere in which a collective commitment to a common rather than private good is possible, and instead that we can detect everywhere nothing but the play of private advantage, then it becomes more credible to think that the first condition in a genuine human life being led as distinctly human has not been met. (Stated in the terms of modern political thought: the state of nature must be exited. The "war of all against all" must cease.) So there is something almost pathetic in the final scene when Jake, of all people, encourages Evelyn, "Let the police handle this," a plaintive expression of hope that is immediately and, by this point, compellingly for most viewers, countered by Evelyn: "He *owns* the police."[20]

It would be comforting to think in more straightforward moral and legal terms. Cross is an evil man, and he is a criminal, guilty of tyrannical and unrestrained sexual predation and of corrupting to the point of unrecognizability the public world, making it "his." We might think: At least we could arrest and condemn him, all as a confident rejoinder to "Forget it, Jake; it's Chinatown" (fig. 5.4). But by this point, the film has created that undercurrent of futility, confusion, and paranoia, such that the title of the film should remind us yet again that the problem is not Cross, but "Chinatown." No one who thinks they have found the truth can do anything with such a truth. (Another pathos at the end; Jake screaming all the details of what he has discovered and no one is listening.) No one who thinks they have left Chinatown really has. Jake thought he had left it behind, but he finds himself staring at the same carnage he brought about there; "I was trying to keep someone from being hurt. I ended up making sure she was hurt."[21]

---

20. It is worth noting that, for all of what appear to be Escobar's good intentions, it is still the case that the police in the film end up "doing as little as possible," little that is of any use, at any rate.

21. I do not share what I take to be the "conclusion" the film seems to leave us with. I mean, I think that this *is* its conclusion, but I would prefer to take it as a prophetic warning about the world of late capitalism than as some now view climate change: it is real and it is already too late. There is nothing effective left to be done.

SIX

Love & Class in
Douglas Sirk's *All That Heaven Allows*

But what I fear, what even today one could grasp with one's hands if one felt
like grasping it, is that we modern men are pretty much on the same road; and
every time man starts to discover the extent to which he is playing a role and
the extent to which he *can* be an actor, he *becomes* an actor.

NIETZSCHE, *Gay Science*

I

One sure sign, among many others, that the great melodramas of Douglas
Sirk's time at Universal Studios (1952–59) might not be all they initially seem
is the immediate ambiguity of the titles of many of the most ambitious ones.
For example, the 1955 film *All That Heaven Allows* could suggest "Look at all
that heaven allows in its generosity." And it could mean "Be careful. This paltry
consolation or happiness, and this alone, is all that heaven allows." (In interviews Sirk made it clear he meant the latter, that for him, "heaven is stingy," and
he was amused that the studio gave it the former interpretation. They thought
it a brilliant, uplifting title.)[1] Many other films throughout his American career
have the same double character: *Imitation of Life*, *The Tarnished Angels*, *All I
Desire*, and *There's Always Tomorrow*.

This ambiguity is tied neatly to the famous irony of Sirk's melodramas.
The great ones succeed in narrating both a surface story and, like the titles, an
ironic counterpart. In Sirk's case, the films manage both to indulge the audi-

---

1. Cf. "Or take *All That Heaven Allows*. . . . The studio loved the title; they thought it meant
you could have everything you wanted. I meant it exactly the other way round. As far as I am
concerned, heaven is stingy" (Halliday 1971: 140). Sirk goes on to make similar points about
other titles.

ence's expectations for melodrama, often satisfying them, even as the technique and style exaggerate those conventions, sometimes garishly, often bordering on kitsch, and thereby also expose the self-deceit and fantasy thinking behind those very expectations, both on the part of the characters and the viewers — a crucial Sirkian connection, as we shall see.[2] This has all been much commented on since Sirk ascended to high auteur status among critics and historians of film, something that began first when the *Cahiers du Cinéma* crowd began writing enthusiastically about Sirk already in the mid-1950s,[3] and then more rapidly after the publication of some extraordinary interviews with Jon Halliday in 1971. Until this realization about his irony, the films can be seen, for many years were seen and are often still seen, as straightforward "weepies" or "women's pictures" or "soap operas" by audiences and critics and studio executives alike.

Now, *how* a cinematic style can suggest irony, how what we are shown can suggest how much is not shown, perhaps the contrary of what is shown, is a fascinating topic in itself, and there are many different examples of how it works: Nicholas Ray's *Johnny Guitar*, Josef von Sternberg's *The Scarlet Empress*, and Stanley Kubrick's *Barry Lyndon*, just to name three examples. One thing it does *not* mean, although it is often taken this way, is that what is not shown — or, we might say, "first-viewing" shown, displayed, narratively attended to — is not *seen*. As we shall see in discussing Ron's smirk, the ladies reading Thoreau, their mink coats, the clothes they wear, the décor in Ron's renovated mill — everything is all right there, on the surface, so obvious, so subject to assumptions about melodrama, that they are seen but not noticed.[4] Another thing invoking what irony need not mean is that an appeal is made to two different audiences for a film, a knowing or savvy viewer who sees the point of melodramatic excess, understands it as critique, and a mass audience not in on the joke. On this view, the sympathetic, compassionate, or angry emotional intensity of "mass audience" reactions to the film are based on blindness and gullibility.

2. Borrowing from his time as a theater director, Sirk deliberately created an anti-illusionistic mise-en-scène, even a Brechtian "distancing" effect, and so later, as a film director, rejected the realist conventions for film that were standard for Hollywood in its classic period.

3. It is generally accepted now, especially in film studies, that Sirk managed to create an artifice that made it possible "to comment on the world, as it comments on the means of representation" (Klinger 1994: 9). Klinger's book is indispensable on the various receptions of Sirk and on the significance of that variation.

4. For a fine discussion, see MacDowell 2018 and his book, 2016.

That is often the case, of course. For one thing there are hundreds of terrible, manipulative, thoughtless melodramas. But anyone, however "knowing," who has ever teared up at the closing scene of *Stella Dallas*, or who was stunned and ecstatic at the reappearance of the transformed Bette Davis in *Now, Voyager*, or who felt so terrible for Annie when she shows up at Sarah Jane's school with her rain boots in *Imitation of Life*, knows that this neat division between knowing and unknowing cannot be the whole story.[5] And whether Sirk, in those surprisingly forthcoming interview remarks about his own films, was simply riding the wave of interpretation begun by Truffaut and the *Cahiers* group and intensified by academic interests in the 1970s, or was expressing his own independent views, he did claim that the effect he wanted was a tight connection between genre, structure, and style, on the one hand, and "such themes as failure, impotence, and the impossibility of happiness," on the other,[6] all of which latter require interpretive work to be noticed, even if not "hidden." And to Sirk's list we can add "the precariousness of love in the American social world he depicts," my topic in the following. More specifically, our question will concern first the ways in which the policing of sexual conventions unavoidably intersects with the policing of class boundaries, and all of that will be shown to make the realization of anything like love, at least any love that is not strictly norm-bound, at best terribly fraught, at worst impossible. Second, the hope is to better understand the attractiveness in this kind of social world of the contrasting ideal of authenticity, or related phenomena like genuineness, nonconformism, and self-reliance in American life, and to

5. Klinger 1989 problematizes in a compelling way this facile distinction between a hip, critical audience (presumably immune to emotional involvement in favor of ideological critique) and a gullible mass audience, but she does so in favor of a reception theory approach that pretty much sacrifices the idea of an integral textual meaning. See her summary on p. 20. I don't see any reason why her point should take us that far. She concentrates on the original reception of melodrama in the period between 1950 and 1970, studio publicity, and the differing reactions of the East and West Coast, and what she has compiled and analyzed is fascinating. But Sirk clearly cares about these characters and wants their suffering and especially their aspiration to be felt, acknowledged, and somehow his films work on both the ironic and raw emotional level. What the mass audience is on to and what the studios understand is not wholly a matter of differing communities of interest.

6. This is Klinger's (1994: 9) summary of Halliday's introduction to *Sirk on Sirk*. I tend to give Sirk credit for his independence in the remarks, given his own involvement with avant-garde and left-wing theater in Germany, but nothing I say in the following depends on evidence from the interviews.

explore briefly the naïveté of a common understanding of that ideal and the consequences of that naïveté.[7] Finally, these two topics taken together will raise a different dimension of irony in Sirk's (or the film's) point of view with regard to the events and characters depicted. For just as melodrama is more than a classificatory genre, but rather a narrative form that frames and interrogates such issues as the meaning of suffering, conflict, the absence of satisfying love, and the lack of resolution of basic conflict (it is the modern analogue of tragedy in this respect), so irony is more than a literary or cinematic device. It is a kind of ethical stance as well, a way of bearing such contingency and frustration; a "right" way of coming to terms with our subjection to contingency and failure. (In this, too, it parallels and contrasts with the tragic point of view, as explored, for example, by Hegel and Nietzsche.) This immediately sounds like a recommendation for distance, non-involvement, playful, mere spectatorship.[8] But, as we shall see, that would be superficial and unresponsive to the unique play of irony in the film.

For it would be wrong to suggest that the films are best characterized simply as a negatively ironic depiction of such impossibility. In the first place, the irony is not mocking or sarcastic. Many of the characters are well-meaning and earnest, even if also fit subjects for an ironic treatment, for our never taking at face value what they say and do. That is, aside from the purely visual dimensions of irony—that dimension of artificial color, lighting, and close-up, overheated expressions of emotion—there is a more subtle dimension of such estranging irony. We see characters who sincerely avow what they believe, but who have no substantive idea about what in fact they are actually avowing, what the implications would be (the invocation of clichés—e.g. "to thine own self be true"—is a sure sign of this dim apprehension), or characters whose expressed self-understanding is clearly a manifestation of a self-ignorance;

---

7. This raises the issue of a properly political psychology. For a discussion of the nature of this problematic, see the introduction to Pippin 2010: 1–25.

8. Anticipating a reaction to this linking a discussion of Sirk to Hegel and other weighty thinkers, I note and echo Cavell's remark: "I am not insensitive, whatever defenses I may deploy, of an avenue of outrageousness in considering Hollywood films in the light, from time to time, of major works of thought" (1984: 8). For further discussion, see "Prologue: Film and Philosophy" in Pippin 2017: 1–12. Cavell's philosophical touchstone is Emerson, and to some extent Heidegger and Wittgenstein. In three books on film, my touchstone has been Hegel on the link between self-knowledge, agency, and knowledge of others. (Hegel is not particularly good on the issue of irony. He thinks it must erode the wholeheartedness and reconciliation that is the goal of modern societies in his account.)

again, even if also sincere and well-meaning.[9] Often we simply *see* that they don't understand what they say or feel, that they even confuse themselves. (Jane Wyman's remarkably controlled performance, and her consistent befuddled and confused looks throughout, are the prime examples.)[10] And such irony also functions as a kind of cinematic, reflective interrogation of just why, in that specific world of 1950s America, romantic love and even familial love should be so fraught. That is, a question can be raised by an ironic point of view if it can be cinematically shown that such relationships are fraught, unstable, and sometimes pathological even and especially when the characters refuse to see it that way or simply cannot afford to see it that way. Unknowingness posing as knowingness can be a rich subject for irony, especially if the irony is not patronizing or mocking, as it rarely is in Sirk's films. In *All That Heaven Allows*, Sirk's targeting of a distinctly *American* self-understanding as a sign of social pathology, and so a sign that he is elevating the thematic scope of the film to be far broader than a story about these individual characters, is signaled by his making Thoreau's *Walden* a central text in what seems like an American struggle for "authenticity."[11] It is this focus that, as we shall see, allows the film to be both a genuine melodrama and a reflective interrogation of the form itself as the form most appropriate to illuminating a certain sort of

9. Cf. the remarks in Comolli and Narboli 1971 about an ideology critique internal to a film, otherwise quite conventional: "An internal criticism is taking place which cracks the film apart at the seams. If one reads the film obliquely, looking for symptoms; if one looks beyond its apparent formal coherence, one can see that it is riddled with cracks; it is splitting under an internal tension which is simply not there in an ideologically innocuous film. . . . This is the case with many Hollywood films, for example, which while being completely integrated in the system and the ideology end up by partially dismantling the system from within" (33). See also Willemen 1971 on a "distance between the film and its narrative pretext" (276).

10. Such psychological states also greatly confuse any standard moral assessment of the characters. This confusion arises particularly in Robert Stack's performances in *Written on the Wind* and *The Tarnished Angels*, and in Lana Turner's somewhat willful (and so blamable) ignorance in *Imitation of Life*.

11. Sirk said, ". . . *Walden* by Thoreau. This is ultimately what the film was about . . ." (Halliday 1971: 113; keeping in mind again that interviews are performances). And "about" is equivocal. There is no reason to believe Sirk thinks that Mick, and in his more intuitive way, Ron, has properly understood *Walden*, and plenty of reasons to believe that what they have appropriated is a facile and self-deceived "lesson," one that is not unique to two individuals but broadly shared (whether anyone knows the text or not) in the current age in America. It is interesting that Sirk uses the same type of allusion to a serious general theme about America in *The Tarnished Angels* (1957). There the elevating "touchstone" for the film is Willa Cather's *My Ántonia* (not to mention that the film itself is a cinematic treatment of Faulkner's novel *Pylon*).

sociopolitical world, the modern, bourgeois American world.[12] In that sense, even the designation of melodrama is misleading, since the film is both an invocation of and an ironizing of melodrama as a sense-making form of human experience. They might all be called meta-melodramas.[13]

The characteristics we associate with film melodrama, a form traditionally taken to be a demotic or "low art" form, are feverishly intense suffering, overwhelmingly of women,[14] expressed around a great emotional crisis, usually involving romantic and/or familial love. In many stock melodramas, there are clearly identifiable villains and victims, but in many others, like Sirk's, there are not. That is, the suffering is caused not by villains but by those whom we love. This is all presented in a cinematic style in which such crises are given expression in a way that is hyperbolic, excessive, overwrought, obvious (particularly in the musical score), something that usually prompts complaint about manipulation, at least if the ironic estrangement from the movie world is not noticed. When we point to such excess, we mean that the expression of emotion in film melodrama goes beyond what we find "appropriate." In the simplest sense, this excess embarrasses us now.[15] As noted, in Sirk this excess emotionality is expressed by an unusually intense, bright color palette in sets and clothes (again anti-illusionistic), sometimes almost garish lighting, hypersharp, deep focus, frequent close-ups of such expressivity, a lush, romantic, and quite unsubtle sound track, and transparently phony, and even ominous (because phony), happy endings.

Of course, melodramas have a historical inflection too. Considered as a narrative style, or, as Peter Brooks has argued, "an imaginative mode" and an "inescapable dimension of modern consciousness,"[16] we associate their rise

---

12. There is a helpful account of the historical conditions, and the internal social contradictions so appropriate for melodramatic film, by Rodowick 1987: 268–80.

13. There is an important sense, explored by Cavell, that all Hollywood genres have a meta-generic dimension, that genres are not structures with features to which later instances "add on" features; that genres are occasions for reimagining the genre. See Cavell 1984: 28–30.

14. Predominantly but not exclusively. As Mulvey (1987: 76–77) points out in "Notes on Sirk and Melodrama," *Written on the Wind* and *The Tarnished Angels* stand out because of their treatment of male victims of patriarchal families in capitalism.

15. Philosophy can be melodramatic in this sense too, can elicit such reactions. Nietzsche does. Cavell says, speaking of the fervor in Wittgenstein's formulations, "If there is melodrama here, it is everywhere in the *Investigations*" (2013: 35–36).

16. Brooks 1976: vii. Thomas Elsaesser 1987, in probably the single most influential film studies article on melodrama, summarizes a discussion of melodrama as "a form which carried its own

to prominence first of all with drama, beginning with French drama in the early nineteenth century, with clear innocence and villainy, and unjust, horrific suffering, and then on into twentieth-century dramas of suffering like the plays of Eugene O'Neill. The more contemporary form of serialized literature started in the nineteenth century with such authors as Balzac and Dickens, and even, surprisingly with art treated now as high art, the novels of Henry James (such as *The Portrait of a Lady*) and Marcel Proust's *À la recherche du temps perdu*, a comic melodrama if there ever was one.[17] Dramatic opera also has to count as a paradigm instance of the genre. In film, much of the style obviously owes a debt to silent films, and their need to represent interiority expressively rather than verbally, but it is the historical location of melodrama that raises the most interesting questions. The modern melodramatic way of imagining human conflict seems responsive to a distinctive historical situation.[18] For one thing, in contrast to tragedy, melodramas are bourgeois not heroic dramas; are about the humdrum world of romance, work, family conflict, private wealth. Nothing of great ethical and political consequence hangs on the fate of characters, who, as Hegel puts it, are now mere individuals, not the expression of universal ethical forces like the state, or the public-private distinction, or the metaphysics of finitude and fate.[19] It could also be

---

values and already embodied its own significant content; it served as the literary equivalent of a particular, historical and socially conditioned mode of experience" (49).

17. Sirk (1977–78: 30) thought Shakespeare was a melodramatist.

18. An indispensable summary of the critical and historical literature on melodrama is Catherine Gledhill's "The Melodramatic Field: An Investigation," in her *Home Is Where the Heart Is* collection (1987: 5–39). She rightly notes early on a basic split in auteurist and "mise-en-scène" and neo-structuralist psychoanalytic and ideology critique approaches, and so the contrast between the author's intentions expressed in what is said and done, and meaning carried more visually and ideologically. Part of the attempt here is to begin to demonstrate why this is a false duality, itself based on the assumption of a Cartesian ideology of the private, self-ownership view of individual mindedness, versus some "outside" determination. The great value of Sirk's melodramas especially is to insist on the inseparability of the psychological (including reference to the author's "intentions" as well as in approaches to characters in the film) and the sociohistorical. But showing this without rendering the former a mere appearance or epiphenomenon of or reducible to the latter is the great dialectical difficulty.

19. See Hegel's remarks about modern drama in Hegel 1975: 1231. "But on the other hand the tragic denouement is also displayed as purely the effect of unfortunate circumstances and external accidents which might have turned out otherwise and produced a happy ending. In this case the sole spectacle offered to us is that the modern individual with the non-universal nature of his character, his circumstances, and the complications in which he is involved, is necessarily surrendered to the fragility of all that is mundane and must endure the fate of finitude."

that the overwrought and near-hysterical tone is responsive to the dizzying, often incomprehensibly rapid changes wrought by ever-accelerating modernization itself, with characters living and suffering in unique and demanding situations, equipped only with assumptions and expectations at home in an era now long gone and irrelevant. (This is certainly the case in James and Proust.) Or characters over-invest so much and so desperately in romantic and familial love because of the ever more apparent banality, repetitiveness, and enormous pressure for conformism in the new form of capitalist life. The excess is a form of desperation. (If we are now unresponsive, it may not be because we are cooler or hipper, but because such desperate resistance has gone dead; the intense yearning has been co-opted. Perhaps that is the mark of being cooler and hipper.) One possible explanation for the excess and hysteria could stem from characters expecting far too much of romantic and familial love, the only arenas available for any individual expressiveness genuinely one's own, even if inevitably disappointed. (That inevitable disappointment is our theme below but, again, Sirk's apparent pessimism about friendship and love is deeply historical and locally inflected, as any interrogation of friendship and love should be. Assumptions about gender roles, competition, dependence, and loyalty are all always located by him in a particular social world and class; in this film and many others, in upper-middle-class well-educated America.)[20]

But in Sirk the melodramatic imagination, while linked to such responses as these, has another function too. Expressed simply and in a way often discussed, the social worlds depicted in many of Sirk's melodramas are often all pretense, theater, wholly false, conformist role-playing phoniness.[21] This means, of course, that they are often simply hypocritical, but the important players often seem to believe the theater and see none of their own falseness. The garishness of Sirk's presentation of such worlds always appears to suggest

20. Another way of understanding cinematic melodrama is Hitchcock's (1937) in an early piece: "In the cinema a melodramatic film is one based on a series of sensational incidents. So melodrama, you must admit, had been and is the backbone and lifeblood of cinema." He goes on to say that direct realism would not work for cinema (ordinary events are too banal), and the extraordinary that he shoots for might be called "ultra-realism." He adds that anyone who wants to understand the psychology of mass audiences and what will work, grab their attention, should study daily newspaper editors. "If film-makers understood the public as newspapers do they might hit the mark more often."
21. There is a good discussion of "pretending" as "the main attribute of American middle-class life" in Rushton 2007: 1.

that this world, a clearly artificial world—no natural colors look like the ones we see—a world presented as if a bright ad in a slick magazine, or a television show in early color, is some sort of projection of *the characters' own sense of themselves,* how *they* see themselves, posed with an intensity that intimates a lingering anxiety and so defensiveness about authenticity, genuine individuality, or self-realization, and in the majority of cases, about the possibility of love in such a world. (We shall return to this issue below; this projective feature could be called the cinematic equivalent of what is "free indirect discourse" in literature, a third-person visual narration that describes, or here depicts, as if from a first-person consciousness.) Here we have a projection of a staged, theatrical phoniness, unaware of itself as such. That is a remarkable technical achievement.[22]

What also distinguishes melodramas by Sirk is a feature one certainly finds in other melodramas (for example, some by Vincente Minnelli and Max Ophüls and George Stevens, and a few by the Dardenne brothers like *Lorna's Silence* and *The Unknown Girl*): the establishment of a connection between that element prominent in all melodrama, the suffering of women, with a social critique of that common world; a critique accomplished simply by its ironic, distanced depiction, as a context within which that suffering is both more intelligible, more painful, and almost inevitable. Sirk's focus on what are clearly regarded as the pathologies of Eisenhower's 1950s America is essential to understanding the enormous attractiveness of the promise of love, both romantic and familial, and for Sirk its inevitable failure—a failure at the intimate level shown as to be expected in such a social world, and often masked in self-deceit (as in *Heaven's* bizarre ending). This would then mean that Sirk's critique of the smugness, mutual surveillance, and policing by a community's residents, their conformism and consumerism, which now almost everyone sees in his films, is also connected to what can look like a private redemption *from* such vapidity (a contrasting "genuineness"), but which is infected with the same pathology it thinks of itself as escaping. The vehicle for the possibility of such a delusion is self-deceit, and his audiences can congratulate

---

22. Of course this is not the only effect of such style. Elsaesser (1987, 52) is surely right that the meaning of what we see in family film melodramas and especially in Sirk is to a great degree a matter of décor, lighting, music, camera movement, composition of frame, color and gesture. But seeing such matters as also an analogue of such free indirect discourse helps destabilize the dualism mentioned above in note 18.

themselves for seeing through the town's hypocrisy (they couldn't possibly miss it; the townspeople are portrayed in very broad, caricature-like strokes), and can want so much to believe in such "havens" as love and family, that the ironic treatment of the latter can be much harder to see, and the implications for human happiness are so pessimistic that audiences don't want to see the falseness in what seems to the characters (and the audience) to be true love. The evidence is strong that most of Sirk's audiences and early critics repeat this phony idealization, and just as willfully "look away," as do many of the characters supposedly "in love." This is paradigmatically the case in *All That Heaven Allows*. But we need to turn to the details of the film to understand how this works.

II

As opposed to other fast-paced Sirk films like *Written on the Wind* and *Imitation of Life*, not much actually happens in *All That Heaven Allows*. It seems reasonable to divide the film into four "acts," as it were. In the first act, we are introduced to the small New England town where the action occurs, Stoningham, clearly a very well-off bedroom community likely near New York, and already somewhat of a parody of "small town" or "village" America.[23] The film begins with an aerial shot, a supervisory or monitoring position from a church tower, although religion is never mentioned in the film. There is no priest or minister (that role has been taken over by the doctor), and it is not until very late in the film that we see a cross on the top of the tower, as if to signal its insignificance. We meet right away the main players, Cary Scott (Jane Wyman), a widow with two grown children off at college. (The son comes home on the weekends from Princeton; her daughter goes to Columbia.) Wyman was thirty-eight when the film appeared, but she is styled to look a few years older, and her circle of friends look older. That the romance begins in autumn, with leaves falling off trees, is no doubt her image of her "last chance" at erotic, not companionate love, a first example of the way the film projects a character's self-understanding, and in this case her own somewhat ironic sense of herself. And there is that "smoldering fire" visible as we approach her house (fig. 6.1).

23. Get a new job, move to a small town, and you, too, can be Thoreau. See Harvey 2001: 74. The two Thoreauvians in the film, Ron and Mick, seem to assume that no urban job can be an authentic one, and that unless one lives in a village and has some job connected with the commodification of nature, one is doomed to falseness.

The children are Kay (Gloria Talbott) and the truly odious Ned (William Reynolds). There is Cary's love interest, Ron Kirby (Rock Hudson), a local gardener and beginning tree farmer, and assorted townsfolk: Cary's best friend Sara Warren (Agnes Moorehead), the town gossip with the apposite name of Mona Plash (Jacqueline de Wit), and a pleasant-enough bore named Harvey (Conrad Nagel), who, everyone seems to assume, will one day or another end up marrying Cary. In this act, Cary and Ron meet and there is some sort of spark between them, despite the fact (or perhaps because of it) that Cary is older than Ron, a widow with grown children. The source of the obvious wealth in the community is not acknowledged, not even spoken of by anyone.

In the second act, Cary and Ron grow very quickly much closer, and a real romance begins. Cary discovers that Ron thinks of himself as a nonconformist, a free spirit whose friend Mick reads Thoreau. ("Mick's bible" and, we assume, Ron's as well.)[24] It is hard to miss the irony of Cary, in a somewhat bewildered tone, reading the "quiet desperation passage." Two Hollywood movie stars, highly styled and made-up, read approvingly about silent despair and independence of mind (fig. 6.2).[25]

We learn that Ron has somewhat bohemian friends (at least by the rigidly middle-class attitudes of the town and, more importantly, in their own eyes) and will soon stop gardening and working for the townsfolk and open his own tree farm. He lives in his greenhouse and has a confident but sometimes smug and self-satisfied air about him (the first signs of trouble with this character, as we shall see). Cary seems quite taken by Ron, although it is not clear how much of that has to do with his independent ideas or the sexual charge she clearly feels (for her, always somewhat bewilderingly) when she is first around him. She does not actually embrace his Thoreauvian philosophy and even at one point assumes he will live in her old house, that her life will go on as before with Ron added on. However, we had already heard some complaints from her

24. We are told that Ron doesn't have to read the book; he already lives it. But as we shall see, that is not quite right. He not only lives it, he preaches it, and rather self-righteously too.
25. Harvey 2001: 374. The theme of such independence is introduced in an already qualified way. Alida says that Mick was very unhappy working in the city and their marriage almost split up because of his unhappiness. They moved here to live their Thoreauvian life and all is now well. She never says whether *she* was unhappy in New York, whether she wanted this sort of life, is happier here, etc. While she seems happy enough, her life is a kind of "imitation of life," of Mick's life. The shadow of the war, mentioned a few times (Mick and Ron were wartime buddies), hangs over the narrative too; as if that experience intensifies the need for finding something authentic and genuine in life.

about the issue of convention and its restrictions. When discussing with her daughter the ancient Egyptian custom of burying the wife alive with the dead husband in his tomb, her daughter says that we don't do that anymore, and Cary says sardonically, "At least not in Egypt."[26] This act is the most complicated and involves contrasting evening parties, at the country club and among Ron's happy-go-lucky friends. Of major importance is an old mill near Ron's greenhouse that Cary encourages him to renovate (figs. 6.3 and 6.4). (The relevance of an aging, run-down building, to be renovated by Ron's loving attention, to their romance is not subtle. There is also a Wedgewood teapot, broken, to be lovingly repaired by Ron, which also fills such a romantic function.) Ron eventually proposes, and after several minutes of terrified deliberation, Cary accepts. The couple announce their engagement to the children and to Sara, and all hell breaks loose.

The third act documents this chaos. The children are appalled, and immediately reject the choice of Ron as unworthy of their father's memory and as an invitation to cruel gossip. ("People will say this all started before father died.") Cary's best friend is gentler but still tells her she is making a very bad mistake. The full supervisorial and disciplining techniques in the town for conforming behavior to the norm are called into play. The chief weapons are gossip and catty remarks and Cary's manipulative, self-centered, and self-deceived children. On the son's part, it rises to a promise to break with his mother forever and never return. Note the extraordinary cold-blue palette of that scene (fig. 6.5) and the contrast with the scene with her daughter, which is much more emotional and pained, as she pleads with her mother, in a kind of emotional blackmail, not to marry (fig. 6.6).[27]

The cruelty and insensitivity of the children are the most dramatic and shocking aspects of this part of the movie. (Cary somehow does not ever manage to see clearly the selfishness and thoughtlessness of her children.) Feeble efforts to dress Ron up like a country club type (again Cary is clueless about what she is asking Ron to do, how impossible the theatrical role is that she has assigned him)[28] and to introduce him to that world are catastrophic failures,

26. Later in the film, this fate is suggested by a scene after the breakup that shows Cary behind a window, as if behind bars, as if trapped by them, staring out and weeping, and in that only image where she looks directly at her image, she seems trapped *inside* the television set purchased for her at Christmas by her children, as if, bizarrely, a husband substitute.

27. See the discussion in Mercer and Shingler 2004: 56, 63.

28. See Camper 1971: "In a sense, then, all characters in Sirk are totally blind, surrounded as they are, not by real things but by falseness. There is no question of seeing 'reality' on any level

but not because Ron is standoffish or explicitly judgmental, but because of the thoughtlessness and sarcasm of the townsfolk. Cary finally cannot stand the pressure, caves in, and wants to wait a while to marry. Ron refuses and they break up.

In the fourth act, we see that they are both miserable apart, but each seems too proud to compromise. The break in the stalemate comes, tellingly, from Cary's doctor, a new sort of authority in this world, whom she had gone to see about her general lethargy and headaches. His medical advice is simple, "Marry him, Cary." What's wrong with the repression the town demands is not, he assumes, that it is unjust, conformist, intolerant, or unfair, but simply that it is making Cary sick.[29] This is decisive for Cary, although her vision of the kind of life her children want her to lead, married to the sexless Howard and watching endless hours of television, has clearly already shaken her up as well.

She rushes to Ron's renovated mill but he is out hunting, and she loses her nerve anyway and does not knock. (This is quite an important fact that most viewers, eager for a stereotypical happy ending, can easily miss; can want to miss. It signals in effect that there can be no reconciliation until, as we shall see, Ron is in some sense broken, weakened, brought to the ground.) Ron is returning home, sees her, and frantically tries to signal to her (no hesitation on his part), falling off a high ledge in the process and knocking himself unconscious, seriously injuring himself. In the last scene, as he recovers, they seem reunited, but we recall that she was still afraid to reconcile, and we see an ending that is quite complexly ambiguous. We will look closely at the scene later.

III

I have mentioned that the portrayal of the world of the town of Stoningham is presented in a way that is unmistakably ironic and, in that way, quite critical. The veneer of civility and friendliness is thin. This already suggests the dual nature of the American pathology that Sirk is examining. It is *both* an

---

or attaining any genuine understanding since such concepts are completely excluded by the formal qualities of Sirk's images" (48).

29. The doctor asks: "Do you expect me to give a prescription for life?" This is obviously a rhetorical question, to which the answer is supposed to be no. But he then proceeds to do exactly that: give her a life prescription. The equivalent existential problem for Ron after the breakup is that he "can't shoot straight," and so is "good for nothing." This suggests he can't really be a man occupying the position of a patriarchal relation to Cary. As he probably sees it, he was dumped by her, and so it would be unmanly to make the first move.

anxiety-fueled, defensive, and often ruthless and sadistic obsession with sexual repression and conformism, *as well as* a compensatory Thoreauvian fantasy of self-sufficiency and independence, and the two are clearly linked. That is, Sirk seems to be presenting the love affair as a supposed brave rejection of such conformism, and as embodying the Thoreauvian philosophy behind the rejection, but there is, in the details of the affair, a much more subtle, but equally deep irony, and I want now to develop that basic point, a point I take to concern not just Ron and his friends, but an American self-understanding in general, captured at its best and worst in a facile understanding of Thoreau. This is so, although establishing it with any confidence would require a look at several other Sirk films.[30] The full claim would be that Sirk treats America's deepest understanding of itself, its self-narration, as a kind of melodrama. That is, if there is such a thing as an American imaginary (and there is not much else that could account for a social bond in a nation-state with very little in the way of nation), that imaginary has its own complex psychological roots and dynamics, and essentially involves some collectively understood self-narration; a whence-and-whither structure that informs everything from acceptable social behavior (including marriage norms) and the norms of civility to explicit political discourse. Perhaps it would be safer to say that at least one significant version of such a collective self-understanding is melodramatic, Sirk's. Cinematically, it can also be heroic and so epic, as in Westerns; romantic, as in many musicals; and tragic, as in the depiction of the fate of postwar urban life in film noirs.[31] This is a large topic, but a national self-conception

---

30. There is almost always some indication in Sirk's films of some specific barrier, impediment, to a more humane life of social solidarity and sensitivity. Underneath what the ironic treatment reveals, there is something to be recovered, remembered. In this film the barrier is some sort of anxiety about sexual and class boundaries, treated as linked. In *Imitation of Life*, it is the fantasy of fame or the dominance of celebrity culture (also treated with great pathos in *All I Desire*). In *Written on the Wind*, it is a fantasy about masculinity and status. In *The Tarnished Angels*, an airplane race figures the effects of obsessive competitiveness. In *There's Always Tomorrow*, it is the deadening habits of domesticity itself.

31. For a fuller account of the latter, see Pippin 2012. The ultimate philosophical goal of such an approach is to show the poverty of any social or political philosophy—that is, any evaluation of the organized use of power by one group against others, with a claim to legitimacy—that does not take into account the individual and collective psychological dimensions of allegiance and especially the malformations or even pathologies typically produced in the societal mechanisms used to insure the internalization of such allegiance; here by the American family in its reproduction of the repressive values assumed to be necessary for order and predictability in Eisenhower's America in the 1950s.

as virtuous and authentic (liberated from a corrupt and dissembling Europe) under attack and damaged and misunderstood just because of those virtues, resulting in the typical excess of the melodramatic imagination: paranoia, either a fantasy of grandiosity and triumph, or a paranoia of persecution by hidden conspiratorial forces, an overheated, excessively emotional political rhetoric, wishful and fantasy thinking, an exaggerated sanctification of the family, and so a mistrust of the public or urban sphere, are not unfamiliar to any American, especially now.[32]

In the first act, as I've called it, the important scenes are the first meeting, Cary's coded reaction to it, and her tentative steps toward a romance. When her friend cancels lunch, Cary, on an apparent impulse, invites her gardener, Ron, to that prepared lunch. He accepts a couple of dinner rolls, and she asks him polite questions about tree farming (playing in effect "the clueless female"). The sound track and his story about the Chinese tree tell us there is more going on than a tree lecture, and we see her disappointment flash quickly across her face when Ron has to leave. Throughout, as here, Ron is associated with nature, and so the naturalness of Cary's aroused desire, something she will never quite be able to admit to herself in that form.

We also see in the opening scenes an example of a frequent technique in the film, one much commented on in analyses of Sirk: the use of mirrors to suggest the reflective status of the film itself. We see not only the movie world, we see (or we should see) that it is represented in a way, or we see ourselves seeing in such a distinct way (the cinematic irony has the same effect). The technique also opens the question of whether and if so how the characters see not just their world but how they are taking, imagining that world to be. So we see the chance for, and the lack of, reflection on the part of someone. Cary sits in front of mirrors a few times, but in the scene depicted here and in all the others in front of mirrors, she never looks directly at herself in them (fig. 6.7).

She fits in a sense into Cavell's category of "melodramas of the unknown women,"[33] although in this case, she is profoundly unknown to herself. The

32. These are characteristics of melodrama (which he calls a "version of experience") in Heilman 1968, although not with respect to films, and never with respect to national character.
33. Cavell 1996. I mean it conforms to Cavell's understanding in the following sense. As Cavell puts it, in some melodramas, the woman wants both to know, and that means that she seeks an education, senses there is something she must learn, and especially wants to be known, to be properly acknowledged as separate and independent in her own right. But Cary's inchoate desire to be educated anew in a way of life she is intrigued by and somewhat afraid of (a

one time she does see herself, it is her reflection in the new TV screen, and she sees in effect a vision of the future her children want to consign her to, the modern equivalent of walling the woman up with the dead husband (fig. 6.8).

The effect of this first encounter is Cary's choice of a bright red dress to go to the country club party, a signal of a kind of sexual awakening that is lost on no one. Notice the red scarf on the daughter, as if she is announcing she is on the verge of being sexually active. In this scene we see as well an extraordinarily explicit acting out of Ned's Oedipal interest in his mother's sexuality (fig. 6.9). I mention Kay and the scarf, because when she announces her own engagement, she announces her full awakening in an identical fashion (although she conforms to her brother's anxiety about low-cut dresses) (fig. 6.10).

The fact that Kay naively tries to explain to her mother the Oedipal complex, rather clumsily suggesting out loud that Ned desires his mother sexually and is jealous of Harvey as a rival, does not seem to be incidental. For the nature of Ron's interest in Cary, which is not clear on the surface, could easily be understood as Oedipal, a love for a mother figure, and so correspondingly Cary's interest in Ron could be vaguely and at least symbolically incestuous. (It is striking that there is no mention at all of Ron's mother. People compliment Ron on his father, but it is as if the mother never existed, and she may still be alive. Such an absence cannot be unrelated to his desire for Cary.)[34] This may have something to do with the town's anxiety about Cary and Ron. Their assumption seems to be that there is something "unnatural" about their love, that something about the basic law that distinguishes and rules social

---

life in which she could freely realize her romantic desire) is frustrated. In this sense, Ron is a phony educator, partly because he plays the role of educator so theatrically, and as if he does not need to be educated himself. (Although he inches toward such a realization by trying to fashion a home that Cary will understand and love, a home that can be for both of them.) He is not, though, the Thoreauvian hero he thinks he is, but a commercial tree farmer, and he is uncompromising and dogmatic (not that these traits are completely absent in Thoreau himself). He is not exempt, no one is, from the demands of a ruthless competitive capitalism. It—together with bank loans, competition with other farmers, crop failures, and so forth—is just offstage, as is so much of his life. So she is intrigued by a fantasy Ron has of himself, one that turns out to be a smug, self-satisfied self-image.

34. The only time we hear Ron express why he is attracted to Cary, it is in response to Cary's questioning why he and Mick had been looking at her and laughing when they first met. Ron tells her that he told Mick she had the finest pair of legs he has ever seen. (How would he know, in those dresses?) He is not in the slightest embarrassed at being caught in such locker room banter with his friend, and Cary silently accepts the objectifying compliment, but it is clear that Sirk is making a point about Ron's relation to women.

order, the prohibition against incest, is at stake. (It is also quite striking that while it would be obvious in 1955 that, given Cary's age, there would be almost no chance of children, this issue never comes up, as if it is obvious both that children are out of the question and that Ron feels no qualms about what he is "giving up.")[35] Sirk also takes care to "point out" cinematically that this anxiety is not only irrational (there is no literal or even implicit actual incestuous desire, just a faint reminder of its prohibition), but strictly gendered as well. He inserts a small subplot in which an older man in Stoningham, Tom Allenby, is going to marry a woman young enough to be his daughter, a woman Sara calls "that moron Jo-Ann," who "bagged" Tom. In that case Sara, who has just been so censorious, is *throwing them a party*, the party at which the attempt to "introduce" the class invader, Ron, fails so miserably.

The first act's emphasis on the banality and self-satisfaction of the country club set well prepares us for Cary's dive into romance, her escape. When they first kiss, however, we begin to notice (probably on a second or third viewing) something uncomfortable about Ron. The air of confidence and masculinity (of a sort) that clearly attracts Cary also borders on and sometimes falls into smugness and condescension, another kind of policing of Cary. Ron appears to be smirking with self-satisfaction. And the bewildered expression on Cary's face, also something we have seen and will see throughout, is telling (figs. 6.11 and 6.12).

Ron's smugness continues when they return home. When she tries to beg off seeing him again when he returns from a trip, we see him patronizingly insist, "I'll see you," again with the smirk. The fact that Rock Hudson is so huge compared to Jane Wyman helps sustain this rather ominous mood, and in all their close scenes together, he looms over her, often with that smirk. And throughout, their embraces and kisses are, while intimate, oddly passionless, even a bit sexless. (It cannot be incidental to making *Walden* a kind of intellectual touchstone in the film, that Thoreau's world is also sexless.) Cary doesn't smile much, always appears stunned and confused rather than liberated and happy.[36]

---

35. As with Oedipus, the prospect of generating children (having generated children) with one's mother is horrific to contemplate, subverting both the family and political life. It could be said to be an attempt to return to and to become one's own origin, the progenitor of oneself, in the ultimate act of autonomy, autochthony. I am grateful to Glenn Most and Ben Jeffery for an exchange about this issue.

36. Harvey 2001: 375–76. Note also Harvey's reports of Sirk's impatience with "sentimentality," a trait that should surprise the early critics of his melodramas.

The contrast between the two evening parties, a raucous celebration, full of genuine good feeling with Ron's friends, and the staid, quiet, gossipy, and phony country club party and Sara's reception could not be clearer (figs. 6.13 and 6.14). And, apart from the decidedly upper-middle-class look of Mick's apartment and Alida's clothes, that contrast is subject to no ironic distancing. Cary is as genuinely happy at Ron's party as we ever see her, and there is no question that the film tilts sympathetically toward Ron and his friends and their Thoreauvian ideals.[37] But Cary's capacity to find happiness is not the same thing as *marrying* Ron, crossing lines of both class and sex conventions, marrying not only "her gardener" but also someone much younger. Marrying Ron (as opposed specially to marrying Harvey) is like shouting to everyone that she is still capable of sexual desire and romantic attachment. But when Ron asks her to marry him, it is clear she has not thought that far ahead and when she does, she is terrified. Cary's reaction is predictably panicked, but she is also asking for help from Ron in imagining a new life, concerns about *her* that he is indifferent to, insisting simply that she can do whatever she wants to do. This is all the language of authenticity and genuineness in a life, as the Thoreauvian idea reemerges, but she is making the plausible point that "being herself" will also, must, carry along in its wake many other people, her children, her close friends. She seems to realize that there might be no compromise allowed between the bourgeois world and the art-, nature-, and artisan-oriented crowd she will join and that she will be "turning her back on everything she knows." Cary initially rejects the idea, goes to leave, breaks the Wedgewood teapot, as she breaks Ron's heart (the breakage seems to help her realize this),[38] weakens at the door, and they reconcile.

37. There is an extremely subtle, almost invisible, indication of the persistence of class and ethnic lines being maintained in the group. When we see Cary introduced to Manuel and his family at this party, we see a lovely young girl, his daughter Marguerita. Cary, who has already been taken aback by the presence of what she takes to be an obvious and far too formidable rival, the Andersons' niece, Mary Ann, completely ignores Marguerita. But Sirk always keeps Marguerita in the background or at the edge of the frame in the party scenes, and clearly directs her to look glum, sullen, and even angry throughout, presumably that the handsome bachelor Ron is ignoring her in favor of a much older woman. (She is the only one at the party who never smiles or gets into the swing of things.) It is as if she knows that a Latina woman could never have a chance with Ron (Mary Ann is always flirting with him), and Cary seems to take that for granted too.
38. Another subtle mark of the fate of their relationship: the precious teapot, which has been identified with Cary's world, is broken so badly that it can never be repaired. It would be a different film altogether if the final scene had included a shot of it fully repaired.

As they come closer to making their engagement public, Sirk makes a point about the gendered nature of the enforcement of class and sexual boundaries; that is, the enforcement falls heavily on the woman, not the man, and the very definition of genuineness Ron imagines for himself is an option only for men. Ron continually asks her not to care about what people think, but it never seems to dawn on him that he gives no quarter in demanding that she think like him; in effect, that it is "my way or the highway." It simply means, he says, "being a man." We see Cary hesitate and then accept the characterization, that being herself, Ron's great ideal, will mean "being a man," not at all being herself. (Earlier in the film, Cary had seemed to us as a woman with an ironic dimension, as when she says, "At least not in Egypt," and in the way she talks about Harvey. She seems now to be imitating Ron's self-seriousness, and Ron of course is totally without irony. This issue will return in the last section.)

We see this even more dramatically through the bourgeois toleration of a predatory male in their midst, Howard Hoffer, who is guilty of far worse than marrying someone younger. (We are thereby also reminded that the town's reaction would very likely not occur, in fact does not occur, when the gender roles are reversed. As noted earlier, the party at Sara's is in celebration of just such a December-May marriage.) Howard clearly assumes that Cary, by, in his eyes, trumpeting to the world that she is still interested in sex, has opened the door to him, and, drunk and disorderly, he ruins the reception at which Ron was supposed to have been introduced to Cary's world.

Cary's children turn out to be petulant, whining self-involved brats, who do what they can to express disgust at the prospect of their mother's marriage. Ned, like Howard, like everyone, assumes and has the gall to say to his own mother that she is interested only in a "set of muscles," or that she is giving in to brute animal lust, and that if she goes through with it, he will never visit her again. (There is never a full reconciliation scene with her children, and after bemoaning the loss of their familial home, the two will later abandon it anyway and disappear from the film. They exit unredeemed and unredeemable.)[39] Finally Cary succumbs to the pressure and tries to convince Ron to wait, to move into her house and to live in her world. Ron refuses, and we then see

---

39. There is a feeble apology from Kay, when she announces her own marriage and seems to have some very dim awareness of how much pain she has caused her mother, but Cary reiterates that it is "too late," and there is no warm reconciliation. The scene maintains a tonality of sadness.

two firsts: Cary exercising some real independence and Ron losing that facade of self-confidence that had so often slipped into self-satisfaction (fig. 6.15).

The children return for Christmas (their condition having been met), and everything has changed. They pressured their mother to give up her fiancé, but then, it turns out, they are moving away and urge Cary to sell the very house Ned had proclaimed so sacred to the family tradition. And they buy her a TV set so she won't be lonely, perhaps the bitterest irony in a film full of irony. As noted above, this is clearly meant to be the modern version of walling the widow up in the tomb.

The reconciliation scene with Ron is prepared for by two scenes that are telling. In Ron's case, we return to a reminder about gender and power in both worlds, Ron's and Cary's, and in Cary's, as noted, her initiative is a matter of health, as "prescribed" by her doctor. In Ron's, the jocular Mick tells Ron that women do not want to make up their own mind; they want a man to make up their minds for them (so much for "to thine own self be true"), and he encourages Ron to do so.

Cary's doctor tells her, insightfully, that she was ready for a love affair, not love. And we see that much of Cary's hesitation has had to do with her anxiety about being older. She has been secretly worried since Mick's party that Alida's blond, young, attractive cousin would be hard for Ron to resist and that he must have taken up with her. When she finds out the cousin is marrying someone else, her inner hesitation is resolved and she drives out to the mill, but again her resolve falters and she drives away without knocking. Ron sees this and tries to call out to her, but loses his footing and suffers a bad fall, is seriously injured. (As noted earlier, given that she turns away from the door, it is crucial that any reconciliation seems therefore to *require* Ron's fall and injury.) This begins the final scene in the film.

Several things are visually important in the last scene. First the mill has been made over to look like what James Harvey has called an extreme version of *Better Homes and Gardens*, Cary's world, only glossier and pushed "to almost lunatic extremes of elaboration and rich deadness—in color."[40] The second is that the familiar visual geometry of Ron looming over Cary is reversed, as Cary is now overlooking him, injured, broken in effect, and in bed, passive

40. Harvey 2001: 374. As noted earlier, this is a little extreme. Ron had been content in his greenhouse, and he is clearly trying to appoint the new space with taste, in some sense a tastefulness he thinks Cary should recognize. And she does; that it was all made over "with love."

(fig. 6.16). It is very tempting to think that this reversal represents not only what makes possible the reconciliation (that Cary now has the "upper" hand, with the injured Ron "diminished") but that their future will now *maintain* such a relationship. Their new world will still have upper-middle-class types like Mick and Alida in it, and the redecorating of the mill means a reduplication of Cary's old world, with some idea of their own authenticity projected on it all. The romance had begun in autumn and is now resolved in some way or other in the dead of winter. This either presages that spring will soon arrive, or that the lack of warmth and the somewhat fraught sexual passion we had seen in their scenes together figures their romantic fate together. All the signs point to the latter. And a deer we had seen before returns. Previously it had seemed to figure Ron's "nourishing" Cary's need for love, her dependence on him, but now it seems not to figure as Cary's dependence on Ron, but the reverse, and somehow Sirk has managed to have the deer seem confused and stunned a bit, as if to remind us that Ron has no idea what he is in for, will be in the same state for some time.[41] Nothing we have seen suggests that the town will change, or even that Cary will change very much. What looks like the reunion of two now independent, self-reliant souls is simply one more way of compromising with the requirements of bourgeois life. Ron has been diminished in power and authority, will continue to turn trees into commodities, and Cary, we expect, will manage to find a way, most likely through self-deceit, to imagine that what they do together will be authentic and their own, even as it reproduces the norms that we have seen enforced throughout.

Much of the dialogue and Ron's injury itself seem tinged with irony. The doctor, in telling Cary that Ron's recovery will take time, that he will need her help, that it will last a while, seems just as much to be describing what Ron will face in hitching himself to a well-meaning but still very conventional woman, how much "help" he will need in getting over his "injury," recovering from his

---

41. Harvey (2001: 376) notes that the deer seems trapped between the picture window and the painted landscape behind it. Schatz (1981: 251) also notes the irony that the "alternate" lifestyle of Mick and Alida (apparently the model for Ron's renovation) is hardly a departure from Cary's upper-middle-class style. One might also add that the notion of the deer trapped could parallel the different way nature is manifest after picture windows became part of American architecture: framed, almost posed, and hardly any longer nature as it meant to Thoreau. And even in Thoreau, once nature *is taken up* as significant and "for us," it is already no longer mere nature. This parallels the authenticity point made here. I am indebted to Tom Gunning for a discussion about this issue.

"broken" status. (This "needing help" scene mirrors an earlier one after the proposal when Ron also pleads that he will need help adjusting.) If they are to reunite, it will at least at the outset be with Cary in a conventional role, nurse and mother. What will happen when Ron is well is left unclear. Cary had been persuaded and perhaps a bit intimidated by Ron into marrying him; she had been bullied out of marrying him by her children; she had been embarrassed into reconciling with him by the doctor, only to fail at the last minute; and she is now moved by concern and pity to nurse him back to health, but we sense no fundamental transformation or new resolve. There is now nothing left of her "red dress" announcement of sexual desire and availability, something that may make their relationship much more acceptable in town, and so to Cary as well.[42] And Ron, of course, cannot act on Mick's advice either, "to make up Cary's mind for her." All he could do to bring this about was fall off a cliff. This kind of stalemate is what we should expect given Sirk's sentiments about the American bourgeoisie, that their "homes are prisons," and that "they are imprisoned even by the tastes of the society in which they live."[43] In the final scene, we note at the very end the effect of the deer as a near-perfect embodiment of Sirk's unique version of cinematic irony. Somehow the poor confused deer figures for us what has become of the self-consciously virile, "my way or the highway" Ron (fig. 6.17).

IV

The film ends, leaving us with two general issues raised. I mentioned at the beginning that the film establishes some sort of connection between the anxious policing of class boundaries and the policing of sexual conventions. As I have been noting, it is unsurprising that we should find explorations of this intersection in so many melodramas. So many deal with the two elemental desires of modern bourgeois life: the desire to love and be loved, and the desire for success, material security, on the one hand, and some measure of status, standing, respect, on the other. There is little reason to believe that these desires sit easily with each other, something starkly manifest in films like *Stella Dallas* (1937), *Caught* (1949), *A Place in the Sun* (1951), *Ruby Gentry* (1952), *All*

42. See Mulvey's (1987: 79) apposite summation of where Cary finds herself.
43. Quoted in Schatz 1981: 253.

That Heaven Allows (1955), and *Imitation of Life* (1959). But beyond this, by the enforcing of such conformism, I also mean to refer to a conformism familiar in nineteenth- and twentieth-century fiction; one could call it "Girardian."[44] In the absence of any substantive common value, we anxiously watch each other for signs of what is worth wanting, and take some comfort in following the lead of "most people," or "most people in our social class," for signs of what ought to be done, or to be thought or to be desired. If we were to question that, we would be in uncharted waters, a source of great anxiety because we sense we would have lost all standards. Another aspect of the general anxiety is obvious. While class differences rest on real inequality, on money and the access to power that it provides, the idea of class as a kind of exclusionary norm, or the idea that members of it are therewith entitled to live a different life, exists as such only in being asserted and acknowledged and internalized, especially by those who are excluded. (Once it is successfully internalized, it can paradoxically become almost invisible, as evinced by the infrequency of its invocation in American political discourse.) Sustaining it requires the policing of perception and desire as well as the maintenance of real material power. So it is one thing to have a fling with your gardener, which Mona and the other town gossips vicariously believe for a while Cary is doing, seeming to take some pleasure in the spectacle.[45] It is another to attempt to ignore a class boundary and thus class privilege for the sake of love, to establish legally a precedent or model that others could follow. Cary is therefore directly challenging the idea that class is a mark of some significant differentiator in human life, and by acting as she does, she treats it as the fantasy it is. Class in this latter sense, as an entitlement to special privilege and a requirement to marry your "kind," is in itself "nothing" at all, nothing real. (It has as much "reality" as the belief that the blood of aristocrats is distinctive.) Cary is on the verge of exposing that and so stands as a potential "traitor to her class."[46]

---

44. Girard 1961. See especially the first chapter, "Triangular Desire," 1–52. This structure might just as well be called Hegelian.

45. Cary is presented as multiply policed. Mona patrols the boundaries of sexual propriety, Sara the class rules, and the children, rather than being progressive agents of change, are the most conservative police force, mindlessly demanding the status quo; a sure sign of a pathological society. See Halliday 1971: 59–65.

46. I realize that the topic of class opens on to several complicated controversies, in this case especially the relation between objective and subjective dimensions of class position and

However, Cary's ultimate timidity and apparent inability to place herself outside the conventions she has known and accepted all her life and Ron's self-congratulatory sense of autonomy and nonconformist rigidity both descend from an American social imaginary dealt with in all Sirk's great melodramas and represent contrasting poles of the dialectic of dependence and independence that that imaginary requires. Such a tension would understandably make any deviation from marriage norms fraught with anxiety and confusion. Ron can maintain his sense of himself only by drawing Cary wholly into his world, and Cary can keep her relations with her friends and family, not to mention her Wedgewood china, three strings of pearls, country club membership, and mink coat, only by somehow or other pulling Ron into her orbit, and that is possible only after Ron has "fallen."[47] Or, in another version of a dialectic that can become a paradox, the bourgeois marriage understands itself as a product of passionate romantic love, but can only be properly realized by contract and an impossible legal promise to love. But who writes the contract?

A final general theme is that issue of authenticity, Ron's "answer," his guiding lodestar. In the conformist world of Stoningham, perhaps of America in general, it is certainly understandable that such genuineness would emerge as some sort of virtue. And for many philosophers, starting with Rousseau and Diderot, and extending through Kierkegaard, Tocqueville, Nietzsche, Heidegger, and Sartre, it is treated as a kind of new master virtue, the trait of character that is the most crucial in the emerging modern mass-consumer societies.

But the first problem with Ron's self-conscious embodiment of such an ideal is evident in his air of smug self-satisfaction and in his "be a man" homily. For, to invoke a familiar figure for such a notion, one assumes that one has "found" oneself and now must find a way of remaining true to what one

---

whether class positions are determined by relation to the means of production, Weberian "life chances," or Bourdieu's cultural capital notion, or even whether class identity has become so fractured and indeterminate as to be useless. That is all easily a topic for several book-length discussions, especially with regard to film theory. A great start: James and Berg 1996, especially James's excellent introduction to that volume, "Is There a Class in This Text?" (1–25).

47. It is difficult to imagine a social life for the two that could combine both the country club crowd and the Mick-Alida community. Dinner parties with Sara or Mona at Mick's place are hard to picture. It might be tempting to see some possibility as even conceivable because Ron has in effect *sacrificed* himself for Cary, that his broken state is something he is willing to do for her. But he actually does nothing; he stumbles and falls accidentally. One can imagine him coming out of his concussion and returning to the Ron we saw in their breakup scene.

has found. But in the philosophical treatments of the ideal in Kierkegaard, Nietzsche, Heidegger, and in Emerson and Thoreau (as interpreted by Cavell), the emphasis is on the enormous *difficulty* of any such "finding." The intricacies of social dependence in modern mass-consumer societies, the near-feudal power of managers in corporate empires, and a heightened awareness of the difference between public personae and private attitudes make any settled sense of just "being" oneself immediately naive. (Compare Kierkegaard's sense that in the modern age the only true Christians are those who cannot be Christians and know they cannot be.) Or any such sense ought to inspire a different sort of skepticism than one about the external world or other minds, but about one's sense of oneself. This would be the kind of irony mentioned earlier here, a kind of ethical stance. As in Cavell's treatment, this is not a skepticism that demands or intimates a "solution," as if a philosophical problem, but a fate to be borne. And bearing it cannot be a matter of resigning oneself to an inevitable self-deceit (as is typified in Sartre on bad faith), or to a kind of cynical playfulness, but simply a lived-out realization of the great difficulty (not the impossibility) of any "finding" and "being" who one "genuinely" is. There is no model or principle to guide any such recovered life. Any such picture or formulation would be subject to infinite qualifications and endless nuances. But there are characters in novels and films who have arrived somewhere, found something, reached some state of mind that can at least be suggestive, provide some sort of illumination. Or the absence of such characters (and there are none in Sirk's Universal melodramas) can also imply something determinate about what is missing or still hidden, forgotten.[48]

It is important, too, that we are shown that the naïveté of Ron's sense of what authenticity requires is linked to his constant avoidance of the dialectic of dependence and independence that is often raised by the film's point of view, by what our attention is directed to. His sense of himself is self-certifying, closed to any sense of how he seems to others, a sense that might have awakened him to the difficulty he is simplifying. Cary must think for herself as long as she thinks like him, about marriage, where to live, and what friends to have. He is in effect "broken" by her refusal to do so, but we sense he is likely to think

48. Cavell's (1984) examples of remarriages would be a good place to start, especially with Jean, Barbara Stanwyck's character in *The Lady Eve* (1941), at the end of her journey from con artist to genuine lover.

of it all as a compromise, even a sacrifice of himself for her, and that, too, is self-congratulatory rather than genuinely reflective. What he never realizes is that authenticity is a cooperative or a social virtue.[49]

Finally, the idea of authenticity as some sort of *goal to be sought* can easily seem paradoxical, as it does in this film, with Ron wavering between dogmatic, smug self-assertion and broken submission, as if "true" to a new but now dependent self that he will never be able to acknowledge as such. This whole situation can be greatly compounded by self-deceit; one knows that one is not able to, not allowed to, represent oneself as who one is, but can manage, over even a lifetime, to hide that somehow from oneself. (Most audiences, I think, accept this temptation in Sirk's films.)

Put another way, the more authenticity, or the avoidance of such self-deceit, needed, as modern mass-consumer societies took shape, to be praised as a virtue, the more suspicious its expression became (that is, just as it became part of a conscious social *strategy*). Once it became publicly acknowledged as a virtue or even as significant, it became suspicious, a strategic means, if only to self-congratulation, as is the case with Ron. *Being* authentic is one thing; *trying to be* and especially *trying to be seen* as authentic immediately borders on the theatrical.[50]

No aspect of this way of looking at what Sirk's film shows us should be understood as a *moral* critique of Ron's smugness or Cary's fear. The ambiguous and somewhat ominous fate of Ron and Cary's love affair, perhaps of the fate of love itself in such a world, is nowhere treated by Sirk as the failure of individuals to live up to their own convictions or to have the courage to risk ostracism and gossip. Any aspiration to the intimacy, vulnerability, and deep reciprocity of love and friendship can come to mean what it does to the agents, can come to require what it does, can run the enormous risks it does, only in a specific social and historical world; and in the world Sirk shows us, the American modern bourgeois world in the immediate postwar years, there is not much hope that such aspirations can ever be realized. As Sirk put it, "Heaven is stingy."

49. I explore this notion further in Pippin 2008: chaps. 6 and 7; see also chapter 7, below.
50. Ron has his own philosophy, formulates it explicitly, and is thought of by others as embodying this expressed philosophy. He is also willing to lecture people solemnly about its tenets. His standing as a character would be much different if Ron were played by, say, Gary Cooper in his prime; laconic, a man of few or no words, simply *being* himself. See also Trilling 1973 for similar Hegelian points, and my treatment of Fried's Diderotian problematic in Pippin 2005.

V

There is one last philosophical dimension to Sirkian irony that is worth mentioning. That the world of Stoningham is treated ironically simply means at a first level that we are shown that things are not as they seem, either to the viewers of the film (most viewers, I suspect), or, especially, to the inhabitants, the players of the theatrical social game of status seeking and boundary policing. Their moral judgments are staged strategies of self-serving protectiveness. That can seem obvious, but it can appear to be the singular traits of self-involved, thoughtless people, and that is not what it seems. But there is yet another level to the irony. Since the irony is not destructive or cynical, we are also being called on to attend to what it would be to live without such theatricality and falseness. And part of what a philosophical reading of a film, one attentive to this difference and to the generality of the problem, can accomplish is to call to mind, however indistinctly at first, whatever is missing in the lives we see — call it mutuality, reciprocity and respect, love, socially realized freedom, genuineness, or, following Cavell, "the ordinary."[51] In Cavell's treatments, what is hidden, very hard to recover, is so because layered over with ossified habits of mind, with too much taken for granted, habits that make it hard even to notice that anything might be missing. In a fine phrase, he once called what is missing an "intimacy lost."[52] (Hegel would call the goal of such proper, corrective attending "the actual" or "the concrete"; also, he thinks, lost in the world he saw coming into being.) The attention to class differences and the role of gender and age policing in the community are treated in the film as the most important sources of the distortion, the ossified and unreflective habits of mind, the loss of what would otherwise be possible, what the intense aspiration to love, understood as a kind of inchoate resistance, aspires to. As noted, class is treated in the film as a cultural and social norm, and Sirk keeps the material sources of class power markedly hidden, as hidden and undiscussed as they tend to be in modern American life. Aside from Ron and Mick, no one ever talks about what they do in the male world of New York that every professional man in the town gets on a train to attend to every morning. Sirk's orientation is certainly focused on the real interests of the socially and economically powerful

---

51. The theme is, of course, everywhere in Cavell, but I am thinking here of the special bearing on this film of Cavell 2013 and Cavell 1991 and more generally in Cavell 1999.
52. Cavell 1982: 161.

(see *Written on the Wind*), but those interests are treated in their social and especially psychological manifestations; in snobbery, the jealous guarding of privilege, anxiety about the fragility of such privilege. Characters like Mona Plash, and what she and her friends represent, are at home in Sirk just as they would be in the novels of James and Proust, rather than in the context of a Dreiser novel (or in Stevens's cinematic treatment, *A Place in the Sun*) or in films by, say, Elia Kazan.[53] At least Sirk's radical leftist past in Germany, his obvious fascination with the nature of these distortions and fantasies in the American experience, and of course the details of the film in question make it reasonable to attribute to him such a concern in these terms. Given the hiddenness mentioned above, this treatment hardly gives us the full picture of class, power, and the consequences of such a social order on the intimacies of daily life, but his treatment allows him, along with directors like Nicholas Ray, Max Ophüls, Alfred Hitchcock, and a few others, to produce something distinctive in Hollywood commercial film—a politics of American emotional life.

53. The role of irony also means that, whatever cinema's role in ideological socialization, that role is here self-consciously attended to, rather than invoked, participated in. That is, we are shown what we have come to want, to desire, in love and marriage (and in melodramas) and the ways in which what we desire functions in the maintenance of a gendered and class-structured social order. This means that we are shown what we normally do not see in melodrama and that showing is thereby critique.

SECTION IV

Irony & Mutuality

SEVEN

Cinematic Irony: The Strange Case of Nicholas Ray's *Johnny Guitar*

I. WESTERNS AND "WESTERNS"

There is little question that Nicholas Ray's *Johnny Guitar* (1954) is immediately recognizable as an instance of a genre that had become quite important to Hollywood well into the 1950s: the Western. It is set in the West in the post–Civil War nineteenth century (probably in New Mexico; Albuquerque is mentioned a couple of times); people ride horses, drink whiskey in saloons, dress in the usual Western clothes, and wear six-shooters. There are recognizable character types: the saloon woman (i.e., prostitute and/or madam), the gunslinger, the young gun eager to prove himself, an incorrigible, thoroughly evil villain (in a black hat, no less), a vengeful posse (also all in black, as if some horde of ancient furies).[1] The gunslinger is also a recognizable subtype; one who no longer wears his guns and appears to be trying to quit, in the manner of Gregory Peck in Henry King's *The Gunfighter* (1950), and Gary Cooper in Anthony Mann's *Man of the West* (1958).[2] There are the crimes we associate with Westerns: the stagecoach holdup, the bank robbery. There is the familiar, final, decisive shootout between two principals; and there is a horrific lynch-

---

1. As with everything else, they seem so "ironically." They are actually easily intimidated by Emma, more sheep than *Eumenides*.

2. This will turn out to be an illusion. Johnny Guitar, we come to learn, is, always was, and always will be "gun crazy."

ing. (Yet none of these mythic types is a cliché. Each element is presented rapidly and so directly as to be blunt, but in a highly stylized way, a stylization that marks it immediately as a Nicholas Ray film, a presentation of emotional life that is discomfortingly raw.) And there is the invocation of elements of the mythic narrative form common in many Westerns.[3] That is, "the railroad is coming," and everyone in the frontier community realizes that this will change everything, creating a situation both of anxiety and opportunity. Usually this event presages a fundamental transition from a situation with weak or no rule of law to a full integration into modern commercial and law-abiding society (with its families, schools, churches, small farmers, and shopkeepers), and it is resisted by large landowners and cattlemen, who exist as feudal barons and are unwilling to surrender authority. (The paradigm here could be King Vidor's *Duel in the Sun* [1946]. There are similar elements in John Ford's *The Man Who Shot Liberty Valance* [1962].) This is often the epochal transition that gives the Western at once its mythic universality and its specific inflection in an American experience of the frontier and of its disappearance.

In this film, the theme is pictorially invoked, or, to introduce the main theme in the following, rather more "cited" imagistically as a theme than straightforwardly assumed. The presence of the images seems too self-conscious to be "natural." For instance, over the back of the bar there is a large replica of a railroad engine (fig. 7.1) — the future, it would seem. Over the entryway to the kitchen, on the other hand, there is a replica of a stagecoach (fig. 7.2).

The present and past, perhaps, but again rather self-consciously displayed, as if primarily decorative, but also obviously figures for one of the main themes of the film. (Again, in typical Ray fashion, that theme, the uncertainty that "the railroad" and progress bring, is expressed psychologically, mostly by the overheated, extreme anxiety and hysteria of a character, Emma.) The reference also seems to *address* audience expectations about classic Westerns, foregrounded as such, rather than simply to permit a Western narrative framework to shape audience expectations.

Moreover, if we start with this last element and work through these familiar elements, virtually every aspect of this traditional framework is present, but "off" in some way, so much so that the excess emotion, elaborate, self-conscious emphasis on costumes, posed and theatrical sets and staging, have seemed to some to cross the line over into camp, or at least near self-parody. At

3. For more on the "founding myth" central to many great Westerns, see Pippin 2010.

the very least, one can say that these major "Westerns" conventions seem, very much like Sirkian irony in the last chapter, more "quoted" or "mentioned" than simply invoked or used, and therein lie issues deeper than genre conventions alone. For example, the railroad is coming, but the work of constructing it is not presented in the usual way, as an opening from the civilized East, but rather as a closing of the West. When the robber gang at the end tries to escape (the leader says they are headed for California; that is, they are headed west), they find that construction has temporarily closed the pass in that direction. This construction is presented as a series of spectacular explosions that seal off the direction that at one point in American history seemed ever available — west.[4] Moreover, in this film what the railroad is bringing is not so much "the East" in the sense of culture, domesticity, boundaries, the rule of law, and so forth, but rather, in the starkest terms, a new social reality built on money, the world of speculation, investment, and thus the kind of social mobility eagerly embraced by Vienna, the ex-prostitute played by Joan Crawford. (How "ex" she is, is not all that clear; the stereotype is that a woman running a saloon is a madam, but we never see any other women; we don't even see many customers. The saloon is eerily devoid of the usual bustle; seems so still as to be dead.) This is a new world where a clever ex-prostitute might quickly become the richest person in town, prompting a corresponding anxiety among the forces of traditional rectitude, so oddly led in this movie by a woman so hysterical, hateful, and bloodthirsty that she seems more like some psychological force of nature than human, Emma Small (Mercedes McCambridge).

The central social conflict in the film is one between the townspeople, led by Emma and to some extent by a cattleman, John McIvers (Ward Bond), and the saloon owner, Vienna, who, more than anyone in the town, is pro-railroad. Toward the very end of the film, Emma does (finally) invoke the archetypal fear of the coming of the railroad ("they'll push us out," bring "farmers, dirt farmers, squatters," "barbed wire and fence posts"), but by this point it is obvious that this is somewhat pro forma, again, strangely, as if quoted, not meant; what characters say at some point in a Western like this, although she says it with unusual crudeness and honesty. This impression is heightened because the logic of her claim is absurd on the face of it; as if killing Vienna and destroy-

---

4. I assume that, as was the case with early transcontinental railroads, the builders built from both directions and that the Kid's desire to head for California is mentioned so that we would understand that the construction is headed for the town from the West.

ing her saloon will have any effect at all on the massive railroad enterprise inexorably making its way toward the area. Her "view" is beyond neurotic. And this doesn't seem any part of her real motivation anyway, which is much more complicated and much darker. For, by the end of the film, we have seen for nearly two hours that the townspeople have allowed themselves to be led by Emma against Vienna because of Emma's personal and intense hatred of Vienna (much more on that to come) and because of what appears to be, on the part of everyone else, resentment and envy that Vienna has acted cleverly, far more cleverly than they have, by buying real estate and building her emporium right smack in the path of the coming railroad. This explains the otherwise bizarre totally isolated location of the saloon. She stands to get very rich either if she sells or continues to build in the area that will soon be a depot. (She has, like a modern urban planner, an elaborate mockup of the whole town she envisions coming soon to her doorstep. Our sense of her strength, authority, and, above all, commercial competence is never challenged in the film.)

So Vienna is only a "saloon owner" strategically; in essence, she is an investor and speculator, and clearly a very good one. (One could say that she gives the old cliché of "a prostitute with *a heart of gold*" a whole new meaning. She is already rich.) Soon after we first see her, we find her having dinner with a railroad executive. She is trying to persuade him to invest with her in more local real estate before the railroad arrives and prices escalate. Despite the fact that there is indeed a very great deal of money to be made (when Vienna asks him how much her property will be worth, he responds, "How much is Albuquerq' worth?"), he has already sensed that there are many in the town who violently object to Vienna, and he clearly does not have the courage for such a fight (courage that Vienna has), and he declines. But what is obvious in the scene is that he genuinely respects Vienna—as a business equal, or even superior—for her acumen and strength. Given the usual treatment of the "saloon woman," the scene is also remarkable for how desexualized and professional it all is.[5] No flirting, no cajoling, and this even though Vienna has no qualms about, is not embarrassed about, admitting without qualification that she got her information about the railroad's route from sleeping with the

5. It is true that the dining area where they are seated opens directly onto her bedroom, and her large bed is visible several times during the scene. Nevertheless, Vienna never alludes to any "reward" for Andrews if he cooperates. Perhaps the bed is there to indicate that Vienna is in principle willing to go to any lengths necessary to realize her plan. (She does try to give him more wine, but who doesn't at a business meeting?) What we see is that it just would not have helped in this case.

surveyor who planned the route.[6] ("We exchanged confidences," she says; what we would call "insider trading.")

The "townsfolk," or the anonymous mass that follows Emma and McIvers around (it includes a well-meaning but, typically for "pre-railroad Westerns," weak and ineffective marshal),[7] also seem responsive to Emma's nearly psychotic hatred of Vienna's "loose" virtue. It is obvious that Vienna is a former prostitute and has from many years of plying that trade built up the considerable stake required to buy the land and build the saloon. (Crawford was in her mid-forties when the movie was made in 1953, and there is no real pretense in the film that she is any younger.) This is infuriating enough to Emma and apparently the townsfolk. (Emma says to Vienna, "You're nothing but a railroad tramp; not fit to live among decent people.") But it appears to be especially infuriating that Vienna is not ashamed of her past, does not deny it, and thereby angers everyone exponentially; even, as we shall see, her former and perhaps future lover, Johnny Guitar (Sterling Hayden). The stark and ironic truth of her fundamental claim—that she is no different than they are, or even that she is much better at "what they are" *than they are*—is what seems so infuriating; what must be repressed, silenced. This is not to say that, finally, bourgeois respectability is not important to Vienna. It certainly is. "Vienna" is likely a pseudonym and already expresses her desire for Old World status and standing.[8] As Victor Perkins has pointed out, this aspiration is embodied by the elaborate and somewhat out-of-place chandelier in the saloon, the one Emma intuitively realizes must be destroyed.[9] But Vienna clearly wants to buy that standing, on the assumption that money is always the real basis of social status. One could say that Vienna believes in, is the representation of, absolute exchange value (both as a prostitute and as an investor), and when

6. Like everything else having to do with motivation, the railroad executive's response could be understood to be more layered. Vienna is asking him for help with the townspeople. She may not last long enough to deal with the railroad. Given that Vienna is a formidable businesswoman, it is not entirely clear that it would be in Andrews's interest to deal with her, rather than someone else in town. It might be better for him if she is "run off." It is my impression that there is some sort of knowing undercurrent in their conversation that acknowledges this; some sort of "I know what you are thinking, and know that you know that I know." But that is not the sort of claim that can be easily demonstrated.

7. Also typically, the weak marshal finally does rise to the occasion, stops allowing himself to be ordered around by the forces of money and power, and promptly dies for his efforts.

8. To the puritanical townsfolk, this would probably suggest not sophistication and social standing, but the decadence of "old Europe."

9. Perkins 2013.

she is posed against the representation of bourgeois moral rectitude (home, school, church, law) in the person of Emma, remarkably our sympathies are with the honest, unapologetic speculator, not the hypocritical, resentment-fueled townsfolk. They are either self-deceived or hypocritical about their motives, and those real motives are ugly.

The successful saloon woman is not unheard of in Westerns but is not often associated with Vienna's frankness and her psychological strength, her command of herself.[10] But this variation, almost inversion, rather than straightforward invocation of the "railroad arrival" theme and all that it suggests, and the unusual complexity of the psychological motivation of the characters, is only the beginning of what is "off," what is both Western mythology, and at the same time its citation and inversion. Most obviously, the main character, Vienna, is a woman, and even more unusually, her main opponent is also a woman, Emma. The climactic duel, the final decisive shootout, is *theirs*. This is hardly the traditional dénouement.[11] There were other actresses from the 1930s and 1940s who could credibly play the lead in a Western (Barbara Stanwyck in Samuel Fuller's *Forty Guns* [1957], for example; or Stanwyck again in Anthony Mann's *The Furies* [1950], or perhaps Marlene Dietrich in Fritz Lang's *Rancho Notorious* [1952]); and there are earlier examples (Lillian Gish in Victor Sjöström's *The Wind* [1928]), and later (in some ways, Claudia Cardinale in Sergio Leone's *Once Upon a Time in the West* [1968]), but none with Crawford's total self-assertiveness and command,[12] and none in such a fundamental, to-the-death struggle with another woman.

10. This steely command breaks only once in the film. After her tense late-night conversation with Johnny, at one point she stops the ironic posturing, seems to physically relax or even soften, says she has "waited for him," and embraces him. The movie conventions of the day tell us that she then sleeps with him. See also Perkins's interesting remark that there is an "undertow of panic in Crawford's self-assertion" (1996: 224). I am much indebted to this article throughout the following.

11. Women certainly take part in the final shootout, as the Grace Kelly character does in *High Noon*, but this woman-against-woman duel is, I think, almost unique. "Almost" because (so I learned from Tom Gunning) there is at least one other, in the 1953 movie *The Woman They Almost Lynched*.

12. The contrast and comparison with Dietrich (fifty-one at the time of the Lang film) would require considerably more discussion. Almost everything Dietrich did with Sternberg was done with some element of irony or self-parody, but she plays it largely straight in Lang's *Rancho Notorious*, and still dominates every scene she is in. One similarity with the strange tone of *Johnny Guitar* is the baffling "voice-over song," "Chuck-a-Luck," that narrates what we are seeing with wildly overdone expressiveness.

Vienna is clearly the heroine of the movie.[13] She is wronged but never wrongs, treats her employees with dignity and unusual equality (if they put in their money, she will split evenly with them), and goes to what seems certain death with great bravery and even a kind of hauteur. (This is all so, even though, if we ask a typical "Westerns-like" question—what is all this heroism in the service of?—the clearest answer is simply: profit, her own interest, what she regards, correctly, obviously, as what is rightly hers.) Her former boyfriend, the Dancin' Kid (Scott Brady), is often petty, lacks any of Vienna's gravitas, and is childish (the way a child might reason: "If they are going to accuse us of a crime, let's at least commit the crime and get the money"); and Johnny Guitar, we are told with authority twice by Vienna, remains "gun crazy." This is apparently a polite term for "seriously disturbed," given that when he hears Turkey (Ben Cooper), the young gun, demonstrating his shooting prowess, he rushes in wildly (as if stimulated by some Pavlovian response), firing rapidly, and, according to Vienna, he would have recklessly killed the boy had Vienna not stepped between them. Later, after she appears to believe he has changed, he offers to pick off a few of the posse, shoot them from ambush, to weaken their will to go on. Disappointed, she notes yet again, that he is "gun crazy."[14]

There are very few characters in Hollywood movies, and certainly nothing remotely similar in other Westerns, as over-the-top insane with sexual jealousy and repressed sexuality as McCambridge's Emma.[15] Ray is willing to go right up to the line of absurdity and parody in his treatment of her. She never simply speaks; she rather hysterically rasps virtually every line, cowing the men around her, none of whom really stands up to her. Much of what she actually charges is simply ludicrous. In the first "invasion" of the townsfolk

13. As always, one has to say "heroine," not simply *heroine*. She owes her success to prostitution and a kind of "insider trading," making use of the information she got in bed from the surveyor. Whether Ray considers that a qualification on her heroism or another feature of her honesty (prostitution being perhaps not an anomaly but paradigmatic of capitalist exchange values) is unclear. See Clark 1996: 79, 102–3, on the theme with respect to Manet's *Olympia*.
14. He does not, however, end up shooting anyone. His one important act is to cut down Vienna at the hanging. Other than that, it is all talk and music. Johnny and Vienna, a killer and a prostitute, are both treated sympathetically because, as Perkins 1963 points out, they are both isolated, vulnerable, wounded people, trying to find their way back to a shared world; Vienna looking to come "down" from her upstairs loneliness, and Johnny trying to come "in" from his endless, rootless wandering. They both realize that the way to do that is first to find their way back to each other.
15. Lee Marvin's portrayal of Liberty Valance comes close.

into the saloon, after a stagecoach robbery in which Emma's brother is killed, when Emma is trying to make a case that it was the Dancin' Kid and his gang who committed the crime, she argues that the Kid "was always eyein' me," and that he, the Kid, staged the robbery so that he could kill the protective brother, and so "now he thinks he can get me." She says all this in such a crazy, deluded way that it is impossible to believe that anyone takes it seriously. It is widely and rightly assumed that the Kid has eyes only for Vienna. Indeed, the Kid and Vienna clearly think it is funny that Emma has such a complicated fantasy about the Kid going on and that she doesn't seem to realize it.[16] (This is all, of course, before the implications of that fantasy, much of which must also involve a dose of self-hatred, become deadly.) The injustice of her attacks on Vienna—there is never a shred of evidence until, by bad luck, misleading evidence at the end—is always obvious, but never noted by anyone. McIver's announcement that he, as if an all-powerful tyrant, will simply pass a law that will forbid Vienna's place from opening, is not seriously challenged by anyone except Vienna.[17] And so until the very end and the final duel, Emma actually succeeds, comes within seconds of hanging Vienna.

Finally, moving closer to the surface strangeness of the movie, there are the names, the sets, and the music. The first time Johnny Guitar has to tell someone his name, he pauses a beat and almost smiles ironically when he says (again rather quotes, or says in irony quotes) his new surname. His real name is Johnny Logan, and he is a very famous and deadly gunfighter (fig. 7.3).

When he is asked why he does not wear his guns, he again quotes a phrase as if "from a Western," as if in ironic quotes: "because I'm not the fastest gun west of the Pecos." (He quotes rather than speaks a line later too, outside the bank being robbed: "Besides, I'm a stranger here myself.")[18] And a tough guy,

16. Another possibility is that Emma's self-hatred, redirected outward at the Kid, is actually or also self-hatred at herself for her desire for Vienna. In the clearest expression of her hatred of Vienna, when she says, "I'm going to kill you" to Vienna—about the only line she delivers softly—and Vienna responds, "I know, but not if I kill you first," Vienna is standing on the stairway, and Emma has begun to ascend, standing very close to her, but with her face therefore in a particularly intimate position in relation to Vienna's lower body. The erotic dimension of her hatred is noted by Perkins 1972: 77–79; 1996: 228; and 2013.
17. The marshal mumbles a slight reservation. The brutal injustice of the "rule of the town" is never clearer than in the case of Turkey, who is told he will be spared and tried if he implicates Vienna. He does. They hang him anyway. No one in the mob protests.
18. The phrase became the title of the 1975 documentary about Ray by David Helpern, and in it, Ray says that the phrase was the working title of every movie he ever made.

macho leader named the Dancin' Kid? The women are going to have a fight to the death, and the two male counterparts are "of the arts"? There is a kind of sly knowingness between the men about their names, but Johnny really does play the guitar and, lo and behold, the Kid really does dance! In fact, to mock what every intelligent character seems to realize is Emma's true motivation—hatred of Vienna because the man Emma, in self-denial, lusts after prefers Vienna—he demonstrates his talent by dancing with Emma. And she lets him! She does not pull or wrestle herself away but sweeps across the floor with the Kid for some time, clearly both bothered and thrilled. The two male names in other words are so flamboyantly non-macho that their use seems to cite ironically the Western tradition of nicknames (the Ringo Kid, Billy the Kid, Buffalo Bill, the Sundance Kid) only to mock them.

Most of the first thirty-five minutes of the movie take place in the main room of Vienna's saloon and gambling parlor. The setting is immediately eerie. It is empty and deathly quiet when Johnny enters, even though there are two croupiers and a barman at work, or at least ready to work. And, as noted, we are never given any reason to believe there are ever any customers other than the Kid and his gang. The employees are hardly welcoming and seem overtly hostile to the newcomer. It is as if Johnny has walked onto the stage of some absurdist drama. (The feeling that we are watching a filmed version of a stage play is hard to avoid when the scene is either of the two interiors, the saloon and the hideout. This again contributes to the feeling of a certain staginess, a self-consciousness about conventions, in the film's representational style. Movies can easily tolerate this "double vision," wherein we see at the same time the same object as both "Nicholas Ray's set" and "Vienna's saloon," but in this film, the former is more pronounced than usual.) The saloon has been built into an ocher rock formation, and that rock has been left exposed at the rear of the saloon. This is likely some indication of Vienna's tenacity; her insistence that she is anchored to that spot and is not going anywhere.[19] And there is that elaborate chandelier and Vienna's piano, both of which will play an important role later. The set is also huge, much larger than conventional movie portrayals of a saloon. The effect of this is rather more opera than theater, especially since so many different sorts of elements of the mise-en-scène are also so "outsized" and flamboyant. This goes for the costumes too, which are in bold, even extrav-

19. Cf. Perkins 1996: 224 on the "fortress" quality of the saloon and its relation to "the owner's quest for security."

agant, bright colors. The costume changes for Vienna are the most elaborate
and dramatically important. She goes from a conventionally mannish black-
shirted pants outfit, complete with six-shooter (when defending herself from
the townsfolk; fig. 7.4), to a red, alluring evening outfit (the old Vienna perhaps, in her late-night and decisive conversation with Johnny; fig. 7.5), to a kind
of neutral gray and brown utilitarian outfit (during a period when a normal life
with Johnny seemed fleetingly possible; fig. 7.6), to that famous spectacular
white dress, a final and self-consciously ironic (virginal) gesture (fig. 7.7).[20]

It is also her final insistence that not only was she a prostitute, but that there
was nothing at all wrong in having been one. In moral terms, her conscience is
clear; that is, absolutely clear, pure, white as the driven snow. All these codes
seem so explicit that the film's romantic and ironic expressivism often dominates any traditional realism.

And as if all this weren't enough exaggeration, irony, self-reference, and
deliberate theatricality, there is a striking moment in the opening scene in the
saloon that is clearly intended to upset normal expectations and to encourage
the "double vision" just mentioned. After witnessing the stagecoach robbery in
which Emma's brother is killed (Johnny is too far away to identify anyone),[21]
Johnny rides up to Vienna's (he has been sent for by her after an absence of five
years) in a violent dust storm. It is an appropriate opening image for the emotional turmoil, confusion, and unclarity we will see between the two romantic
leads. But it prompts Vienna to tell Sam, one of her employees, to light a lan-
tern and hang it outside so that potential customers can see their way to the
saloon. (Given the violence of the storm and the thickness of the dust, this is
pretty useless, but it is a mark of Vienna's optimism, for all her hardheaded-
ness and world-weariness.) Ray has Sam walk directly toward the camera and
complain about working for a woman, all while looking directly *at* the camera;
that is, at the viewer, violating the first rule of movie acting and destroying any

20. Vienna finally ends up dressed in some old clothes of the executed young boy in the gang,
Turkey (Ben Cooper), whom she had treated maternally and whom she had encouraged to
lie, to incriminate and doom her, when they both believed Emma's and McIver's promises that
such a lie would spare Turkey's life. There is no particular reason that Ray had to have her
change yet again and into these clothes, suggesting a kind of identification (or guilt), but its
significance is unclear, at least to me.
21. Johnny's distance from the events, the impossibility of his intervention, and even his complete disinterestedness—that is, beginning a Western with "inaction" and passivity—is also
quite odd. Cf. the interesting remarks about this issue and about Ray's play with Western
typologies, his inversions of traditional types, in Durgnat 1971: 188ff.

illusion of unobserved observers.[22] Ray then, in effect, "corrects" this by show-ing us that it was a point-of-view shot, that Sam was walking toward and speak-ing to Tom (John Carradine),[23] Vienna's trusted kitchen employee (fig. 7.8).

But the damage has been done, and at the very least the problem of the film's realism has been raised right at the outset. I would say that here again the effect is that the movie itself, as a "Western," has been attended to as such, cited, quoted, mentioned, thematized, not allowed to simply play out conven-tionally and unproblematically.

Victor Young's music often makes use of the "Johnny Guitar" theme, the song we only hear finally sung with lyrics by Peggy Lee over the closing scene. When that refrain is not playing, the music is as "overdone" as much else in the movie, "cuing" our responses too obviously, always opting for lush when spare would have been just as, if not more, effective.[24] But the "Johnny Guitar" theme and the romantic and sometimes melancholic mood set by the music is a reminder that the conflict between Emma and Vienna is only one aspect of the movie's focus.[25] The other is a love story, or a love that, as Vienna says, "burned up" and was left in "ashes." And that element of the plot, a melodrama inside a Western, functions itself like some resistance to the Western frame-work, forcing it into near-parodic self-reference.

Near to parody, but it never crosses the line. André Bazin is right when he notes that "not once does Ray adopt a condescending or paternalist attitude toward his film. He may have fun with it, but he is not making fun of it."[26] So what *is* he doing? Why make a Western that works *against* simply being a Western, that exposes a kind of conflict between content and form, that seems

22. Cf. Perkins's (1996: 226) account of the scene, which is different from that presented here.
23. Tom is party to another parody, this time of homespun Westerns wisdom. Johnny remarks to Tom, in clear anticipation that what he really wants, needs, cannot live without, is Vienna, that all a man *really* needs is "just a smoke and a cup of coffee." Later, after Johnny and Vienna have clearly slept together, Tom remembers the words and repeats them in even clearer irony, *as if* all a man would really need is a smoke and coffee, and not love and sexual intimacy (in the way teenagers used to say "as if").
24. There is an interesting "overture"-like movement over the opening credits. The music begins with an ominous martial sound and then transitions to the lush "Johnny Guitar" theme, as if to introduce the two halves of the film: the violent confrontation between Emma and the townsfolk, on the one hand, and Vienna/Johnny, on the other. I take it to be the chief task of any interpreter to understand the relation between these two parts.
25. For important remarks on the importance of the music in the film, and especially of the main theme, see Perkins 1996: 225ff.
26. Bazin, cited in Wilmington 1974: 20.

at least to upset the "balance" that Perkins has claimed is an ideal in a film, between "what is shown and the way of showing"?[27]

II. GENRE-BENDING

There is no question that our expectations and interpretive assumptions are mainly shaped by the film's surface conformity to the Western genre conventions. But not exclusively so. The wise-cracking, laconic Johnny Guitar character, unable to free himself from Vienna, and the gambling theme invoke film noir conventions.[28] The sets and costumes and choral movements of the posse suggest the conventions of a movie musical.[29] But the excess, even hysterical emotional expressivism also suggests melodrama, a most unusual combination with presumably "masculinist" Westerns. There is no space here to sketch even a crude view about the genre conventions of film melodrama. I will just assume that it is safe to say that there are many types, and that besides, say, Cavell's "melodrama of the unknown woman,"[30] there is at least something like the "melodrama of the wronged, suffering, unjustly judged woman," known or unknown, and that what such a fate (the quality of being wronged) mostly prevents (in these films, at any rate) is the realization of the possibility of love, the very state often believed to count as some sort of redemption and overcoming of such fate, a second chance or a new beginning, the American hope. The emotional register of the suffering and the hope is intense in melodramas, "boosted" by music and gesture, sometimes said to be exaggerated, even as noted, bordering on camp.[31] Another way to say this is that often lovers in melodramas struggle against what appears to be the very bad hands they have been dealt by fate, a fate they can defeat if they can become and remain lovers, despite it all. In this typically melodramatic case: Can a woman

---

27. Perkins 1972: 78.
28. There is something, a good deal actually, of the "Gilda-Johnny" relationship from Charles Vidor's 1946 noir, *Gilda*, in the Vienna-Johnny pairing.
29. Richard Neer (2011) has also pointed out that there are even elements of the fairy tale in the staging of the secret hideout, enterable only through what appears to be a magical wall of water. See the reference to Truffaut below, in note 39.
30. Cavell 1996.
31. Viewed in this way, perhaps the master of melodrama would be Douglas Sirk, although films by George Cukor and Vincente Minnelli or Michael Curtiz's *Mildred Pierce* (1945) could stand as good examples.

once a prostitute ever be anything other than an "*ex*-prostitute"? Can a man who killed other men be anything more than "a killer" who now (or at least recently) no longer kills? Can each forgive the other for their pasts? Under what conditions? Only if a killer can truly become an ex-killer? A prostitute an ex-prostitute? Finally, melodramas, especially Ray's romantic (*In a Lonely Place, On Dangerous Ground*) or familial melodramas (*Bigger than Life*), portray characters so profoundly invested in their love, that no real relationship could ever "contain" it. There is excess emotional turmoil everywhere, destabilizing, undermining, enraging.

Their initial banter makes clear that this is no joyous reunion, even though Vienna has sent for him, and Johnny has come at her bidding. They both initially pretend, perhaps also to themselves, that it is just a business relationship. But a deep hostility, and so a deep emotional connection, is apparent immediately. They clearly each feel betrayed by the other,[32] but the fact that they are together again in itself also indicates *some* hope for a new start, even though neither is willing to admit that hope to the other. In a movie where almost every other line is dripping with irony, the first unmistakable indication of the tonality Ray wants to create between the two is a line of Vienna's. Johnny is to play something on his guitar and asks for requests. She tells him, with a clear trace of bitterness, that whatever he plays, "just put a lot of love in it." She obviously means: "You're so good at pretending to love, at 'performing' love, and then betraying, leaving." But of course she also means, as is often the case with irony, *exactly what she says*: please *do* put a lot of love in it, return to loving me. What the music helps her recall is ultimately too intense for her to maintain her ironic stance, and she asks him to stop. (Perhaps the ultimate ironic line in the film occurs after the villain Bart [Ernest Borgnine] kills Corey [Royal Dano], brutally stabbing him in the back, and then says simply and self-righteously, "Some people just don't listen.") In a later conversation, Johnny reveals that he had had some hope of a reunion, but he is so clumsy and maladroit in expressing himself that he succeeds only in infuriating Vienna. He says, "A man's gotta stop somewhere; this is as good a place as any." A "touching" proposal, Vienna responds; and yet again the irony: "I'm overwhelmed."

---

32. From what we learn of their breakup, there is no reason for Johnny to feel this way. In his own mind, he apparently feels betrayed because Vienna didn't sit around patiently, knitting or something, until he deigned to return. This is another factor that would lead one to doubt they can really reconcile, as the ending suggests.

But the heart of the (noirish) melodrama plot—ex-lovers who have
been burned badly but cannot help wanting to reignite the flame, however
dangerous—is revealed in an extraordinary late-night scene in the saloon.
Johnny cannot sleep and has been drinking. Vienna clearly cannot sleep either
and comes downstairs in her out-of-the-past scarlet evening dress (or negligée) getup. Things don't start off well. Johnny gets right to the point that he
cannot get over, asking bluntly: "How many men have you forgotten?" The
obvious absurdity of the question (it's like asking a crowd: how many people
are not here? one can't remember a number if one has forgotten the men)
is some indication that there is no resolution, no reassuring answer, for the
problem Johnny has. Vienna *has* slept with a lot of men. And she responds,
"As many women as you remembered." That is, you are no innocent either
and, perhaps she means, at least I have forgotten those men; they were not
important. But then Johnny asks her to tell him something nice. "Lie to me,"
he requests, and she does. He gives her lines to say and she robotically repeats
them, in effect negating them, blocking their pragmatic force, by the way she
says them. She says them but clearly does not mean what she says; she in effect
expresses the opposite of what is said. Or at least performs this negation. At
some level she probably does mean them, doubling the irony (fig. 7.9).

"All these years I've waited."

"I would have died if you hadn't come back."

"I still love you like you love me."

So a theatrical display in a film full of theater, posturing, and ironic reversals; taking back with one hand what is given with the other.[33] Here Vienna
enacts some of the pathos of an ironic stance; she speaks only in quotations
(Johnny's), cannot be "in" the lines herself. This seems another indication that

33. A clever final example of this stylistic oddity resulting from the sort of irony attendant on
hyper-self-consciousness: when Emma and the posse find Vienna in white at the piano, she
plays the "Johnny Guitar" theme as if sampling it, not playing it, or rather playing around it,
playing with it; not simply playing it. (Perkins 1996: 225 says that she plays it "in the reflective vein of a nocturne.") The theme too, as played in such a way, is not *meant* as much as it is
said. It is as if Vienna is exploring the meaning of the theme reflectively, not directly meaning
the theme.

there is nothing in their attempts at mutual explanation and exculpation that will be of any use in overcoming their impasse; certainly not mere words said now. Perhaps they will all sound like someone else's words, quotations. Johnny bolted when Vienna suggested settling down and remains "gun crazy"; she did not quietly wait for him to return, but used her talents to build a budding empire, making clear that she did not need him, could live without him. (There is no question of what she had to do to acquire the necessary capital. She tries to tell Johnny what "every board, every plank, every beam" in the place cost her in dignity and self-respect, but Johnny doesn't want to hear.) Neither of these facts can be changed or explained away.

But in an impulsive moment, they briefly indulge the fantasy that the past and the doubts it creates can simply be willed away, willfully forgotten. Johnny asks her to imagine it is her wedding day; she breaks down and admits she has been carrying a torch for him; they embrace and the strings swell, the "Johnny Guitar" theme washes over them and us.

Events unfold very quickly from this point on. They are inadvertently caught up in the Kid's bank robbery so that suspicion is cast on them and they have to escape the posse. This is when Johnny makes his proposal to pick off a few posse members and Vienna knows that he will always be "gun crazy." They separate; she tells him that it was a mistake to have sent for him; he should stop by and pick up his pay.

The posse arrives at Vienna's. Emma and McIvers trick Turkey into falsely implicating, betraying, Vienna. Emma shoots down the chandelier with a shotgun, and Vienna's saloon burns in a spectacular fire (fig. 7.10). They hang Turkey[34] and are about to hang Vienna. Johnny has not abandoned Vienna but has hidden and climbed to the top of the hanging tree, and he cuts Vienna loose just as Emma (who else?) whacks the horse carrying Vienna in the hanging noose. They escape through a mineshaft and make their way to the Kid's lair, where the posse also tracks them. There is a final shootout between Vienna and Emma. Emma shoots the Kid between the eyes as he calls out Vienna's name and is then herself shot and killed by Vienna, who is wounded. She and

---

34. The interrogation of Turkey is clearly designed to echo everything from Soviet show trials to the McCarthy witch hunts. See Eisenschitz 1993: 212. The betrayal is staged by Ray with, somehow, both sympathy and condemnation. One of the most interesting but relatively unexplored confluence of themes in the film is the link between the posse's (or the mob's) willingness to be led against Vienna, the nature of the enmity they bear against her, and Emma's transparently sexual repression and its resulting hatred.

Johnny walk through the waterfall that hides the lair and happily embrace. This is when we finally hear the lyrics for the "Johnny Guitar" theme, sung in a wistful, melancholic tone by Peggy Lee (fig. 7.11).

> What if you go, what if you stay,
> I love you.
> What if you're cruel, you can be kind,
> I know.
> There was never a man like my Johnny,
> Like the one they call Johnny Guitar.

The contrast is striking. This uncertainty ("what if you go or what if you stay") and melancholy ("what if you're cruel") stands in counterpoint to what looks like a Hollywood happy ending, the embrace. But of course, nothing has changed. Vienna's last assessment of their relationship, that Johnny was still gun crazy and that it was a mistake to have sent for him, is no doubt still true. Vienna had said that she would not kill to protect what she has, and perhaps she has learned otherwise and so now accepts the need for a bit of gun craziness, but that is not discussed. Perhaps, with those lyrics, all one can conclude is that the status of their relationship remains highly uncertain.

III. COUNTERPOINT

Let us say that there are two senses of "not meaning what one says," the traditional understanding of irony. There is a knowing form, and this is predominant in all the cracking wise in the film. Vienna's "I'm overwhelmed" in reaction to Johnny's "proposal" is typical, as are her mere recitations of the lines Johnny feeds her. There is also an unknowing form. We might say that someone ironically reveals (even, in some very complicated way, intends to reveal) the opposite of what they deliberately or consciously intend to reveal by what they say.[35]

Emma says that the Kid is always eyeing her, but that is not what she "really means." Unbeknownst to her, unconsciously or in self-deceit, she really means

---

35. The most important discussion of this issue is Cavell's (2002c), the article by that name in the collection. The essays in this collection raise a number of issues of relevance to Ray's films, as I try to show in chapter 8.

she is always eyeing *him*, lusting after him. (What she really means to say when she says to Vienna, "That's big talk for a little gun," is anyone's guess.) The townsfolk say that their motives in attacking Vienna are moral considerations, but what they really mean to do is, unknowingly but effectively, strike out against the new world of money, speculation, and social mobility that she represents; or they partly mean to protect themselves from their own desires, which Vienna excites; or simply *they* want the property Vienna has cleverly secured and are acting out of envy. As we have seen, sometimes a single statement can embody both forms, as when Vienna says, "Put a little love in it," knowingly not meaning that, meaning to say Johnny has no love to give, and yet unknowingly meaning the request literally. (Admittedly, the "unknowing" side of this is extremely controversial in philosophy. There are many who will say that they cannot understand what the claim even means. In this limited context, I can only suggest that we would be restricting our interpretive capacity in an extreme way if we must believe either that Emma means exactly what she says, or that she knows perfectly well what she really means but is simply a hypocrite.) In the melodrama plot, this is all intensified by what is clearly a great reservoir of hate and resentment motivating what the two principals say, even as feelings of love and aspirations for reunion also motivate what they say and do, a kind of psychological complexity that is something of a trademark for Ray's films. This can all make even a single small phrase unusually complicated. When Johnny and Vienna are arguing and Johnny returns to his absurd "Why didn't you wait for me?" theme and notes that between the time they separated and now, there must have been other men, Vienna coyly smiles, almost coquettishly, and says, "Enough." What did she mean to communicate by saying this in that way? That she was proud of the fact? Inadvertently revealing that she enjoys having many lovers? Is she boasting that there were enough (scores, hundreds) to pay for her saloon? Is she simply defiant in the face of his accusations? Unconcerned about his reaction? All of the above?

At any rate, this is often the situation—unknowingness, misunderstanding, missed signals, honest expression but in a state of self-deceit—that is typical of intense melodramas.[36] What I want to conclude by noting is that it is all not typical of conventional Westerns, and that this helps explain why the Western framework in such a situation cannot "mean what it says," why the

36. Cf., for example, the greatest of film melodramas, Max Ophüls's *Letter from an Unknown Woman* (1948).

expectations and meaning intended by narrating within such a frame cannot but point instead *to* those expectations and *to* that framework, rather than that the frame just *creates* the expectations or orders the plot.

There are of course Westerns with love stories at their center. *The Man Who Shot Liberty Valance* concerns a love triangle. There is also a triangle in *High Noon* (1952) and *Shane* (1953) and even in another very fine "quasi-Western," I suppose we have to say, also directed by Ray, *The Lusty Men* (1952). But the meaning of the love stories within the Western is intertwined with the mythic elements of the plot and are bereft of either sort of irony. When Hallie chooses the educated Ranse over the small rancher Tom in *The Man Who Shot Liberty Valance*, there is no emotionally charged, or as we say "melodramatic," scene (in fact, the choice happens offstage), and there is no suggestion of complicated mixed motives or self-deceit. She probably, much later, considered it a mistake, or at least has some regrets, but she knew she was also choosing a way of life—simple literacy for one thing—but also culture, travel, sophisticated politics, and our appreciation of what that sacrifice of Tom cost her could not be as keen as it is if the emotional undercurrents were as complicated as they are in *Johnny Guitar*.

It would be far too simple to say by contrast that in these epic Westerns people say what they mean and mean what they say, but it is true that there is usually not this melodramatic potential for misunderstanding, and the general drift of such a characterization would not be wrong. And in that context, the context of myth at both a universal and historical level, this is not a limitation. The elemental psychological issues raised—love of one's own, fear of death, pride, vengeance—are profoundly important and quite complicated. But it is another sort of complication that confronts the Western's characters, having mostly to do with the taming, education, direction of the political passions, and not with, let us say, first of all, interpretation, the problem of meaning. When the latter becomes central, the Western framework cannot contain the issues and the framework looks ironic.

This means that there is a large issue to discuss here, too large for this context. Put it this way: the Western at its best is a classical narrative framework, in league with the epic, and often with the tragic (*The Searchers, The Man Who Shot Liberty Valance, The Gunfighter, Shane*). In melodrama, neither the inevitable "objective" conflicts in what social roles require nor the subjective crises stemming from having to determine what to do (the sources of ancient and modern tragedy) propels the action. And it is *because* no great principles are at

stake, are credible (given, perhaps, what we "now" believe about psychological motivation), that love and being loved assume the role of such principles
of significance, a role they cannot bear, producing the hysteria and excess of
melodrama.

This is partly why, when in *Johnny Guitar* someone voices what would be, in
a typical Western, a typical motivation relevant to the epic context, we notice
the framework; our attention is directed to the narrative pattern rather than
carried along by the narration, because we have seen enough to know that it
"can't be that simple." As noted, a paradigmatic instance of this is when Emma
invoked finally the "cattlemen-farmer" archetypal conflict as a reason for her
hostility to Vienna and all that she represents.

It is as if Ray had set down, perhaps as a kind of experiment, inside a classic
Western setting, the much later historical world of Sirk, or even the world of
Dix and Laurel from *In a Lonely Place* (1950), and then let us watch the grat-
ing, anomalous implications roll out.[37] (Ray does just about everything he can
to say: This may be a Western movie, but these are not Western characters.
For example, Corey, one of the Kid's band, is several times shown reading a
book; not a common occupation in Westerns.) Somebody in some Western
might be able to say, "All a man needs is just a smoke and a cup of coffee," but
among these ironists, the quotation marks are almost visible.[38] The seriousness and the sheer "adultness," one might say, of Vienna's defense of herself
to Johnny (and her withering destruction, in her "if a woman just slips once"
speech, of the male double standard on which many Western "virtues" were
built) and the sophistication of her analysis fit uneasily into the archetypal
purposes of the classical Western. This makes that lack of archetypal fit visible and the Western frame more cited than used, and so to seem like a narrative structure and set of problems no longer relevant to subjects of this level
of self-consciousness. And even more strikingly, the characters *seem to know
this*; this seems to be the meaning of their air of wise-guy knowingness, at least
on the part of Vienna, the Kid, and Johnny, none of whom ever met a wise-
crack they didn't like. One can quite plausibly imagine Vienna simply saying,

37. Wilmington (1974: 21) says that the film "reshapes the poetry and the myth [of Westerns]
to fit an essentially modern situation." I would say that the whole point, what is most interesting about the experiment, is that the content does not "fit" the form.
38. The same could be said for stock "cowboy" lines such as "I never shake hands with a left-
handed draw." Or "Luck had nothing to do with it."

"Oh for God's sake, Emma. Stop with all this 'public morals, collusion with the Kid in crime, hooray for bourgeois domesticity, the railroad will destroy our traditional way of life' crap. You want to kill me because the Kid prefers me to you and you hate yourself for desiring him (and maybe for desiring me)." (She actually does say something close to this.) Or, more imaginatively, one can picture the Kid saying to his colleagues, "Well, we look and talk like an outlaw band; you've all seen Westerns. We must *be* an outlaw band. Let's finally act like it."

A dominant "knowing irony" can suggest the kind of uncertainty or reluctance to take any side in some important dispute, which is inconsistent with the high seriousness and mythic ambition of great Westerns. In the crisis situations portrayed in Westerns, indulge such an irony and you begin to sound like a Lee Marvin character, a cynic. The great problem in great Westerns is the possibility and the nature and especially the cost of civilized life itself. Such a film cannot do everything and so cannot portray as well the problems that arise at a much more intimate and self-conscious level, a level not tied to the basic problem of safety from decline into the state of nature. Those problems include the "unknowing irony" that make stable romantic relations so highly individualized and thus ungeneralizable and that make the sociopolitical issues much harder to manage. The relationship between Johnny and Vienna doesn't *mean* anything of some mythic importance in the way the relation between Hallie and Ranse in *Liberty Valance* does, or between Marshal Kane and his wife, Amy, in *High Noon*, or between Shane and Marian in *Shane*, or between Dan Evans and Emmy in Delmer Daves's *3:10 to Yuma* (1957) or between Ben Stride and Annie Greer in Budd Boetticher's *Seven Men from Now* (1956).

If this is so, then it means that the melodramatic and romantic world of a Nicholas Ray film serves rather as a counterpoint to the assumptions and ends of a traditional Western, not an instance of them, even though, in a brilliant move on Ray's part, it is formally presented that way. It is in this sense that a Western, as treated by Ray, cannot mean what it says, must become, as a mere form, visible and thus mannered or perhaps "baroque," a form that cannot contain the melodrama "within" it.[39]

---

39. Perkins 2013, in "Acting on Objects," has noted that the film has an "aura of the baroque." Andrew 1991 reports (without citation) that "Ray himself regarded the film as baroque," and he cites Truffaut's characterizations of the film as "a fairy tale, a hallucinatory Western, a Western Dream" (71). Wilmington (1974: 20) attributes to Bertolucci the description of *Johnny Guitar* as "the first of the baroque Westerns."

But if this is the right way to begin to understand the ironic dialogue, the studied self-consciousness of the Kid and Johnny and Vienna, the melodramatically exaggerated sets, costumes, and music, the occasional flirtation with self-parody, the inversions of character types, the intense hate-love nature of the central love story, and the appeal to psychological motivation like repressed sexuality,[40] then it all obviously returns us to the most important and difficult question posed in the first section above. Why would Nicholas Ray make a Western that cannot be what it is without a great deal of irony, given what he asks it to contain? Why bring that issue, the lack of fit between form and content, so much to the foreground?

Whatever answer there is to this question, it is present in the film only by implication, and drawing out such implications is difficult. We can though notice what is not present, what is conspicuously absent, in *Johnny Guitar*. The great epic Westerns all have some ethical and often a straightforwardly political dimension. The central question usually concerns some dimension of the problem of justice, whether as a question about the relation between justice and vengeance, or the legitimacy of some act of violence, about the relation between violence and the rule of law, or about the conquest and near extermination of native peoples, or about the injustice of some form of historical memory, or about the psychological costs of the founding of a civil order in a context where it was absent. As we have been noting, by and large this sort of framework of meaning is absent or present only ironically in *Johnny Guitar*. I have said that the love affair between Johnny and Vienna doesn't mean anything epic or mythic, carries no larger significance. But one could also say that the central events in the other plot, the attacks on Vienna by Emma, McIvers, and the townsfolk, do not draw our attention to any social or political issue larger than anxiety about social change and expression of envy. (The exception is the clear reference to the McCarthy witch hunts and thus to forced confessions, self-serving, erroneous accusations, and mob behavior. But even that already suggests a context of corrupt or failed politics; that is, a hypocritical, posed politics, behind which there is only self-aggrandizement, self-interest, and venality. McCarthy's and Nixon's speeches were both phony, and unknowingly, ironically self-revealing. The framework of national security politics contained the reality of hysteria and power lust.)

Moreover, there is nothing unusual in Westerns about the portrayal of "ordinary citizens" as easily cowed, acting like a mob. *High Noon* comes to

---

40. Cf. such a theme in *Stagecoach*, *The Far Country*, and *Ride Lonesome*.

mind immediately. But that crowd expressed its timidity by inaction; this one by becoming a lynch mob. What, though, is the great issue animating their intense hatred of Vienna? That she is in league with the Dancin' Kid and his group? This just on the basis of the fact that they drink at her place on Fridays? That she is not respectable? For that matter, what is McIvers's motivation? Before he becomes part of the group accusing Vienna of complicity with the stagecoach robbery, he seems to have already formed some resolve to join with Emma and get rid of Vienna. (McIvers and Emma are said to be the two largest landowners in town and to have the most cattle.) The only possible explanation is the one Vienna gives: that he cannot stand for her to make such a profit and so eventually enjoy such influence in the post-railroad town.[41] But that is venal, petty; that is, *private* (which doesn't, of course, mean it isn't true), and when joined with Emma's bizarre sexual and violent fantasies, and the fact that there is no character in the film who defends any principle higher or more complicated than individual entitlement, one could venture the guess that the nearly explicit inappropriateness of the Western's frame appears motivated by a general skepticism about that political dimension of human life in general, a skepticism that is in this film most often expressed by irony. If this is so, one might venture far out onto a thin limb and suggest that this skepticism touches on the problematic link between the political psychology required by capitalism and that required by liberal democracy. The latter requires some commitment to a common good; some allegiance to the community that is more than merely strategic. The questions about justice noted above as typical of classical Westerns are not in play if we restrict the basic question of the political bond to "You can get yours if I can get mine." Yet the "political" rhetoric of "the town," of Emma and McIver, is mere appearance; the motivational reality is darker or transparently self-serving. The former, a speculative market economy, requires competitive individualism, often a ruthless form that sets everyone off against the other in a zero-sum game and foments paranoia, justifiably so in Vienna's case. I don't mean that Ray's film means to raise this issue as a question, but rather that the "Western's" ironic status in the film

41. It is true, though, that in the closing scene, Ray allows the camera to linger significantly on McIver's expression as he stands over the body of Emma and looks up to Johnny and Vienna descending from the hideout. What we see is unquestionably regret and even shame at how far he had indulged his venal concerns, now with Turkey, Corey, Bart, the Kid, and Emma all dead. He no longer, in other words, considers himself righteous. Just his expression alone concedes that the language of righteousness and justice was a façade for his own envy and greed.

is an indication that he thinks the issue *is settled*. Vienna's shrewdness is the future; the ostensibly countering political rhetoric is phony, an excuse for the prosecution of private interests. Thus Johnny's extraordinarily unusual (for a Western) cynicism and cold indifference to the conflicts around him. To him, Vienna is a mercenary who will do anything for status and money (though he still loves her, after his fashion), the townsfolk are hypocrites, and the Dancin' Kid's gang are children, or the Western equivalent of unserious fraternity boys.

What we have instead is typical of Ray's much more psychologically than politically complex films; that is, we have a great investiture of importance in love and being loved as the central human problem,[42] or, we should probably say, we have what has become the central and most difficult human problem, since the Western is now noticeably of historical rather than thematic significance. This is so even though Ray was certainly aware, as few directors ever were or are, of the nearly certain impossibility of such redemption. And yet this does not mean that the film should be characterized as another of the more "psychological" Westerns, such as those by Anthony Mann or Budd Boetticher. It is fair to say that those Westerns explore more self-consciously the psychological costs of the frontier-town transition or the legal/extra-legal violence problem, than the "objective" problem itself. But the Western framework itself is secure, just given a different, more-psychological-than-epic inflection. A question like "What really *is* the difference between a sheriff and a bounty hunter, if any?" might be explored by asking, "What does it mean for this individual (the Jimmy Stewart character in Mann's Westerns) to face that challenge?" But it is still the classical question at issue. We are still within the generic language and concerns of the Western.

There is one more element that connects the love story melodrama with the "Western" plot. Put simply, both raise the question of the possibility of "new beginnings," a sort of escape from, or reconciliation with, the past. As in many epic Westerns, the question is whether a "second founding" for the country, after the hatred and brutality of the Civil War, is possible; in this as in other films, whether the refounding of a modern commercial republic is possible in the shadow of that hatred and brutality, in a context of virtual lawlessness. The Vienna-Johnny relationship poses at a personal and psychological level a similar sort of question about a new beginning, shadowed by the bitterness of their breakup. Vienna has "become" an entrepreneur and insists

42. And in other films, home, the family.

on being so treated, and for all of Johnny's persistent "gun craziness," he has, after all, changed his name, trying for a new identity, his guns are in his saddlebags, and he carries a guitar instead. The surface image at the end—the purification by water, or the waters of forgetfulness—suggests that they have succeeded. But, one final time, we cannot escape the irony of the embrace. Vienna had thought once before that Johnny was over his "gun craziness" and had been disappointed, likely will be again, perhaps the same sort of disappointment the "gun-crazy" country seems to experience regularly in trying to hold together its fragile union.

EIGHT

Passive & Active Skepticism in Nicholas Ray's *In a Lonely Place*

Who is it that can tell me who I am?
King Lear (I.iv.238)

I

In a Lonely Place (1950), while often characterized as a film noir,[1] also has the emotional intensity, the sense of intimacy, the tenderness in its treatment of very flawed characters, and the psychological complexity that one associates with a film by Nicholas Ray. It presents as well an intense focus on romantic love, or at least on the possibility of romantic love, that in standard noirs would be a matter of obsessive attachment to, or mostly submission to, a murderous femme fatale, and so a relationship contaminated by an underlying struggle for power. The movie is modest in scale and seems offered as material for reflection; as if it poses a question rather than just narrates and resolves a story. There is much more conversation than action, heightening its more reflective aspects.

---

1. It is included, for example, in the excellent anthology by Cameron 1992, and the film is the subject there of a brilliant article by Perkins 1992 in that collection. And it exhibits the modest "B movie" production values associated with the genre, as well as the thematic issues of fatalism (characters who cannot seem to make their own fate, seem doomed from the start), paranoia (police spying is a central element of the plot), and moral ambiguity (we are as attracted to what seems like the integrity, honesty, and forthrightness of Dix Steele, the Humphrey Bogart character, even as we begin to suspect he may be capable of murder). And it is a study, a fairly intricate study, of failure; here the failure of love. See Pippin 2012 for more on the philosophical dimensions of the noir genre.

It is reflective in another sense too, and I will come to that in a moment. There are two intertwining narrative threads in the plot. In the main plot, a bitter, apparently burned-out Hollywood scriptwriter, Dixon Steele (Humphrey Bogart), is accidentally connected with a murder victim, one Mildred Atkinson (Martha Stewart), a hatcheck girl from his favorite restaurant, whom he had asked home after work to tell him the plot of a popular book he has been asked to adapt for the screen. Since Dix was the last person known to have seen Mildred alive, and since he has a long record of fights, attacks on others, even perhaps domestic abuse, the police figure him for a violent character and suspect him of the murder. As in many noirs, one has to pause often in plot summaries. This last bit—that Dix has been "known for violence"—may not be what it seems. As Victor Perkins points out, the police captain in charge of the investigation, Captain Lochner (Carl Benton Reid), is shown recounting, very slowly and solemnly for dictation, almost comically so—as if his belief in what he is saying is comical—the list of Dix's scrapes, but he is clearly reading from press clippings, not from police records.[2] (Any movie audience could be expected to know all about press agents and their problematic relation to the truth.)[3] But Dix has an alibi. One Laurel Gray (Gloria Grahame, still Ray's wife at the time), an unemployed starlet, is a new neighbor of Dix's and had happened to come home at the same time as Dix and Mildred (a spectacular entrance, close to the femme fatale appearances that doom so many noir heroes; it won't take long before we learn she has a suspicious past, with "gold digger" associations). She swears that she also saw Mildred leave Dix's apartment, alone. (Another interruption: it is of some importance that this claim is not supported by what the viewer is allowed to see. All we view of what Laurel sees is that Dix has partially disrobed, is in a dressing gown, alone in his apartment after midnight with a young woman, and we surmise that she must have heard Mildred loudly yelling twice for help.[4] Mildred is enthusiastically acting out a part from the book, but Laurel does not know this, does

2. Lochner has a kind of superego role in the film, the Supreme Father, for Brub and Laurel and to some extent Dix. His distaste for Dix is obvious as he reads out the incidents, making clear that he is as much condemning Dix as reciting facts.

3. Mel says early on, "It is much easier to get people's names into the paper than to keep them out," reminding us of the press agent's role.

4. Ray takes care later in the film to establish that sounds from Dix's apartment can easily be heard throughout the complex. When asked if he just lets his phone ring and ring, he replies that he does and his neighbors will confirm that fact. ("Just ask my neighbors.")

not mention the screaming for "help" to the police, she never asks Dix about it, and we never hear this lacuna explained from her point of view.) We do not of course *know* that she has not seen this, but we are given no confirmation. Moreover, later, when people are trying hard to convince her that Dix did do it, she never replies resolutely, "Look, I *saw* her leave alone." And by the end of the film she is clearly convinced that he could have done it, which has to mean that she did not see Mildred leave alone.[5]

Dix and Laurel fall in love, and immediately Dix can write again. His own life now has a "plot," with love at the center, and he can write himself and Laurel into it. (This also suggests, at the reflective level again, that they may be trapped by Hollywood expectations, by Dix's "script" for them too. Lauren's main function in their relationship is as the transcriber of *his* words. As we shall see, the last lines of the movie, her lines, are from Dix's script.) But from the beginning of their romance, the police put a lot of pressure on Dix, plant a lot of doubts in Laurel's mind, and that, and what Dix (rightly) regards as several violations of his trust, and the exhibition of his own terrible temper, doom their relationship.[6] At the end of the film, after their nearly violent breakup (Dix appears to be intent on strangling her until the phone rings), they learn that the real murderer has been caught and that Dix is in the clear. Laurel says that this news would have meant everything had they heard about it the day before, but now it is too late, again as if they are typical film noir victims of mere chance.[7]

In this, the major plot, it is obvious that the question the characters are struggling with, and so the one addressed to us, as viewers, is something like "what do we really know when we claim to understand someone, or to under-

5. Polan (1993: 65) notes this. It is an extraordinarily important piece of information in the film—that all along, from the very beginning, Laurel had been lying to the police about their chief suspect, a man she does not know, and whom she decides to protect (decisively) on the spur of the moment, because she liked his face. (This already tells us a great deal about Laurel.) Extraordinarily important, but, typical for Ray, this fact is only silently present throughout the rest of the film.

6. Another interruption: this is at least what the surface narration seems to indicate, the explanation we are invited to accept: that sheer bad luck, the murder, dooms the relationship. As we shall see, the psychological reality of the film is much more complicated.

7. We are invited to accept this too, but that would be another mistake. It is not so much that her fears about Dix would have been assuaged if only she had known the truth earlier. As in many such cases, her *needing* to have them assuaged already means they cannot ever go back to where they were before she began to find such fears credible.

stand their 'character' or 'true self' or who they really are, especially to the extent necessary (whatever extent that is) to trust someone, and so expose oneself to possible betrayal?"[8] Or "what is the right way to acknowledge and live out the implications of realizing that we will very likely *never* be in a position to resolve such issues?" Everyone—Laurel, Dix's agent, Mel Lippman (Art Smith); Dix's improbably named army buddy, Brub Nicolai (Frank Lovejoy), who is also the police detective working the Mildred murder case; Brub's very conventional and suspicious, even hostile wife, Sylvia (Jeff Donnell); and Captain Lochner—they all want to know whether Dix is *capable* of murder. The usual tropes and figures come to mind: they want to know what is "inside" him, want to know the real, if hidden, Dix. The issue is naturally most important to Laurel, since she is in an intimate relation of trust with Dix; exposed to him, to his supposed instability, and to his potential violence, as it were. As we shall see though, once she allows the question of whether this trust and faith are justified to arise, the possibility of answering it immediately changes, as her relation to Dix has just changed; he notes the change, is wounded, *he changes*, and then, and only then, does he begin to evince what could be, and are taken to be, indications that he really *is* "capable of murder." The movie, in other words, introduces us to a reflection on one dimension of the philosophical problem of "skepticism about other minds," but in a distinctly practical register (perhaps the only appropriate register, as we shall see). In the modern period (and it seems to be an exclusively modern problem), the most general form of the issue is "how do I know that other apparently human beings *are* actually human beings (at least are human beings like me), and not automata, and so forth?"; and the most common focus for the discussion is the experience of pain and its relation to pain behavior. That is: "I only see, know, can be sure of, another's expressions, presumably of pain. How do I know the other person experiences what I experience when I experience pain?" But our inability to enter and "have" another's experience, or in some other way know what they experience in the way we experience what we do, gives rise to many forms of doubt or skepticism, most famously in cases like Othello's, and is certainly at issue in this film.[9]

8. This is complicated for us, the viewers too, because by 1950, we certainly think we "know" Humphrey Bogart, know what a Bogart character is. But he is very much not that character in this film. Perkins (1992: 226) notes that Bogart's biographer, Joe Hyams, reported that Bogart disliked the film, perhaps realizing how vulnerable and so untypical and unheroic he looked.
9. We seem pressed to a kind of holism in such understanding. I might come to understand another's dispositions, commitments, beliefs and anxieties, and so forth; that is, understand

There is an interconnected subplot too, and that suggests that other level of reflectiveness mentioned earlier. This concerns the "Hollywood plot." Dix, we are told, "hasn't written anything good since before the war," now some time back. His own reason for this, which we are invited to share and sympathize with (up to a point), is that this is because of his integrity, his refusal to churn out the schlock that Hollywood requires.[10] We are several times shown Dix befriending an alcoholic actor friend, Charlie Waterman (Robert Warick), clearly a Shakespearean actor of the "old school," genuinely trained as an actor, familiar with the classics, who later actually recites Shakespeare's "When in disgrace with fortune and men's eyes" sonnet. This seems to suggest that there *was* a time when movies aspired to something real and honest, whereas they are now made by what Dix calls "popcorn salesmen." Everything we see of the movie industry, often from what seems to be Dix's point of view, is of a soulless mass-culture machine, geared to the "Mildred Atkinson tastes" of the public.[11] There are many other "internal" references to the industry in the Ray film itself. I mean not in the plot but in what can be taken as references by Ray to himself in Dix (the apartment complex is the one Ray lived in when he came to Hollywood), to Bogart and Bogart's reputation, to studio heads and so forth.[12] But if the problem *in* the film is sincerity and trust, the problem *of* the film (as a film) is very similar. Dix wants everyone to know that Hollywood

---

the content of such states. But I would not thereby really understand what they mean to her, how they fit into some unique psychological economy. To understand that, I must simply have come to understand her. But that can't be formulated in any propositional content. It is to understand how she does and would go on in all sorts of ways.

10. This appears to be his stance/excuse now. It is clear from conversations with a movie director at a bar that Dix *had* been willing to write what the studios wanted. Not anymore, though; so he claims.

11. Another interruption: so much for the surface plot again. Paradoxically, even though Dix's eventual script contemptuously ignored the book on which it was to be based—just as Ray did with Dorothy Hughes's novel—the supposedly corrupt movie producer is actually crazy about its quality and wants to start production right away. This could mean either that Dix was wrong; quality films *can* still be made, like the one we are watching perhaps; or that Dix was wrong about his high-brow ambitions. Maybe he thought he had written *Citizen Kane*, but he ended up with another good way to sell popcorn. Perkins (1992: 224) suggests that an association between Dix and Herman J. Mankiewicz may be deliberate. For more on the "Hollywood frame" for the narrative, and the suggestion that the "lonely place" referred to in the title is Hollywood itself, see Eisenschitz 1993: 133–46. Polan (1993: 12) notes the interesting noir narrational theme: "forward motion combined with the undoing of confident progress by a paranoid looking back. . . ."

12. Again, many of these references are pointed out by Perkins 1992.

films are false, dishonest, pandering, and in that sense "insincere." So if the former problem concerns what it would mean, how it would be possible, to know someone well enough to trust him or her, to trust not just that they are honest but that their own (sincere) "presentation of themselves" is not itself a self-deceived fantasy, is reliable, this latter concerns what it is for a film (or a work of art) to be "genuine" too, to prove Dix's skepticism about the movies wrong. This was partly at issue in the "interruptions" above; feeling sufficiently assured that the "formula plots" we are apparently invited to invoke are inadequate, that the film has rejected such satisfactions, would invite us to closer attention; something that is itself, at the outset, an act of faith by the viewer, based on some sort of trust.

There is a visual embodiment of both levels of reflection in the opening credits. The first thing we see are Dix's eyes in the car's rearview mirror, and so the problem of both our knowing him (the eyes being windows to the soul) and *his* knowledge of himself, or anyone's knowledge of themselves, is introduced. (It is probably deliberate and important that at no point in the opening shot does Dix look at himself in the mirror or even check the mirror. If though, as this avoidance might indicate, he knows himself poorly, then his remaining "true to himself" and all his clinging to fiercely held ideals of integrity will carry a different weight in what follows.) But we are also at this point not just watching Dix *in the movie*; the credits are rolling by, so we are also attending *to the movie*, not what it represents. (We are in effect seeing a movie screen—the mirror—within a movie screen.)[13] And since the movie is itself, or presents itself as, a mirror to the events, "reflecting" them (not just their visibility but their meaning) realistically, the question of the film's reflective honesty or genuineness is also at issue, perhaps problematically at issue if the same doubts about what the film (any film, implicitly) "purports to be" can be raised as about Dix's self-knowledge (fig. 8.1).

II

At this point I will need to introduce some philosophical apparatus in order to develop what has been introduced. Given the framework already presented (skepticism, other minds, genuineness, fraudulence, revelation,

---

13. Eisenschitz (1993: 135) calls this "the fragmentation of the screen that was to assume obsessional form in Ray's work."

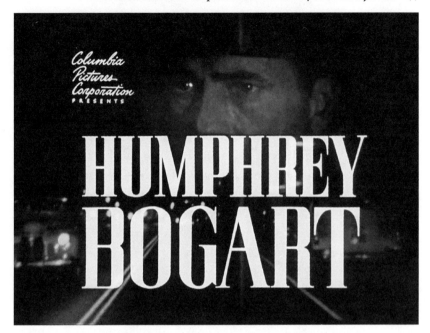

FIGURE 8.1

acknowledgment), it should come as no surprise that the approach I will take up is Stanley Cavell's discussion of the problem of skepticism in *The Claim of Reason*, and his own use of his approach in essays like "Knowing and Acknowledging" and "The Avoidance of Love" in *Must We Mean What We Say?* and "Othello and the Stake of the Other," originally the closing discussion in *The Claim of Reason* and reprinted in *Disowning Knowledge in Seven Plays of Shakespeare* (2003). I am interested in Cavell because he provides a different approach to, and an often perspicuous vocabulary for, discussing a Hegelian idea that many have found either opaque or dangerously illiberal or both (in Hegel and also in Cavell's source, Wittgenstein): that what it is to know oneself as a subject is wrongly conceived at the outset if understood as some sort of particularly intimate relation between a thinker or an agent and itself, as something essentially "inner" and directed to a particular kind of object. (Both Hegel and Wittgenstein stage their dissatisfactions in terms of rethinking something like the logic of "inner and outer" in philosophical psychology. And so for both, an implication of this rethinking is that "knowing" another can be nothing like the fantasy of looking "inside" them, or telepathically gaining insight into "what *they* experience." And for both, this is because it is the wrong model for the person himself, for his own self-knowledge.)[14] Cavell goes so far as to say the whole notion of a knowledge of others is wrongly framed. The struggle with attempting to understand others requires something other than a special sort of propositional knowledge; it requires instead a certain "acknowledgment" of them, as he puts it. The context in which doubt about what I take to know of another arises is often, in Cavell's discussion, a particularly intimate one; a great deal is at stake in the burden of such doubt and in what is achieved if it can be alleviated. With so much at stake, one manner of self-protection—an unavoidable consideration—is to ensure that each is as exposed as the other, as much at risk, even if no stable form of reassurance about this is ever available. (This is certainly the case in the movie; there is a great deal at stake in Laurel's knowing "what Dix is really capable of"; there is a great deal at stake for Dix in whether Laurel can be trusted, what it "means" that she had been the kept girlfriend of a real estate tycoon.) This means for Cavell that such an attempt to know something about another is inseparable from what he calls "taking up an attitude" toward that other.

I understand what Cavell is trying to say in the following way. And here I will stray a bit from his own formulations, will not be so concerned with global skepticism about the human/non-human distinction, and will try to put his points in my own words. First, that any intimate involvement with others inevitably involves a struggle of some sort, ideally a mutual struggle, to understand each other. This also means that the struggle is necessarily dynamic. That is, knowing each other is not a matter of episodic, punctuated inspections or momentary revelations, but always a struggle over time to understand and be understood, where what is to understand and to be understood is itself at least somewhat unstable, itself changing over time. Second, in the context of one's involvement with another, thinking one knows what, say, another would do in some situation simply amounts to a matter of whether one can trust the other *to do* this or that. Knowing that another will stay loyal in some crisis is, in a practical context, counting on them to stay loyal. (Counting on them is what it is to know them; the former is not based on the latter.) Wanting to know

---

14. Cf. Wittgenstein 1958: 178, "The human body is the best picture of the human soul." And see his more general remark that since the meaning of an expression is not tied to an inner punctuated experience, that even God could not learn, by such inner inspection, what someone meant by "bank" if he had said, "Wait for me by the bank" (217). From Hegel 1991: 140: "Hence what is only something inner, is also thereby external, and what is only external is also only something inner." And "an individual cannot know what he is until he has made himself a reality through action" (Hegel 2018: 230).

whether another loves me is determining what I can expect, count on, from the other. One *makes it true* (even if not in some wholly self-constituting way) that the other is loved by what one does, not by registering a feeling. Hence the link between knowing and taking up an attitude, and any such taking up of an attitude, is an acknowledgment of the other in some way or another, an expression of a resolution of confidence that such and such is the case, or not. Therefore such attempts at acknowledgment are of a sort that can also fail. Ray's film is about such a failure, and while it is certainly not *King Lear* or *Othello* (the scale of the film is much smaller, more intimate), there is much to be learned from it as to why such a failure is a failure.

I do not mean to say that Ray's film in some way exemplifies or supports Cavell's analysis, but that we cannot really understand what that analysis amounts to until we see the issues "alive" in an appropriately complex dramatic or literary context. I take Cavell's own work on literature and film to be guides to how that "realization" (to use Hegel's word) is to be understood.[15] In Cavell's terms, what we see in the film are characters trying to understand what others mean by what they say and do, all under the pressure of a great deal of uncertainty, and the pressure of unavoidable, immanent decisions, and where the stakes in getting matters right or wrong are quite high. This attempt, as Cavell explains it, involves not trying to understand what is literally said, but what is meant by a character's saying what is said, *what he or she means*, not simply "what is meant," or what she meant by doing what she did or did not do.[16] (An obvious example in the film: the police must ask what it means that when Dix learns of Mildred's death, he remains flippant, cracking wise, and apparently indifferent.) This will involve quite a complex activity, though still everyday and familiar, of interpretation, assessment, and, especially, evaluation (rendering ourselves intelligible to each other is inseparable from the way we render ourselves answerable, accountable, to each other),[17]

---

15. See his account of how and why he was "pushed to literature" (and, one assumes, film) "to discover the problem of the other," and to finding it "undiscovered for philosophy (in English)" (Cavell 1999: 476).

16. This is a common theme throughout Cavell 2002. A particularly clear formulation is Cavell 1999: 355. In Cavell 2002a, the theme is introduced by attention to Shakespeare criticism, and in opposition to the idea that there could be differing, distinct emphases; some on "character," some on "words."

17. See Cavell 1999: 256, on Wittgenstein on "attitudes" toward others: ". . . human expressions, the human figure, to be grasped, must be read. To know another mind is to interpret a physiognomy, and the message of this region of the *Investigations* is that this is not a matter

all of which is made even more difficult when the characters are in intimate relations of dependence, exposed emotionally to each other. In those cases, the question must also involve issues like what did he mean by saying that to *me*, then (or doing that, then) and when I have a great stake in his meaning one thing and not another, in his understanding me one way, rather than the other. (The skepticism involved is what Cavell calls a "motivated" skepticism, and we will hear more about it shortly.) If all of this is so, the task of investigating what it is to understand another, another's meaning and deeds, will need to be carried out in some context where the complexity of such factors can be constantly visible and bear on the issues in a credible way. Simple and contrived philosophical "thought experiments" are not going to do the job.[18]

As viewers of filmed drama, all of these issues of what is involved in understanding others are in play for us as well, with a fundamental difference that needs to be worked out: we are not exposed in any way *to* those whom we are trying to understand, and the characters in the drama cannot do anything to make themselves available to us. We cannot struggle together to be understood.[19] However, if what was said above about the nature of the problem of subjects who are "other to each other" and find that otherness unsatisfying and even disturbing is correct, then, in watching the film, we can be said to have come to understand something (if we have) *about that* in some way that cannot be reformulated in an argument or in a more familiar philosophical justification (or not all that well, as in what I am going to say discursively about the film). Something like the compellingness of the narrative will have *illuminated something* in a way again much closer to having *understood someone*, than it is to having *proved something*.[20]

---

of 'mere knowing.'" And: "In no case is such knowledge [of others, of their 'physiognomy'] expressed by a 'mere report.' . . ."

18. "In general, Part II of the *Philosophical Investigations* moves into this region of meaning. It is a region habitually occupied by poetry" (Cavell 2002a: 271).

19. So one merely preliminary version of the special competence humans have in being able to acknowledge other human beings, what Cavell calls "empathic projection," is largely what I am limited to in aesthetic appreciation (though not in social experience; see below). The Cavellian drama of the inseparability between knowing and being-known can occur aesthetically only in the domain of the imagination. For the relevance of the notion to pictorial art, see Fried 2002: 36–39, 226–29; and Fried 2010: 105–6.

20. See Cavell 2002b: 189, on "why it is we treat certain objects, or how we can treat certain objects, in the way normally reserved for treating persons."

III

What I need from Cavell in order to address these issues in the film are three major claims, mostly worked out in *The Claim of Reason*, but present almost everywhere else in his corpus. The first is directly related to what was just mentioned: the nature of the problem. For Cavell claims that skepticism about other minds is really not skepticism but "tragedy," and, as he says, "there is no human alternative to the possibility of tragedy."[21] He establishes this somewhat indirectly, by arguing that such a putative skepticism about other minds cannot at all be made to parallel traditional skepticism about the external world, which, at one major level, can clearly be at least initially formulated as a problem about knowledge.[22] For one thing, the latter cannot be lived out as a form of life; we leave it, like Hume, in the philosopher's study, and treat the world, as we must if we are to avoid injury, as full of real, spatiotemporally located objects. But we *do* have to live out and live with a kind of deep, irremediable uncertainty that we will ever know what we think we need to know in order to deal with other human beings, as well as with a kind of uncertainty about just what *would* ease our anxiety about this situation (a fact that immediately calls into question whether our frustration at the otherness of the other can be understood as product in our finitude in trying to know). We take it as intuitively obvious that each of us occupies an absolutely superior position with regard to our own mindedness, that is, "what it is like to be me." So we are then tempted to think that overcoming skepticism about other minds would be knowing the other's mindedness by occupying just *that* sort of a superior position with respect to *her* mindedness (by "having" *it*). It is *very* unclear what this could be, though.

If I imagine myself with extraordinary telepathic powers, so that I can begin to see and feel things exactly as you do, then either this is incoherent (for *you* don't experience the world as *me* having those experiences as *mine*, as I would, with such powers), or the whole difference or separateness between me and you vanishes (like Cavell's Corsican brothers example in "Knowing and

21. Cavell 1999, 453. There is also lucid summary of this point at 432.
22. "At one level," because at another deeper level, Cavell will want to say that the most intimate or proximate mode of our being in a world, oriented and familiar with it, is not "knowledge," and skepticism is not primarily a matter of the limitations of what could be known, had we more powerful capacities of sentience and sapience.

Acknowledging," one of whom simply has every and only every experience the other has). In that case, we do not have someone knowing another's mind, but the simple collapse of the separateness of persons altogether. We have just one mind, perhaps in this fanciful example, in two bodies; not one mind knowing *another*. So, Cavell says, what we have in this concern with knowing others is not frustration at the limitations of knowledge (an assumption that implies there is some limitation that can be overcome, and we have just seen what the fantasy of overcoming it would amount to), but unavoidable, constant disappointment with what we do have available from the other, disappointment with what is available (all that is available), once we have disabused ourselves of the fantasy of "breaking into" the other's world.[23] However, once we have given up that fantasy, the idea that what we are left with is "insufficient," or a frustrating result of an in-principle surmountable finitude, can no longer get a grip.[24]

Second, with this established, Cavell can introduce an analysis of what is motivating our concern with the other's knowability (once it can be established that the problem cannot be an epistemological or even philosophical problem), suggesting that our enacting our inability to break into the other's world is motivated by ("means") an anxiety that others will be able to break into ours (and so a defense against that) or a fantasy of inexpressiveness about ourselves that insures our unknowability to them, itself a reassuring response to an anxiety about being revealed, available to others' gazes. So, "the block to my vision of the other is not the other's body, but my incapacity or unwillingness to interpret or judge it accurately, to draw the right connections." And ". . . the alternative to my acknowledgement of the other is not my ignorance of him but my avoidance of him, call it my denial of him."[25]

This last point already introduces the third and most important contribution of the book, the differences between, and especially the complementarity and inseparability of, what Cavell calls active and passive skepticism about

---

23. Cavell 1999: 341, 434.

24. There is a clear indication of the role the fantasy of looking "inside" another is playing in the dynamics of the film in a brief bit of dialogue between Dix and Laurel once he notices an oddity in the angles at which their apartments face one another.

DIX: You know, Miss Gray, you're one up on me—you can see into my apartment but I can't see into yours.

LAUREL: I promise you, I won't take advantage of it.

DIX: (*wryly*) I would, if it were the other way around.

Thanks to Richard Moran for discussions about this issue.

25. Cavell 1999: 368, 389.

other minds. The first, active skepticism, just reiterates what we have mostly been focusing on: how can I know another, the true nature of that other's (supposedly) inner life. The latter though is a concern, or an anxiety, about whether *I am ever truly known* ("as I really am") by an other. And the two modalities are interconnected.[26] If we assume, as we should given Cavell's concerns, a domestic, or intimate, or dialogic situation of self and other, where the question is not what "any self" (a human sciences researcher, say) can claim to know about anyone at all, but the everyday struggle to make ourselves intelligible to each other, then in claiming to know something about you, and in claiming this *to you*, I of course risk being misunderstood. I need to make sure that *I* am being understood, not just that my words are intelligible. This requires some effort; it does not just happen. And it comes with emotional risks. And it is often just in those cases where I am trying to convey to someone what I take it I have learned about her, I feel myself badly misunderstood. Feelings are hurt; friendships can fracture. Likewise, in hearing from others what they take themselves to have understood about me, I want to reserve some special authority to acknowledge or reject such claims; I am not just an object to be inspected and reported on.

And the connection is deeper. Insofar as I strive to understand something about another, I must be willing to *make it possible* for that other (or even any other) to understand *me*, or I will not be understood, in the sense just discussed; or, better, in Cavell's way of seeing it, I will have not been able to say what I mean. And insofar as I want to understand myself, I cannot claim that my own understanding is inexpressible, cannot be understood by others. (If that is so, then famously *I* can't be said to have expressed what I mean either.)[27] But this also involves accepting that I have to struggle to make my own putative self-understanding available for others, subjecting to some extent the question of what I mean to say to another's view of what saying that *would* mean.

And just by considering something like the common neighborhood these concepts inhabit, it is clear that such a claim to authority and rejection of a claim can often also be a version of defensive protectiveness against an unpleasant truth (too close to be easily or effectively distinguished), just as the putative claim about me can be motivated, directly or in a self-deceived

---

26. This interconnectedness is the main reason that understanding acknowledgment as "empathic projection," introduced in Cavell 1999: 421, is no longer adequate by 442, where this other (passive) skepticism/anxiety is both introduced and linked to the active form.
27. Wittgenstein 1958: §§244–71.

way, by hostility and an urge to wound. It can be this and also be true, of course, but our question is what *the other* meant by saying what she did. Moreover, the situation is even more difficult if set out, as an intentional task, to get the other to see things as I do.

But then the responses you produce in the other are apt to be directed to the wrong thing, to the part you have enacted, not to yourself. It is as an alternative to the wish to produce the response in the other that I claimed you must let yourself matter to the other.[28]

This leaves us with three complicated levels of complexity. This dynamical picture, especially this link between active and passive skepticism,[29] means that the struggle to understand another must also be a struggle to be understood, and a mutual struggle against suspicions of insincerity, mere seduction, manipulation, simple misunderstanding. But there is a second level of difficulty when we realize that in many contexts sincerity resolves none of the major anxieties, and this because a sincere avowal by an other may be an expression of self-deceit. In some cases I am called on to understand the other better than she understands herself; called on to admit that an other may have understood me better than I understand myself.[30] And third, this struggle goes on over time, at no point in which can there be any resolution once and for all of what provoked the anxiety and uncertainty. Sometimes my very attempt to *question* another's self-representation alters what one *might* have understood about such a person *before* any such interrogation or expression of skepticism. (As we shall see, this certainly happens in the film. Dix's *being* Dix, one might say, changes a great deal under the pressure of everyone's doubts about him. In returning to the film, we shall also return to the question of what it would mean to, as Cavell puts it, "let yourself matter.")

IV

Let us say that the issue of anyone's knowledge of any other is dialectical; not a matter of a subject knowing, or confirming in some way in the face of doubts,

---

28. Cavell 1999: 383; see also 352.

29. See Moran 2011: 250.

30. An implication: if I want to understand the other (in the practical, attitudinal sense, want to count on the other), even direct access to "what she thinks" can be dissatisfying. What *she thinks she thinks* and what *she really thinks* may be quite different.

its knowledge of an object. Moreover, our understanding of such an other subject is often available to us only in terms relevant to that subject's relation to us. It could even be that what we think we understand of an other is a result of that subject's acknowledgment of or engagement with an "us" that was not genuinely or honestly made available for acknowledgment, and this can "distort" the "results." In this and several other senses, acknowledging and being acknowledged are inseparable elements of intersubjectivity, and so subject to these dialectical gymnastics.[31]

In the terms presented by Nicholas Ray's film, the major issue for the police—and for Dix's friend Brub, Brub's wife Sylvia, Laurel, and Dix's agent Mel—is understanding Dix's "temper and potential violence," and, just as Cavell would have it, that issue cannot be isolated as a mere report or a matter even of knowledge. There would be something bizarre about simply "recording" the fact that another "tended to violence." Always? In any circumstance? In what circumstance and why? That is an assessment, a judgment in the normative sense, with consequences for conduct, but it is also not something "seen" or, that is, "provable." And there is a good deal of emphasis by Ray on *the extremely limited* bases for any such judgment, unavoidable as it is. Lochner seems to suspect Dix because Dix is flippant and did not call a taxi for Mildred. Laurel stands up for Dix, perhaps lies for him, because she "likes his face." Brub invokes the cliché that artistic geniuses do not and cannot behave like the rest of us. Sylvia thinks, on the basis of the vividness of Dix's imagination, her "college education," and Dix's unusual behavior that he can be classified as psychologically "abnormal." And this is an issue for the viewers as well, complicated

---

31. Another, very important sense is one explored by Moran 2011. It is that in exploring what knowing others' mindedness would amount to, I have to be oriented from my sense of what it is for me to be known, and this as measured by my superior position with respect to myself. Exploring this further, Moran shows, should lead us to doubt that the issue itself is correctly posed in terms of knowledge. Cf. also this very apt formulation: "With respect to other minds it may seem that the problem is rather to break into another circle of experiences. But the main point is that the objects of external world skepticism do not have a perspective on what it is to be known. The question of their knowability has to be solved on the side of the knower alone, with no 'confirmation' from the side of the known object. The possibility of forms of skepticism both with respect to knowing an other mind (the 'active skeptical recital') and with respect to being known by an other mind (the 'passive skeptical recital'), will turn out to be crucial for understanding the instabilities in the idea of an Outsider in other minds skepticism, and for understanding what may be distorting in seeing the problem of others as a problem of knowledge in the first place" (246). I discuss the implications of this distinction below.

even more for us by the fact that this is Humphrey Bogart, and I think it is fair to say that we, or most viewers, accept the early indications of his violent tendencies as marks of Bogart's toughness, integrity, and unwillingness to suffer fools gladly. As the movie goes on, however, those early explanations become less and less credible, and the questions about the meaning of Dix's conduct become much more complicated, as if *we* are being called to some account for our own early "acceptance" of the incidents.

This all has something to do with the ease, one might say, of a straightforward reading of the plot. Ray is clearly aware of this and is somehow referring to rather than invoking this expectation. A man, a war veteran, with a hair-trigger temper is suspected of murder. A woman saves him with an alibi of sorts; she is probably lying, because she is immediately infatuated with him, as is he with her. Their love suffers from the continued police scrutiny and her growing doubts about Dix. These doubts prove justified. He seems eventually to snap and attacks her. But, thanks to a lucky phone call, he does not injure her, and they learn "too late" that he has been cleared.

The hold of such a reading can be very strong, and I believe it is connected with a kind of default hermeneutic in understanding other people: that when someone does something startling or dramatic or hitherto unexpected or objectionable (violently beating a motorist after an accident, say), we are justified in saying: *We now* know *he is the type who would do such things.* In one sense this is a trivial and obvious tautology; he did it. In another sense, it is profoundly misleading and is under sustained attack in this film. (If the phone call had occurred before the beach scene, Dix would not have been such a type? Someone can be such a type without ever expressing his type?) The same doubt is being cast on the typological explanations mentioned above. That is, this appeal has something to do with the deeply misleading and just as deeply entrenched reliance on *ex ante* elements like fully transparent, determinate intentions, character traits, dispositions, and the like, in the explanation of actions, and, by contrast, what is actually the essentially retrospective or belated nature of self-knowledge and the knowledge of others unavoidably linked to such self-knowledge.[32]

There are two clear indications in the film of Dix's possible violence. After these, the near fight in the street at the beginning and the bar fight, the turning

32. See Pippin 2012 and 2008.

FIGURE 8.2

point of the movie occurs at a beach picnic, and the character and meaning of "the violence" change dramatically (figs. 8.2 and 8.3).

These first scenes raise no suspicions about Dix/Bogart (they are "in character" for a Bogart character),[33] but everything changes with the most important scene in the movie, a friendly beach picnic the Nicolais had arranged with Dix and Laurel. Laurel had been called in to Lochner's office for more questioning, or more pressure, since Lochner suspects she is lying about the alibi. At the interview she learns that Brub's dinner for his friend Dix had *also* been part of the investigation, a confidence we hear Brub had explicitly asked Lochner not to reveal. (Again, exposure, betrayal of intimacy, as a strategy in a struggle for control of the agenda is made visible.) Laurel does not tell Dix about the added interview, nor about the minor but still significant betrayal by Brub of his friendship. She thus enters into a collusion with the Nicolais, and from here on, Dix's violence is a reaction, each of the next three

33. They are "both linked to the Hollywood environment and stressing the rage it arouses in Dix Steele" (Eisenschitz 1993: 136).

FIGURE 8.3

times, to his learning of such a betrayal; actions by people he trusts, trying to find out something about him without asking him, or to act in a way that is hidden from him, indicating a distrust of his honesty and a certain objectification of the object of their study.[34] This attitude toward Dix arrogates a certain position of superior power to those who adopt it, and part of what Dix's violence means, intends, is a rejection of such power, something not ever understood or even considered by Lochner or the Nicolais or Laurel. And it is hard to exaggerate the importance of Sylvia's revelation. It is the pivot on which everything in the film turns. It leads to the car accident, the fight, a catastrophic collapse of Laurel's trust in Dix, her panic, her attempted flight, and

---

34. Right after apparently realizing that she "should have told" Dix about the interview, and apparently willing to heed his advice to "ask him" if she wants to know something, Laurel shows up at Sylvia's house, again discussing Dix in worried tones. She knows whose wife Sylvia is, and so reaching out to her has to count as a form of disloyalty. (Sylvia's motives are also interesting. The Freudian slip seems intended to ruin the marriage she is ostensibly encouraging. Is she jealous of what Laurel has? Attracted to Dix? Dissatisfied with her "average" husband?) I am grateful to Michael Fried for this point about Sylvia's possible motivations.

FIGURE 8.4

Dix's paranoid reaction to all that, and eventually to the irrelevance of Dix being cleared (fig. 8.4).

We are prepared for the intensity of these reactions by a scene in which Dix's vulnerability, his fear of "letting himself be known," in Cavell's words, is painfully visible. The extent of his need to be known and loved (to finally escape his "lonely place"), the extent to which he is not theatricalizing the self he presents to Laurel, and so the palpable fear of the exposure and rejection of himself as *he* understands himself, all amount to the extent to which he is enraged at finding himself treated in such a third- and not second-person way, let us say.[35] Here is the scene, as much against the Bogart type, especially at the beginning, as one will see. There is also a kind of anticipatory, defensive, somewhat scary reaction to his own fear, an ominous foreshadowing. (Call it the "murderousness of love.") Watch the positions of his hands and listen to

35. Sylvia's slip also touches another nerve. Brub and Sylvia and Laurel had all been talking about a matter of great intimacy and importance to Dix—his marriage—all without consulting him.

the foreboding undercurrent in the music. I think that part of what is so intense about Dix's speech in this love scene is that the viewer senses how deep is his hope that someone will finally be able to tell him who he is, that his loneliness has not been a matter of his being always by himself but that, being alone, there was nothing for him to be, or be with, at all. (This is connected with the fact that Dix now switches to a kind of overheated movie-script language, elevating and formalizing his address.) I would guess that for most viewers it is only on a second viewing that we sense the great imbalance in the scene, how silent Laurel is, how less desperate. Compare what you hear here from Dix with what is on her side: "I'm interested."

So what appears to be this desperate desire to be loved is dangerously close to a massive fear—great to the point of implied violence—that he *will* be intimately known, unguarded. His gesture of tenderness is also, at the same time, murderous. It is also oddly photographed for a love scene, with him standing and her sitting, something that may signal that Dix believes he is in charge, running the show, however vulnerable. It turns out to be an ironic pose (fig. 8.5). Compare this now with the scene near the end when Dix learns that Laurel had been planning to flee and begins to attack her. The position of his hands clearly couples both scenes (fig. 8.6).

And throughout these developments, the meta-movie issues reappear as well. At a dinner with the Nicolais, as they discuss the case, Dix stages a reenactment for them and assumes the role of film director, setting up the set, positioning the actors, explaining their motivations, and indicating how easily we can be made to believe the "truth" of dramatic representations, how vulnerable we are to the conventions of screenwriters. (We have already seen, and will see throughout, the reliance of characters on clichés, stereotypes, hasty, stock generalizations for interpretation, and this scene dramatizes how powerfully "movie logic" can fill the role once played by traditional roles, social hierarchies, natural order, and so forth.) The continuity of this scene with the opening credits is established by lighting, which highlights Dix's eyes, just as they were in the mirror. While we may be surprised at the effectiveness of Dix's direction, the scene ends with a nice irony. The person who most confuses image with reality (is most susceptible to the confusion) is the "average" middle-class Brub, who, it turns out, begins actually to strangle his wife. Ray seems both to be identifying with Dix's talent, and so identifying his movie with powerful scenes like this, and keeping some ironic distance. Dix begins to look positively insane in the scene, although there is an unmistakable pleasure

FIGURE 8.5

FIGURE 8.6

on his part in theatrically terrifying Sylvia, perhaps having sensed her suspicions of him. Ray seems to be playing along with Dix, garishly highlighting his "insane" eyes (fig. 8.7).

I have said that Sylvia's betrayal of a confidence is *the* central dramatic explosion in the film's narrative. Afterward, everything in Dix's relation to his friends and to Laurel changes, and because of that everything about the attempt "to understand Dix," especially by Laurel, has to change as well. That which results from trying to know someone is a function of what one allows of *oneself* to be known (often based on a fragile and self-deceived sense of what there is to be known), and that this dialectic is inseparable from issues of control and fear of exposure is prominently on view from now on in the film. When Laurel says that "we" didn't want to upset you, so we kept the meeting with Lochner from you, we should feel a chill of betrayal. Up to this point, what has Dix done to deserve this infantilizing, disloyal treatment? He had counted on them believing him and in him; that is, he trusted them, and they had been false. They were all reserving judgment on whether he could be guilty of murder. The "Dix" we see from here on out in relation to these intimates can hardly be called "the true Dix coming out," however genuinely

FIGURE 8.7

dangerous he has become. (Nothing in anything we have seen or heard about him suggests the nearly homicidal rages he is *now* subject to. Does this prove that the suspicions were correct? That he "was capable of murder"?)

But Sylvia does not initiate everything; the spark she provides finds pretty combustible material. Everyone agrees that Dix is "not normal," that he has an aura of unpredictability and a sometimes violent refusal to compromise that attracts attention and erotic interest. (Mel, who loves him most and perhaps best, explains that you just have to take all this on if you want closeness to Dix.) Laurel's first contact with him, after all, is as a murder suspect, and she must be harboring doubts and anxieties that are easily brought to active life. Those doubts are very near the surface and after the road rage incident are uncontrollably present. When she visits Sylvia after the fateful picnic (another act of disloyalty; Dix had insisted that people stop talking about him behind his back), she admires their cozy house and says that this is what she wants, domesticity and kids; normalcy. Laurel? With Dix? We have heard none of this before, and it rings completely false. She is already trying to escape and concocting self-deluded fantasies about herself to justify it. We have also already seen that Sylvia and Brub have "converted" sexual passion into marital or domesticated love by means of several normalizing strategies. Sylvia gets to be the smart one, for example, Brub, the "average one." Nothing about their domestic situation makes them look appealing as the "future" of Dix and Laurel. Marriage, the bedrock, foundational bourgeois institution, the contract to love and so the heart of the system that maintains that all the human passions can be contracted into submission and control, thus assumes a kind of metonymic role for the social order, and greatly elevates the stakes in the issue of whether Dix and Laurel will, or can, marry. In their post-dinner conversation (when Sylvia tells Brub that she is glad he is "normal" and "not a genius"), the suppressed hostility and self-deceit is on view in this picture of a "normal" marriage.[36]

---

36. Now, the great subject of nineteenth-century prosaic literature, the novel and drama, is marriage. This is appropriate; it is the central institution of bourgeois society: marriage represents *the* compromise between passion and law, or contract: the improbable unity of contracted passion. (I promise to love you forever.) I am not dealing with the issue the same way he does, but I assume that my enormous debt to Cavell's pioneering pair of books is obvious: 1984 and 1996. There is accordingly always a great anxiety about this; whether the unity required in marriages built on romantic love between individuals is a fantasy or ideological. (If it is, then perhaps all contractual constraints are; say, property; contractual restraints on takings.) That is why the central plot in such novels is adultery. (And why the subject of gay

And similar doubts about Laurel had been suggested throughout the film, and we learn, in the restaurant scene when Dix hits Mel, that he, too, has been thinking all along of what appears to have been something close to concubinage between Laurel and the real estate tycoon, "Baker." In one of the strangest scenes in the film, the point seems to be to reveal to us Laurel's "secret life" in the past; how little available for Dix she had really been. In the scene, the relation with her masseuse, Martha, seems "coded" for a lesbian relationship. Martha calls Laurel "angel," the tone of the conversation is of a jilted lover's and is aimed clearly at "breaking up" Laurel and Dix, and she says later, "I'm all you have." (In fact, Ray has obviously set up a clear parallel love-match in each of the two cases, two same-sex friendships, between Mel and Dix, and between Martha and Laurel, that are more stable, perhaps even deeper and more intimate than the heterosexual love affair, although both are also based on some very implausible, fatalistic conviction that the loved one, Dix or Laurel, has a fixed nature that must be wholly and uncompromisingly accepted in love.)[37]

Both of them, in other words, Dix and Laurel, have created, in all sincerity, a fantasy of intimacy and love (a Hollywood fantasy, one might say) that most viewers have largely bought in to, and both of them are subject to intense panic and retreat and even violence when that fragile fantasy begins to collapse. Of course, to make things even more complex, as complex as they are, it is not unheard of for human beings to formulate for themselves some ideal goal and

---

marriage touches such a nerve of anxiety in modern American society. Varying its contractual conditions seems to many to open a disturbing set of questions about what marriage itself is. If we are able to vary its contractual conditions, where can it stop? The people who are anxious think: Those in favor of varying the contract think there is no such objective, real, "natural" thing as marriage, and they are right.) But the topic of marriage also requires some collective understanding of how persons enter marriage; how we pick our partners, by means of intense romantic love. And there is the same kind of anxiety. Is there such a thing? And this depends on what we take it to be. One profoundly influential form of understanding (instructing us as to how to understand it, and assuming several conventions in projecting it back to us) is Hollywood film. Romantic love is a form of engagement with others that can be haunted by its own form of skepticism. In this film, a central element in that mythology is on view. Laurel likes Dix's face. Dix sees her in the courtyard for a second. And we also see in both how much they expect such a romantic relationship to do for them, how religiously Dix, at least, expects to be saved, as well as the lived-out implications of such a structure of understanding. 37. It is also the case that much of the film is suffused with an air of paranoia and the constant surveillance and pressure exerted by the commercial interests of Hollywood and the police. In this scene the "world of women," pressured and dominated by the much more powerful "world of men," is also visible. There are some remarks relevant to this issue by Polan 1993: 39–41.

invest so heavily in its achievement and what they expect from it that they ensure that they cannot achieve it. Practical contradictions like this are the natural home of "real" contradictions. Some of the intensity and overwrought investment in what they expect from being in love is framed by the fact that both live "inside" the movie world and *its* fantasies. Some of this resonates with Cavell's themes in another, even deeper way. If it is true that Dix and Laurel have jointly formulated a kind of goal that ensures they will fail, then that failure means they have also achieved a form of self-protection and can in that sense (Cavell's "avoidance" sense) be said to have intended to fail. That an agent can be doomed, *can doom himself*, by what he does to escape doom, is the stuff of tragedy both ancient and modern.[38]

The film builds to a conclusion in a powerful scene, full of undercurrents and double meaning. Dix, sensing that Laurel is drawing away (she cannot sleep, has been taking pills), suddenly proposes marriage, and this in a manic, impatient way that contrasts all the more with Laurel's sleeping-pill haze and her own clear hesitations. Bogart gives as powerful a performance here as he ever did, suggesting by the business of his action, and his air of unease, and the pace of his speech, that he knows everything is falling apart, and that he is simply refusing to see it, wants instead to push forward before it is too late. (As you will see, he is trying to "straighten out" something already crooked.) Laurel, for her part, enacts a Cavellian theme, but in a slightly different register. She has not "let herself be known" by Dix, let herself matter to him, but this is because she doesn't know what she should reveal or how. Her lack of self-knowledge, which we saw when she spouted her pieties about domesticity, is on view here, as she seems unable to look into one mirror, and then, as if to make the point again, she turns to another mirror, and again fails to see her

---

38. I don't mean that each of them has cynically, or simply out of fear, withheld themselves. *How* could Dix "explain" his past violence and expect to be understood, rather than even more suspected? (When he does try once, saying that he will not allow the other driver or anyone to call him names like this, Laurel recalls that the grave insult was "blind knuckle-headed squirrel.") Extraordinarily, though, Laurel knows why he is angry but never apologizes, as if conceding that explaining *herself* would be impossible. And it is simplistic in the extreme to suggest that she should have "told Dix all about Martha and Baker." As we have seen, it would take some superhuman talent to find a way to break through the conventional language of "abnormal," "unstable," "gold digger," "unemployed starlet," "kept woman," and so forth. As noted, there is something here of what Cavell finds in *Lear*: the characters *avoid* trying to do something like this, and that can be called "the avoidance of love." But it is much more credible here, in this world, to say that they *can't* "let themselves be known," not merely that they won't.

reflection (all of course an echo of the opening credits). And Dix enacts the domesticity she says she wants, but, as you'll see, clumsily. Here is the scene. The irony of Dix's description of their own love scene, that it is like his movie script, is true but (a) that also means it is posed, that just as in a fiction film, it is staged by both of them as they both suspect things have fallen apart, and (b) ironic because there is actually no real love anymore. The irrelevance of what they simply "tell" each other is also a point made, but it has a different meaning than the one Dix intends. Bogart has never been better, as, when he sits on the couch for breakfast and Laurel comes toward him, the fleeting expressions on his face register at once what he knows, but what he also will not admit (figs. 8.8 and 8.9).

This all serves as prelude for Dix's final violent attack on Laurel, interrupted by a phone call that will announce he is cleared. Ray is willing to go very far in this scene to suggest that what has happened is not the result of mistakes, moral failures, correctable blindness. He stages the aftermath to suggest that their last nearly deadly physical encounter[39] was also at the same time something like the last time they made love, suggesting, too, that the violence and the love are intertwined, given what we have seen of the complex demands — almost impossible demands — made on these lovers, and by these lovers.[40] That intertwining is unmistakably and rather startlingly suggested by Laurel's dishabille (fig. 8.10).

That closing line, "I lived a few weeks while you loved me," brings together many of the themes of the movie and, appropriately, leaves a good

39. This ending was improvised on the set. The original script, which they filmed, has Dix murder Laurel just as Brub arrives to tell him he is in the clear for Mildred's murder, and so has to arrest him for Laurel's. In an interview, Ray remarked, "I just can't do it! Romances don't have to end that way. . . . Let the audience make up its own mind about what's going to happen to Bogie when he goes outside the apartment area . . ." (quoted from Ray's documentary portrait *I'm a Stranger Here Myself*, in Eisenschitz 1993: 144 and in Polan 1993: 61, who notes that the original ending was shot, and that Ray ordered a closed set for the next day and reshot with the ending we have).

40. Perkins (1992: 225) notes that the "investment in love" on both sides is "excessive," and so the relationship is "doomed." The reasons for such an excessive investment amount to the great theme of nineteenth-century novels, such as *Madame Bovary*, *Anna Karenina*, and *Effi Briest*. Bourgeois marriage often serves as a great figure for bourgeois domesticity and convention itself (that is, ordinary life), and romantic adventure, adultery, as a kind of salvation or liberation from such a fate; there as here an illusory salvation. The great cinematic treatment of such fantasies about love: Max Ophüls's *Reckless Moment* and *Caught* make much the same point.

FIGURE 8.8

FIGURE 8.9

FIGURE 8.10

deal unsettled. Laurel is quoting a line from Dix's new movie, lines that Dix had already expressed as if a foreshadowing of the end of their own affair. ("I was born when she kissed me; I lived a few weeks while she loved me. I died when she left me.") There is, first, genuine pathos in the line; they, Laurel especially, *had* missed their chance for "life." There is, second, the fact that Laurel expresses herself in a line from a film, not her own words, and so that second level of reflectivity returns: the movie's relation to the audience, its own genuineness or honesty, and so here the question of its quotability, or the meaning of Laurel's use of it to express herself.[41] (She sees herself in lines provided by a movie, and this could mean either that the movie script has captured something genuine, or that Laurel is as "real" as a character from a film.) Third, there is her alteration, changing the third person (she) to the first (me). Laurel seems to realize that Dix's "leaving her" is as much a result of her distrust and

41. It is a Hollywood line, not Shakespeare, but I don't think Ray is ironizing its use here. I assume we are meant to understand that it does express both the pathos of the moment, Laurel's reliance on *Dix's* words (the closest she'll get to *self*-knowledge), and her own realization of who has done what to whom.

that she is back where she began, a starlet with a shady past. Astonishingly, in her mind, *Dix left her*. ("I died when you left me" would be the continuation); they did not break up—all an odd way to put it after what we have just seen.

Stanley Cavell has argued that skepticism about other minds, while an expression of uncertainty about another, is not properly skepticism in the philosophical sense but tragedy, and that there is no human alternative to tragedy. I think Nicholas Ray would agree.

Agency & Meaning

NINE

Vernacular Metaphysics:
On Terrence Malick's *The Thin Red Line*

I

The narrative conventions that make the Hollywood war movie a recognizable genre are among the most familiar, fixed, and predictable of any genre conventions, so much so that even variations or inversions of the conventions are just as familiar.[1] War movies from different wars are also all different, but at the heart of the most familiar species of the war movie genre, the Hollywood World War II movie, there is almost always some sort of group dynamic that is broadly egalitarian. A cast of colorful characters from various parts of the country and various social classes are thrown together in a combat unit and destined in the course of the movie to face some great test. Likable, wise-cracking minor characters are usually the first to die, increasing our emotional stake in the fate of the rest of the crew. There is some crusty lifer, a sergeant or chief, who is inconceivable in any walk of life other than the military and who is usually a comic character, often a supposedly amusing alcoholic. No well-known war movie in the twentieth century is about a professional army

---

1. And there are several species. There is the boot camp transformation movie; the impossible objective movie; the prisoner of war and escape movie; the daring, reckless fly-boy movie; the war as seen by children movie; the coming-of-age war movie; the underground resistance movie; the patriotic propaganda movie; and so forth.

or about mercenaries. World War II or Korea or Vietnam movies are naturally about a citizen's army of draftees or volunteers who yearn to return to their civilian lives, hate the army, but do their duty. Their memories of home (and sometimes what we see of their home life) and what they will do after the war are among the most frequent topics of conversation, are what sustain them, give what they do meaning (they are protecting home). Loyalty to their new friends, the revelation of the unique power of relationships forged in wartime, as well as the emergence of great courage from unexpected characters are all familiar themes within the genre.[2]

As noted, the variations in the formula are just as familiar. The most frequent violation of the straight "ordinary" or "democratic heroism" theme concerns ambitious and thereby corrupt career officers who see the war as a means of advancement and so are far more indifferent to the risks and suffering of their men than any humane perspective should tolerate. *Paths of Glory* (dir. Stanley Kubrick, 1957) is perhaps the most famous example of such a film.[3] (Sometimes, though, the ambition, while clear, is also linked to qualities of great military leadership on an epic scale, as in *Patton* [dir. Franklin J. Schaffner, 1970].) Another variation or inversion, very prominent in Vietnam-era war films, concerns the pointlessness, even the absurdity, of the war itself, a meaningless project concocted by distant politicians, requiring enormous sacrifices for goals that no sane, ordinary soldier can possibly accept or even understand, with psychological costs that are incalculable. (*Apocalypse Now* [dir. Francis Ford Coppola, 1979] can serve as the paradigm of such movies. The soldiers whistling the theme of *The Mickey Mouse Club* at the end of *Full Metal Jacket* [dir. Kubrick, 1987] could serve as well.) In both the formula and the variations, then, an underlying theme emerges: how (or whether) ordinary citizens of a commercial republic, whose daily lives involve no exposure to physical danger or violence, can come to be able to participate wholeheartedly in acts of nearly unimaginable ferocity and deal with the psychological trauma of constant death, often of buddies loved in a way not permitted to

2. Since genres exist for the sake of variations, even in more traditional Hollywood war movies, this then can have a kind of inverse presentation, too. That is, the loyalty and love that grows among men can also be a great difficulty for the group's particular or national purpose. In *The Thin Red Line*, that is certainly the case for Captain James Staros (Elias Koteas), when he decides not to attack. A fine treatment, one might even say a study, of such a theme is Anthony Mann's *Men in War* (1957).

3. Another impressive example would be Robert Aldrich's *Attack!* (1956).

men in any other context, often for geopolitical purposes that seem pointless. An underlying, often implicit question is: What do men need to believe, what do they need to understand, to endure such an ordeal?

In many of Terrence Malick's films, various genre conventions of Hollywood movies like these are invoked and structure much of the narration.[4] This is especially true of his 1998 film, *The Thin Red Line*, which has many of the elements of a Hollywood World War II movie. But, as in his other films, these genre conventions create expectations and suggest explanations that are then undermined, refused, left open, made to seem irrelevant, made mysterious, or even ironized.

The implication is unavoidable that, therefore, these conventions about motivation and value are no longer available, no longer credible, and the viewer has to struggle to find some point of orientation. This sense of being lost, once these conventions are invoked and then refused, is the main effect on any viewer and seems a major point of the film itself. Genre considerations can be said to provide a common or even a mythic structure of intelligibility in film, and in this genre that means the narrative and even visual structure concern how we, as modern viewers of the movie, have come to understand war. War movies both purport to instruct us on how to understand war (and so sometimes raise questions like whether war is avoidable or evil or natural) and rely on what is already assumed to be our settled conventions about the issue. However, especially in this war movie, Malick's two quite dramatic technical innovations—his almost devout concentration on the visual beauty, magisterial indifference, and sublimity of the natural world, and the unusual meditative interior monologue voice-overs by individual characters—violate not only genre conventions but many narrative, dramatic, and psychological elements of realist fiction films.[5] (They have also been intensely criticized.)

---

4. The outlaw road movie; the social class/romantic triangle movie; the settlement/aboriginal movie; the war movie; the coming-of-age movie.

5. There are few films for which George Wilson's apposite remarks about the perils of heavy reliance on plot exposition alone in understanding the film are more appropriate. (Although, there are certainly many Hollywood films for which the remarks are just as apposite, as Wilson shows better than anyone ever has. Malick is just making the issue exceptionally clear.) I mean remarks like these: "Perhaps it is the confused idea that film is the most 'direct and immediate' way of narrating a story which has led most viewers, professional and otherwise, to suppose that the requirements of plot exposition confine a film's significance. . . . Viewers dispose their attention toward the 'focus' of the story's ultimate resolution. They are perceptually set to follow the evolution of those plot conflicts that are marked out to be the subject

Malick often composes his movies with contrasting and interlocking visualizations of, or visual embodiments of, or allegorical allusions to, or even visual contrasts with, voiced reflective meditations.[6] The visual narrative always seems to be inflected, in a number of different ways, by the content and tonality of these meditations (more than by requirements of the plot alone) and framed in some way by shots of the living, natural world that are for the most part not required by, and are often independent of, the plot. That is, to say the least, an unusual mode of filmic composition. It is a kind of genre for which there are few conventions except those that appear in Malick's other films.[7]

There *is* of course a gripping war narrative in *The Thin Red Line*, driven by the planning for and anticipation of a horrific frontal assault on an entrenched position, followed by further attacks on Japanese positions, and the development of two sets of complex character relationships. But that narrative, and even much of the character conflict, while clearly important, can often seem secondary to Malick's novel compositional approach. Neither the narrative nor the character development bears the meaning of the film in the significant way that the visual compositions and their related voiced reflections do.[8]

---

of an audience's most immediate and engaged regard. Indeed, it is the normal goal of narrative strategies to make this temptation effectively irresistible" (Wilson 1986: 10).

6. This takes up in a different way an important suggestion by Richard Neer 2011 in his fine piece on *The New World* (dir. Malick, 2005), when he says: "More specifically, there is at any given moment in *The New World* a reciprocal relation between the narrative of discovery on the one hand, and the declaration of the film's own possibilities on the other." This reciprocal relation assumes a number of different forms in *The Thin Red Line*, only some of which can be explored here.

7. One could make a case for the relevance of Kon Ichikawa's *Fires on the Plain* (1959). There are voice-overs in the film (more monologues than meditative), non-narrative concentration on animals and nature (insects, dogs, birds), and the visual emphasis on the emaciated state of the Japanese; this widespread insanity and desperation is echoed in Malick's depiction of the Japanese on Guadalcanal.

8. It is fair to say that Malick's use of the voice-overs has changed over the course of his career. In his first two films, it is different from later experiments. In *Badlands* (1973), Holly's commentary (Sissy Spacek) is largely *counterpoint*, dissociated from, rather than reflected in, the scenes we view. (We see murder; she wants to talk about what they ate.) In *Days of Heaven* (1978), Linda's voice-over (Linda Manz) is both knowing and innocent at the same time. Her flat, almost affectless narration, rather than help reveal the psychology of the characters, renders the drama more opaque and strange. After *The Thin Red Line*, John Smith's voiced musings (Colin Farrell's character in *The New World*) is more politically tinged, but very much in character, not generally reflective, and Pocahontas's is more religious (in the vague sense of

(At the most one could say that the narrative and character developments are only one of the four main structuring elements of the film, along with the shots of nature, the voice-overs, and the music.)[9] The aim of this chapter is to understand the relation between these narratological, visual, and psychological innovations and the thematic developments in the film, most of which concern that traditional war movie theme: how ordinary citizens of commercial republics can both come to participate in acts of extreme violence and come to understand in some way what they are doing, come to confront, much more vividly than they do in ordinary life, that they will kill other humans beings and that they may die.

II

There are two central pairs of characters in the film. The first sergeant, Welsh (Sean Penn), and the enigmatic, moody soldier, Witt (Jim Caviezel), form the first pair. And Lt. Colonel Tall (Nick Nolte, in an extraordinary, riveting performance) and Captain Staros (Elias Koteas) form the other. But we are given very little time or sufficient background or dialogue to know very much about these characters as individuals, and the other characters in the infantry company appear on-screen so randomly and disappear so quickly that none of the usual war movie group dynamics that we expect can even begin. For a long time, it is completely impossible, even for someone who has read the James Jones novel, to link up characters with individual names. We do not, except

"spiritual"). In *The Tree of Life* (2011), the technique is much more like that in *The Thin Red Line*. Malick is clearly experimenting with the right relation between what we might call being inside the (and our own) narration and being outside. And that is itself a complicated issue because, while we need to believe that we can both inhabit an inside, and also step back and assess things from outside, there is obviously no outside.

9. The intended meaning of the musical soundtrack is a very interesting issue in itself. After the Arvo Pärt opening chord, the idyllic scenes are accompanied, as if in counterpart, by a requiem, Gabriel Fauré's, but to add to the complexity it is the "In Paradisum" section that we hear. A counterpoint choral song (and the chorus is something connected to the solidarity-isolation theme to appear shortly), the Melanesians', is then heard (Arsenije Jovanovic's "The Prophecy from the Village of Kremnus"). Perhaps the most interesting piece of music, the title of which directly addresses the many interrogative moments in the film, is Charles Ives's "The Unanswered Question," played during and after the Japanese camp has been overrun, perhaps the most violent sequence in the film.

for two isolated instances, get to see their home life, so there is little to fill out their characters.[10] The camera does not follow them for sufficient stretches of time for the normal association and identification to occur within the plot of the movie, and the central dramatic event of the film, the frontal assault up Hill 210, held by the Japanese, is not photographed in a way that allows us to follow the action, anticipate what might happen, or properly identify who is at what risk and why. This difficulty of identifying individuals is also greatly compounded by the fact that the spoken monologues are unattributed. The ubiquitous southern accents do not help either. We often do not know with any certainty who is speaking the voice-overs, so it is hard to place a monologue in the plot. Why some particular character would be thinking just *this* or *that* then is as impossible to determine as who is speaking. This is uniquely disorienting, even more so than that so many characters look alike, especially when wearing their helmets. We are prevented from any normal psychological identification of the voices and so from any normal inference about the motives and implications of what is said. At one extreme point, we even hear one character's musings, a character named Train (John Dee Smith), voice "over" a kind of *visual* monologue clearly imagined by *another* character, Bell (Ben Chaplin).

The result of this is the most radical departure from what could be called the main convention of war films: the creation of solidarity between men, a solidarity of such profundity that nothing in ordinary life (certainly not politics) comes close, and that is usually offered as an explanation for the acts of selfless heroism that we see.[11] There is no such solidarity here, and there is instead a great deal of emphasis on isolation, alienation from others, and loneliness.[12] (Welsh at one point insists that the best a man can do is "to make himself an island." And we also hear: "War don't ennoble men. It turns 'em into dogs. Poisons the soul.")[13] War, the ever-present possibility of death and

<hr>

10. The exceptions are Bell's memories of his wife and a brief memory by Witt of his mother's death and his childhood. Both instances are dreamlike and do not contribute much to any standard psychological profile of a character.

11. A good example of the formation of such a cohesive group is the patriotic (and very British) Carol Reed wartime vehicle, *The Immortal Battalion* (aka *The Way Ahead*) (1944). There is an especially explicit concentration here on the particular challenges of a citizen's army in democratic societies, although the tone is naively optimistic about the issue throughout.

12. This issue is one of the main themes of Chion 2004.

13. All quotations from the film are from *The Thin Red Line*, dir. Malick (1998; New York, 2010, DVD).

killing, forces on everyone the question of death, the unavoidable need to make some sense of it, to learn how to live with a possibility we easily ignore in daily life. And this pressure, we see, isolates everyone from everyone else, rather than creating a new community. (As the difficulty of tracking characters already suggests, however, such isolation, remarkably, does not in itself mean an *individualization*. The visual, voiced, and even psychological identities of characters can seem porous, shifting, and unstable, even though no new group unity is created. And since the voice-overs are unattributed by visual cues or anything else, the thoughts seem to float in logical space, as if they could visit any character or be shared by, be thought by, anyone.) When, near the end of the film, the new company commander, Bosche (George Clooney), does describe their group as a "family," the irony, given what we have just seen for two hours, is almost unbearable, and Welsh, interspersed in the new captain's palaver, thinks to himself in voice-over, "Everything a lie; everything you hear, everything you see; they just keep coming, one after another; . . . they want you dead or in their lie." More subtly, when Staros invokes the family image as he departs, relieved of command, he too says, "You are my sons, my dear sons; you'll live inside me now. I'll carry you wherever I go." Here the tone is pathos, not irony. For he has *not* been able to act as their father, to "protect" them, defend them. He had to yield command to their military father, Tall, and so he obviously needs to believe in a familial bond that was never actually possible.[14]

III

This profound isolation is a sense heightened by the most untraditional and controversial technique in the film, those reflective voice-overs, which are not addressed to anyone and are in effect monologues. They thus bear some resemblance to dramatic monologues in stage plays, when a character says what he thinks out loud, to himself. But Malick's monologues are rarely tied to any specific event in the action, are not reflections about what one should do and why, and do not provide information about a character's view of what has just happened or will happen. Even some dialogues are in effect, ironi-

---

14. In Welsh's first conversation with Witt, Welsh had already made clear that any such claim by Staros would have to be a fantasy. Welsh says, "This is C Company, of which I'm First Sergeant. I run this outfit. Now, Captain Staros, he's the CO, but I'm the guy who runs it. Nobody's gonna foul that up."

cally, monologues: those between the Japanese and Americans, each speaking their own language, sometimes at length and in bizarre indifference to the obvious incomprehension of the other.[15] Welsh mentions the isolation theme several times in his monologues, especially when he describes everyone as mere "moving boxes," as if all shut up "inside," prevented from any real contact with an "outside." And the dramatic action plays out such a theme. A character swears to a dying comrade that he will write the man's wife, then immediately recoils in horror from what he promised, saying he won't do it. Another character, Storm (John C. Reilly), admits to Welsh, "I look at that boy dying, I don't feel nothing. I don't care about nothing anymore." And it is not irrelevant that Guadalcanal is an island. Witt of course is the great exception, but his love of the men and for Welsh seems independent of, prior to, even indifferent or resistant to, the experience of war, not inspired by it. (The war also creates an even vaster gulf between the Americans and the Japanese prisoners, whom the soldiers treat as animals or things. The great exception is Witt, and that again raises the question of the meaning of his role in the film, clearly the central one, the thematic center of the movie, however mysterious.)

Malick has also profoundly changed the narrative and characterization in James Jones's novel, all in ways that move the narration further away from any formula (or, one could even say, further away from mere narration).[16] Witt has been changed from a rather stupid Kentucky racist into a kind of meditative warrior and spiritual center of the movie. Scenes that took many pages for Jones to fill out and motivate are dropped briefly into the film without development, as if sections of film that did explain them have been simply cut out. For example, in the film we see a *very* brief couple of scenes on the ship before landing in which a character, Doll (Dash Mihok), says he will steal a pistol, and we then see him doing it. The reasons for this desire and what it means, developed at length in the novel, are not given. We just see Doll later using the pistol. (The same is true of the machine gun Welsh carries in the film.) We sense in the film only that *some* sort of standard moral constraint is already wearing

15. In a scene at the beginning of the campaign on the islands, the American troops pass by a Melanesian man, and neither side does very much to register the other's presence. Nothing in the film is dispositive about anything, however. Later we see a Melanesian man tenderly helping the American wounded.

16. A good summary of the relation between the novel and the film can be found in Power 2003: 148–59.

away, but not why or who this character is. Or, in the film, we know far too little about Sergeant Keck (Woody Harrelson) to understand the significance of his falling on a grenade to protect his men, after Keck had accidentally pulled the pin and thrown the pin, not the grenade. Sergeant McCron (John Savage) goes mad in the assault after having lost his entire squad and begins to rave about how we are all dirt, but who is Sergeant McCron and why do we only know him in his madness?[17] Dale (Arie Verveen) desecrates bodies, stealing gold teeth, and torments a prisoner (as if the prisoner understands English), but we know virtually nothing about Dale, and it is very difficult to identify him later when he sits alone, shirtless in the rain in obvious, intense psychological pain. Welsh is a deep cynic in the novel, convinced that the entire war is about property, something he goes on about at great length. In the film, though, we only hear this once from Welsh. Mysteriously, and in a way unmotivated by anything we have seen, it is after he has risked nearly certain death in an act of great beneficence that has nothing to do with property. He rushes head-long into withering fire in order to get morphine to a dying soldier.[18] (Also, before a major assault, a soldier complains that he has stomach cramps and cannot proceed. His sergeant is about to force him to go when our supposed cynic, Welsh, again mysteriously, in a kind of gratuitous act of sympathy, allows the soldier, likely a cowardly malingerer, to return to the rear and sick bay.) Very famous movie stars, like John Travolta and Clooney, and relatively major stars like John Cusack and Woody Harrelson, are briefly introduced only to disappear (thus defeating the predictability and familiarity that comes from the Hollywood star system). Major characters in the novel, like Fife (Adrien Brody), are also reduced to cameo roles in the film, and therewith one of the most important themes in the novel, one focused mostly on Fife and elab-orated at length in the novel, physical homosexual love among the men, is eliminated.[19] All of this functions to interrupt any genre-based expectations about narrative and that great forward movement of Hollywood narratives we have become so used to in American films since the likes of D. W. Griffith and others discovered how to control and accelerate narrative pace. I want to

17. The fact that the actor is John Savage suggests yet another intertextual reference, this time to Savage's character in *The Deer Hunter* (dir. Michael Cimino, 1978).

18. The tenderness of the soldier's dying good-bye is one of the film's most poignant and effec-tive small moments.

19. There is one very tender scene of a Japanese soldier cradling a comrade as if a lover, but nothing is made of it.

say that all of this is quite deliberate and shifts our attention to the alternate compositional method alluded to above.

Moreover, and as already noted, in the most unusual departure, whatever we do learn about these characters is through the voice-overs, and what we learn is not at all standard psychological detail about their ordinary lives. The voiced monologues have a figurative, meditative, poetic form totally at odds with any war movie convention. Indeed, it would be fair to say, now that Malick has released other films since his return to filmmaking with *The Thin Red Line*, that his use of these meditative voice-overs by individual characters and the very sweeping philosophical and religious scope of these voice-overs (in effect asking what could the context be within which these sorts of events could have any significance) have most divided audiences and critics. Some viewers (like me) clearly find them engrossing and successful, the key to the films' great distinctiveness; others find them pretentious, unmotivated in the film, anti-cinematic, and off-putting.

IV

But the voice-overs also introduce a great deal of narrative and thematic tension into the film's visual narration, and if we begin by noticing these unusual tensions, we can better appreciate how the underlying theme of so many movies about twentieth-century warfare is being addressed (and in a way negated) by Malick. I mean that large question mentioned earlier: How is it possible for citizen soldiers of at least putatively pacific commercial republics[20] to come to suffer the trauma and engage in the killing required by modern warfare, especially in foreign lands, far away from their own homes and families? This is of course simply a question for any human being who must do what war requires, but Malick's focus on the Tall-Staros conflict, and the necessity for contemporary men to understand in some way what their predicament means, without a conventional appeal to "the mysteries of God's plan" (never an issue cited in

---

20. "Putatively" because the American republic has so often been at war during its relatively short history. The traditional American war movie treats war as episodic and unusual, but here the voice-overs by Train elevate such violence and destruction to permanent metaphysical status. This is another reason why the narrative framework of the genre is invoked only to be refused.

the film; no character avows any conventional theodicy, apart from temptations to Manicheanism) or the protection of the nation (never mentioned in the film), gives the film its distinctive character.

I mean such things as the following. The film opens on a scene of Witt and another soldier in what appears to be a kind of peaceful island paradise of Melanesians, playing with children and swimming through beautiful crystal-clear ocean water. Several things are strange though, upon reflection. Witt, throughout the film, avows a great love for C Company, volunteering to return to the fight after his exile into a medical support unit. (In the novel he leaves and returns five times.) We see several times in the film that his avowal is quite genuine. But Witt at the beginning is, after all, AWOL. He has left the fight to others, abandoning them until he is caught and brought back in the brig.[21] He says he is "twice the man" Welsh is, and he clearly means in bravery and soldiering, but his (in effect) brief desertion (in battlefield conditions yet) is never explained.[22] But the unremarked-on fact is very important. Whatever Witt's allegiance to his company is, it is not mediated by political, national, and military institutions. He is certainly not a hypocrite. He *does* love his comrades, but that love has little to do with their common institutional bond, and what Witt is led to do has nothing to do with anything like his duty to them.

Moreover, the Melanesian setting is ambiguous. Witt remarks to a mother that the Melanesian children never fight. The mother corrects him, saying that the children do fight. This correction is a brief signal that all is not, in effect, what it seems, certainly not what it seems to Witt. (Not to mention the ominous crocodile at the very beginning.) Nor is this correction by the mother the first indication of some tension between what we see and what we come to understand. This scene occurs at the very beginning of the voice-overs, as we hear an overpowering, ominous organ chord (Arvo Pärt's "Annum per annum") and see that deadly-looking crocodile, a huge tree and root and enveloping vine system "attacking" the tree, and we hear an unattributed voice intone, "What's this war in the heart of nature? Why does nature vie with

21. The only commentators I have found who notice this odd fact are Leo Bersani and Ulysse Dutoit in their fine chapter on the film in Bersani and Dutoit 2004: 124–78.

22. Not only are many characters in the film hard to identify and reidentify, but it is also hard to connect what a character avows with what they do, upsetting another important dimension of movie logic. Witt loves Company C but is AWOL; Welsh seems a cynic and encourages selfishness but performs a genuinely heroic, altruistic act.

itself? The land contend with the sea? Is there an avenging power in nature? Not one power, but two?" (fig. 9.1).[23]

So now we come to one of the most startling facts about the film. Unless one has an *extremely* sensitive ear, it is almost impossible to realize that this voice we hear at the very beginning—by far the most frequent voice we will continually hear sound the most general reflections and questions about the meaning of war, killing, death, and the place of such violence in nature, and which will voice the last reflection we hear ("All things shining")—belongs *not* to Witt, an almost inescapable attribution on first hearing, but to a character we have barely caught a glimpse of: one Private Edward B. Train, played by John Dee Smith. We have only seen him briefly in the bathroom aboard ship (fig. 9.2). He tells Welsh how afraid he is, that he wants to own an automobile after the war, that "the only thing that's permanent is, is dying and the Lord," and that "this war ain't gonna be the end of me, and it ain't gonna be the end of you neither." He is an unlikely candidate to be the one raising the large questions he does, to say the least. This is confirmed even more strongly when the film circles back to the very same Train at the end, in the landing craft heading back to the ship, and he again babbles away about how life just has to be better for him after all this suffering, that is he older now, not old, but older, and other such banalities. Yet, again, as with narrative conventions, what we think we know about character cues and expressive possibilities are given no purchase or grip in the film, and we are, again, lost. It is not only very difficult to identify Train's voice; it is even more difficult to believe that he could voice such sentiments, could have such an inner life.

All this worry about a violent, warring nature is, nevertheless, in preparation for our being *visually* pulled immediately into the quite *contrary* romantic conventions of native innocence and a harmonious nature, as if, as in the post-Rousseauean convention, it is only the arrival of the civilized world that introduces brutality and violence into a naturally peaceful world (as if the forbidding destroyer belching black smoke is the human avatar of the croco-

23. Throughout a great deal of the second half of the film, a low, humming musical undertone can be heard, occasionally accompanied by the sound of a clock ticking for long stretches, especially in battle scenes. I say *Manichean* here because the tonality is religious, and sometimes second person, but the reflection could certainly be understood in a Freudian way, as Freud came to realize late in his career that there might be a death instinct, as well as eros, a duality for which there is no resolution or synthesis, just a constant struggle, much like the one Train is concerned about. This is something suggested by Bersani and Dutoit 2004.

dile). It is as if we hear what may be true (what *Train thinks may be true*), that a Manichean view is true: there is great beauty and harmony in nature, as well as great violence, chaos, and brutality, and there is no mediation or synthetic point of view possible. Yet we *see* what we are encouraged to think Witt believes or is trying to believe, that the Rousseauean convention is true and that he has discovered the deeper truth about the possibility of natural beauty and true natural harmony. (But even in the opening, idyllic scenes, we hear Fauré's "Requiem" on the soundtrack as a kind of subtle counterpoint, reminding us that, however beautiful and innocent the scene we are seeing, the film will be about death, killing, and sorrow about death, a musical theme sounded over a scene seemingly at odds with it.) Indeed, at the end of the film, we see a very different Melanesian village, more consistent with what we heard from Train, now with violent arguments among the tribe members, suspicious, wary children, disease, stacks of human skulls, and so a hint of cannibalism in the tribe, testifying again to how much of what *we originally see* depends on *what Witt thinks he sees* (or wants to see). There is no suggestion whatsoever that the village has been transformed by the invasion of the Japanese and Americans,[24] and the existence of the skulls is clearly designed to signal that the violence in the tribe is long-standing; they were there but not seen by Witt (and so not by us). This is only the first indication of the many complicated relationships between what we see, what characters avow, and what other characters believe (figs. 9.3 and 9.4). (Nor does this explain the confusing elements of the next scene in the village. Witt looks around, obviously very sad, and we begin to see what appears to be his remembrance of the village as it was—as he thought it was—and we hear a voice-over begin to wonder what had happened to produce these divisions. But the voice is not Witt's. It is Train's again.)

Welsh is the most cynical character in the film, deeply skeptical of the war itself (the whole thing is just for property) and clearly very concerned that Witt's loyalty to the company and fearless dedication will get him killed, pointlessly. ("If you die, it's gonna be for nothing.") At one point, after he tells Witt that there is "just this world"—and this time is not contradicted by Witt, who only looks up to the moon—we see a hellish scene of wild dogs eating corpses of soldiers, as if to confirm Welsh's cynicism (fig. 9.5). But Welsh also clearly loves Witt and so somewhat ironically embodies rather than confounds part of the war movie formula. Even someone who thinks the war effort is corrupt

24. As Bersani and Dutoit 2004 mistakenly surmise; see 157.

and worthless *is* willing, almost gratuitously, despite himself, to take great risks for his comrades and is deeply concerned with Witt's fate. This is a mirror in effect to the fact that Witt, who is introduced to us in pacific scenes, is no pacifist at all (something we would clearly expect) but is willing to fight and kill with intensity without questioning his role in the killing.[25]

Then there is the unusual story of Bell, a soldier who had been an officer but who gave up his commission so he could spend time with his wife before being shipped out again as a private. There are long, idyllic voiced-over scenes of Bell's memories of physical affection with his wife and his intense longing for a total merger with her. (The prominent image is water, a figure throughout the film for harmony, merger, and a common bond of life, especially in the assault scenes, in which the men must fight with inadequate water. This is another way in which the theme of isolation or aloneness is stressed, by emphasis on what is missing, the harmony symbolized by water, as when the men rest in the rear and swim naked together, joyously, in the ocean. The last battle scene, when Witt saves the company by sacrificing himself, takes place as the soldiers wade hip-deep in the waters of a river. Witt sends a badly injured soldier floating away on the water, as if he is returning him to a primary harmony.) We are led to believe that these memories are what sustain him, motivate him to get home, give his life some ultimate meaning, as if, if there is no national or familial community, there is at least a reliable romantic connection with others. But we then learn that these may be imaginative projections, romantic fantasies. He gets a devastating letter from his wife, suddenly asking for a divorce and even, in a sublimated moment of sheer, deep aggression, asking Bell to "help her leave him." She has fallen in love with someone else.[26]

So, while there are other voice-overs, these four are the most frequent: Train's Manichean reflections, Witt's concern with death and facing it calmly,

25. Insofar as a film as a whole can suggest or inspire allegiances, create sympathy, provoke aversion or disgust, one might say that at least this aspect of Witt's relation to war is echoed in the film as a whole, which is not an "antiwar" film at all. Or even a political film, for that matter. The national mission in fighting the Japanese, the "cause of freedom," and so forth are never mentioned.

26. "I drink you" is Bell's closing apostrophe. Later, before he gets her letter, he writes her a kind of hymn to love. "Love. Where does it come from? Who lit this flame in us? No war can put it out, conquer it. I was a prisoner. You set me free." As I am trying to show, the irony (here somewhat bitter) and the unexpected reversal of our standard expectations is not unique but runs through the film from beginning to end.

Welsh's cynicism, and Bell's romantic idealism. And they all introduce various tensions: between what a character does and what he thinks; between the voice-over and what we see and hear; and among the voice-overs themselves, all of which are both integrated into and also somewhat independent of normal plot and character development and war movie conventions.

V

The most significant tension occurs between Tall and Staros and is a more straightforward character conflict, the closest to a war movie genre convention. That is, while we are set up, again by a standard convention, to see Staros as the caring humanist leader whose first concern is for his men and Tall as the egomaniacal careerist, the plot development is quite surprising, perhaps the biggest, though subtly presented, surprise in the film.[27] The Japanese are dug in on the top of a hill, in entrenched machine gun positions that artillery cannot damage. The only option, Tall tells Staros, is a frontal assault. Staros, agonized by the losses his company will suffer, nevertheless dutifully begins the attack. It is indeed horrific. His men are mercilessly cut down, and at a break in the action Staros declines to attack further, telling Tall that it is simply suicidal. (He also explains, in a way that, even if we suspect Tall's careerism and are deeply sympathetic to Staros, we have to regard as oddly out of place,

27. Besides the 1964 Hollywood film of Jones's novel, there is another film about the battle for Guadalcanal, Nicholas Ray's 1951 *Flying Leathernecks*. There is the same sort of confrontation there between a very stern, by-the-book commander (whom we suspect may be a martinet, a prig), played by John Wayne, and his "humanist" second-in-command, played by Robert Ryan. This dynamic plays out in the more formulaic way, as each comes to appreciate what is of value in the other. Wayne really cares deeply (we are allowed to see his home life and tenderness for his children); Ryan comes to understand the burdens of command: he must refuse help to his dying friend and brother-in-law in order to complete the mission. (In a way typical of Ray's films, there is a jolting, unsettling moment at the end of the film when Ryan and Wayne "bond" in a quasi-jocular, now very friendly way, totally at odds with the fact the bond was built over the sacrifice by Ryan of his own brother-in-law.) I am convinced that Malick is referring to and so commenting on this film (there is even the same sort of possibly malingering, reluctant warrior), just as I am that the ending scene of Witt racing through the jungle, a moving camera tracking him as the enemy closes in, is a comment of sorts on Elias's running through the jungle, same camera motion, immediately preceding his death, in Oliver Stone's *Platoon* (1986), but I am not sure any of that can be proven; or compare Malick's dialogue to Elias's comment in *Platoon*, "I love it here at night. The stars. Not good or bad. Just there" (*Platoon*, dir. Oliver Stone [1986; Burbank, 2000, DVD]).

unusually squeamish, and openly so in a battlefield conversation. "We had a man," Staros says, "his gut got shot out on the slope, sir. Uh, created quite an upset." We can imagine Tall thinking: "Your men are *upset*?")

This amounts to a moment in the film very much like Witt's having gone AWOL, that is, a crucial ambiguity not much attended to by critics and commentators and another comforting convention denied us. In short, the heart of *the* dramatic event in the film, the attack on Hill 210 by C-for-Charlie Company, is in effect a mutiny under battlefield conditions by an officer, a refusal to fight on. What is *much* more surprising is that despite our expectations and identification with Staros the humanist, the colonel turns out in the end to have been right; this result is something quite extraordinary, given our invitation to regard Tall as not only heartless but, as is often the case in such movies and characters, incompetent.[28] Tall himself goes to the forward position, standing up bravely, not flinching when an ordnance goes off, apologizing for the lack of water in the assault, and rallying the troops. The men have been able to make it to a ridge that the Japanese have mistakenly left unguarded, and one might argue that this is just a piece of luck that Tall could not have counted on, but the fact remains that Tall turned out to be right that a direct assault, if conducted with a full commitment, could succeed.[29] (Not to mention that he is right when he has to tell Staros: "This is not a court of law; this is a war.") Bell finds an approach that allows a volunteer force to get close enough to the nests to attack and take them out, and the assault succeeds. Tall does not bring

---

28. There are plenty of war movies where the hardness-softness issue is prominent, something one might expect to be more important for citizen armies. A good example is Henry King's *Twelve O'Clock High*, where the problem is given an official name, "Over-identification with the men" (*Twelve O'Clock High*, dir. by Henry King [1949; Burbank, 2007, DVD]). This is a pressing issue in the film since part of Gregory Peck's job as a commander of a unit of bomber pilots is to push the flyers as far as possible so command can learn how many continuous daylight precision bombing raids they can take before they crack.

29. This is not something as clear as it ought to be in discussions of the film. Simon Critchley thinks that Tall has devised an alternative to a frontal assault, but the flanking movement Tall proposes is not the "flanking-through-the-jungle" that Staros had wanted. (We never see the jungle.) It is another route up the hill itself, all of which is exposed to Japanese fire. There is simply a ridge not occupied by the enemy that the men can use to stage a small squad attack. Robert Sinnerbrink thinks that what Tall eventually orders was Staros's idea, and Tall takes it over when he arrives. That is also incorrect. Staros had wanted to avoid an attack up the hill altogether and to flank through the jungle. That is what Tall rejects; see Critchley 2002 and Sinnerbrink 2006: 26–37. For someone who gets it exactly right, see Silverman 2003: 323–42, especially 327, 329.

any charges against Staros but notes that Staros is not really suited to command ("You're too soft") and sends him home. We are inclined by a kind of movie logic to be for Staros, but his question, "Have you ever had anyone die in your arms, sir?" is maudlin and self-congratulatory (and is countered simply by a withering, incredulous stare by Tall), and we end up unsure what to think. (There is also an ominous, growling music on the soundtrack that has been and will be a feature of the film for a while.) Tall is also earlier given a striking voice-over, again contra type, creating a strange moment of sympathy: "Shut up in a tomb; can't lift the lid. Played a role I never conceived." The isolation theme again: he is as trapped as the rest of them by what the war requires.[30]

We are, though, not done with Tall. He has two more extremely important scenes, and after both his status in the film, or our suggested judgment of him, is almost impossible to sort out. After the initial victory, he has a conversation with Captain Gaff (John Cusack), who led the seven-man team that made the initial breach. Gaff is quite worried about the state of the men. They are dehydrated and cannot, he thinks, press on. Tall thinks the men have momentum and spirit and so cannot wait around for water. "If some of the men pass out, well, hell, they'll just have to pass out," he says. Gaff, staring at Tall in an openly judgmental way, reminds Tall that this means some of the men could die. So we have our Staros moment again, as an attractive, humane character pleads for "the men." Tall stays true to form as, on the one hand, a craven careerist, the man who could tell Staros that he must capture the objective because "the Admiral got up at dawn for this." Here he tells Gaff that Gaff has no idea what it feels like to be passed over for a promotion, as if *that* is why the men must press on, and that death could just as easily occur from a sniper. And yet, on the other hand, he is also a ruthless and ultimately successful leader. (Tall's ambition is not great or world historical, like Patton's; it is small-minded and bourgeois. He wants a promotion and respect. But this ambition is not unconnected with the military victory, and the implication seems to be that it, this self-serving, careerist ambition, is all that is left of ancient "spirited-ness,"

30. There are also religious differences between Staros, presumably a Greek Orthodox Christian (the character had been Jewish in Jones's novel), who prays before the battle, "Let me not let You down. Let me not let down my men," and Tall, whose "religion" appears more ancient, more suited to a warrior, not a Christian—that is, for a believer for whom the equal and absolute value of human life makes war a complicated business. Tall invokes Homer, not Christianity. (Not that Tall's Greek ethos is genuine. The invocation is deeply ironic, given that Tall's only real motivation is careerist.)

thymos, the need for distinction, greatness, and glory. The same point is made by Travolta's preening, pompous officer at the beginning of the film.) This next assault *again* succeeds, and what happens again appears to justify Tall's willingness to press on. Yet the moment is personalized, too. Tall—who, throughout, in trying hard to persuade Gaff is clearly trying to persuade himself—tells Gaff that he is like a son to him and, in a way that silently speaks volumes about the powerful and complicated *attraction of war* to many of these modern "domesticated" men, asks Gaff if he knows what his, Tall's, son, does. "My son is a bait salesman," Tall says. Not the usual way, in war movies, of referring to the home front. (It is clear that Gaff does not at all feel this familial bond, so the image of the familial bond in war is undermined again.) Finally, in a way that complicates everything, Tall finally *does* send runners back for water, as if conceding Gaff's point. Again this confounding of genre and narrative and psychological expectations seems quite deliberate and once more leaves us, to some extent, as lost as many of the main characters.

And then, after the scene where he relieves Staros of command, we see Tall sitting alone (dramatically and sadly alone, one has to say), looking at the devastation and death around him. Nolte creates a powerful sense of futility and sadness in a silent, brief scene in which all Tall does is sigh twice very movingly, and he is in effect rehumanized for us yet again in his isolation and obvious self-doubt. We are not, in effect, allowed to mock or simply dismiss him. This is the last we see of him.

So both the voice-overs and the filmed scenes can often seem to take back with one hand what they have given with another, raising expectations and suggesting allegiances that are then undermined or called into some question. And this emerges as the underlying structure of the whole film. In the way negative theology is held to be itself a mode of knowledge about God, Malick's *negation* of narrative and character conventions and patterns of intelligibility, we might say, forces us to see things about the dramatic events and the characters and the visual images in a distinct way, in a kind of fresh strangeness, a strangeness echoed in the photography of nature, as we shall see.

VI

For one thing, these unresolved tensions create an appropriate sense of mystery and bewilderment and a lack of resolution one must simply learn to live with. One such mystery, a major one in the narrative, is the mystery of command itself; some men will actually follow an order, get up, and run straight into machine gun fire. This is not a completely stable, clear-cut matter. Staros does not acknowledge the authority of Tall, and even Staros himself at one point has to ask, "Am I the captain or a goddamn private?" They are of course afraid of the consequences of disobeying, but no war can be won, no assault successful, if that is the only motivation of those who attack. They must in some sense or another invest, ideally wholeheartedly, in the goals of the command. How that happens, how it can be sustained, is something our attention is drawn to several times in the film, especially in the opening charge when a young soldier must order two others to get up and run into almost certain death. They hesitate, but then attack and are immediately killed.

For another, from what we have seen so far, we can say that Malick has again refused us two conventional ways of thinking about this willingness to face death. The politics of the world war are never invoked, and so the question—deeply interesting in itself and explored in different ways in many film genres—of the psychological bases of political and thereby military authority is not raised.[31] And the idea that war creates an emotional bond of love that takes over in critical situations, that the men fight, even to the death, for each other, is also refused. We are not even allowed to come to any coherent sense of what the group is, who is in it, how to identify and track individual characters, or who even *likes* whom. The family image is invoked only to be undermined, and even the deepest connection in the film between Welsh and Witt is fraught with distance and incomprehension.

In effect, the sense we get is that these men are caught up in some vast historical force sweeping them forward to a remote island in the South Pacific, and the issue for them is not how to get themselves to do what they are ordered to do. As we see several times in the assaults up the hill, there is no way out, no option for them. They look around and look forlornly at each other and realize that they have no choice but to go forward. Once engaged, the violence itself has its own dynamic. The more they fight, the more ferocious, even vicious, they become and the more many of them like it. (Doll says: "I killed a man. Nobody can touch me for it.")[32] Malick has largely deemphasized what is tradi-

31. This is something rightly stressed by Bersani and Dutoit 2004. They also note that this refusal is another indication of a lack of commonality in the enterprise of the war. Staros seems completely indifferent, given everything we see, to the strategic importance of Guadalcanal and what it might be worth in lives.

32. This is particularly vivid in the final attack on the Japanese position, staged as if the men had become seized with some collective insanity, shooting unarmed prisoners, looting, and desecrating bodies.

tionally understood to be the psychological issues (especially when compared with the novel, where it is quite prominent) and concentrated on something else. I have claimed that Malick has not allowed the narrative line or even character conflict to carry the primary meaning or the primary significance of what we are seeing and that while he realizes that an associative connection with the conventions of war movies is inevitable for the viewer, he also takes a number of steps to invert those expectations, frustrate them, and ironize them. This implies that we cannot understand war as we previously have; the expectation that we can leads us to expect the genre conventions and then leads to our being lost when they fail us. This can be said to be about both the way movies have rendered human practices intelligible, the way they no longer can, and about the problem of the intelligibility of the events themselves.

To come to the basic issue: Malick instead forces our attention predominantely on motion pictures of nature, framed and panned in a certain characteristic Malick-like way, and he has interrupted any usual narrative flow with very frequent and occasionally difficult-to-attribute voice-overs. This deemphasis on narrative meaning and the anticipation it creates (Who will do what to whom? Why? Do they know why? Are they self-deceived?) shifts our attention to two of the main frameworks Malick allows us for understanding the action we do see: first, the kind of reflective interrogation of meaning, especially of death and killing, voiced in the interior monologues and, second, what he is trying to achieve with photographic effect. And here, especially with the former issue, the voice-overs, he takes very great risks.

First, he is willing to frame the issue that he thinks is most pressing in the situation of war—the ever-present possibility of sudden death—in starkly simple and direct terms. As noted, the issue threading through the main voice-overs is not "What is this death of mine for? Is it worth the cost (for the nation, for my family)?" but "What does it mean in general for my life as a whole that I will die? What is it to live, to direct or lead a life, if it must be led under such a constant certitude? And why, if death is such an evil, is there so much killing, violence?" The consolation we are led to believe the characters need is not political or social but—and here any choice of a word will be inadequate or misleading—philosophical or metaphysical or religious. (I say "led to believe" because the issue depends yet again on the status of Train in the film, about whom we know almost nothing and so depends on the status of his voice-overs.) But this invokes another set of conventions and another set of dangers for Malick.

For when a character in a film engages in what sounds like very general philosophical reflection, we expect the formulations to be equal to the difficulty of the subject matter, and we easily, unproblematically, assume that any such sympathetic character speaks for the maker of the film, the auteur. But we have already seen in *The Thin Red Line* some sort of visual embodiment of, or comment on, or contrast with some aspects of a character's world, and this visual point of view is not necessarily stable, conceived in that way by the character speaking, and in no sense necessarily trumps some other voiced point of view (and world), like Welsh's. (It is a very simple point but one that often seems lost in discussions of this film and *The Tree of Life*. No one speaks for the movie, for the auteur; the characters speak for themselves.) But what is even more striking is that Malick allows these characters to muse over what is happening to them in prose meditations that aspire to a kind of poetic expressiveness strictly within the limitations and background of each character. The musings are not elevated to some sort of canonical status by an attempt to inflate the quality of the prose. When we hear Witt (Witt, finally, and not his near-voice-twin, Train) at the beginning, after Train's introductory questions, we hear what appears to be an ordinary man straining the limits of his powers of expression.

> I remember my mother when she was dying. Looked all shrunk up and gray. I asked her if she was afraid. She just shook her head. I was afraid to touch the death I seen in her. I heard people talk about immortality, but I ain't seen it. I wondered how it'd be when I died. What it'd be like to know that this breath now was the last one you was ever gonna draw. I just hope I can meet it the same way she did. With the same . . . calm. 'Cause that's where it's hidden—the immortality I hadn't seen.

The "death I seen in her," "the immortality I hadn't seen"—the poor grammar and the like make clear we are hearing a *particular* voice, and this is true even when Witt struggles to use figurative language, evocative of Ralph Waldo Emerson. "Maybe all men got one big soul, who everybody's a part of—all faces are the same man, one big self." Or: "Everyone looking for salvation by himself—each like a coal drawn from the fire." The sense we get is that the war can be borne, endured (the prospect of our own death, so terribly heightened by war, can be borne or endured) if the questions addressed in the monologues can get some sort of purchase, can lead to some sort of presentiment about their resolution, but that must happen from the point of view of the ordinary men—men unused to violence and the presence of death, the bourgeoisie at war—who are forced to ask them. This point is relevant to something that Stanley Cavell sometimes says: that there can be no real virtuosity for true philosophy as there is for mathematics or music. It must be something that in some way anyone does, can do (in their own way, of course, as in Emerson on individual genius). What these men need is not politics or love or real fathers or to become a band of brothers but some kind of vernacular speculative position, a vernacular orientation within the whole.

VII

The issue of the content of these reflections, which in one way or another deal with the question of how death and killing can be understood and thereby, perhaps, endured, is linked to the unusual visual composition of the film. Our attention is sometimes drawn to photographed scenes of animal and plant life in a striking, meditative way. For the most part, there is no internal plot-related reason for editing in, at various points, shots of such organic life and sunlight. For the most part, we do not see establishing shots for any point of view and so do not see what characters see in the course of the narrative: animals and plants as obstacles, threats, food, the uncanny, or frightening objects. We do not much see them looking at what the camera is looking at. I've said that what we see often is related to a monologue we've heard, but this need not mean—from the point of view of the character *as such*—that *this* thought of his could be captured by *this* visual image. (For the most part, we know that these objects are not related to the plot because some of the Manichean reflections of Train and the more nihilistic meditations of Welsh are framed in a montage of sublime and mysterious natural violence, as if in confirmation of the monologue: crocodiles, wild dogs, bats, and dying birds.) But both the presence of the non-plot-driven photographs and the seriousness, even solemnity of the attention to such objects (often heightened by the musical score) create a general expectation of a different kind of attention from the viewer, and the seriousness of the tone suggests much more than mere atmospherics. The effect of the sort of framing, attentiveness, and lingering over the living things is to alter what we are actually to be attending to. It is not merely the objects we see when framed this way but rather, given the lingering attention of the camera, if one can put it this way, the *objects in the light of such attention,* photographed as if *seen* in a mode of interrogative attention that, by its very intensity and independence from the plot, detaches the objects from any normal intercourse with viewers and allows some other dimension of meaningfulness (or some different sort of question about life) to emerge visually, and so requires some other stance or attitude to be possible with regard to such a presence. To a large extent that suggested stance is similar in tone to the voice-overs: intensely interrogative and unresolved.

So, looked at this way, we see not the mere beings (one dimensionally, one might say, to retrieve an older term) but see them in the light of the question of what it is for them to be at all, especially to be alive, a presence that cannot be rightly captured as a discursive theme but only in a kind of intimation or disclosure available to a visual art. There is a modern tradition in philosophical reflection on art that holds that artworks can be the bearers of truth, not as making any tacitly assertoric or even discursive claim but rather as disclosive, especially of a kind of truth unavailable discursively. (One could count Hegel, Schiller, Schelling, Schlegel, Schopenhauer, Nietzsche, Heidegger, and Merleau-Ponty as representative of this tradition.) And Malick's photography evokes such a tradition, in the way it resonates with the mute presence and strangeness of such beings, as well as with their silence, a contrastive presence not only with narrative and dialogue but with the inescapable threat of sudden nonbeing or death. But such a disclosure, intuitive and prediscursive, about "the thin red line" between life and death, the meaning of the title in the novel, also somehow announces its own unavailability for any determinate thinking, as if something is also being withheld or hidden from such discursive intelligibility, from what the voice-overs alone could make sense of.

In the film, this sense of ontological attention is often both insisted on and intensified by the emphasis on sunlight. We look up through the water to the sun; we pan up huge trees to the light; sunlight streaming through leaves pervades many of the scenes, as if to suggest that we are seeing not mere objects but objects *in their being illuminated* by this basic ontological question, prompted by their being at all. To emphasize this even more, in Witt's early memory of the bedroom in which his mother was dying, at the end the camera pans up to reveal, quite surprisingly, that there is no ceiling. The room is exposed to the sky and sun, and so we are first introduced to this sort of ontological trope: what it is to see everything, even death, in the light of this interrogation and wonder, in the light of the question of the meaning of their living presence, a question that does not, perhaps cannot arise in our everyday dealings with such organisms (fig. 9.6). (The sunlight image returns at the end, in the last and ultimate conversation between Witt and Welsh in an old plantation. Witt looks up and, again, there is no full ceiling or roof. They are relatively unprotected from the imperative for this sort of attentiveness [fig. 9.7].) Seeing in this way allows us to say that the main structuring element in the organization of the film is then a kind of counterpoint between the primarily aesthetic (in the sense of sensible, intuitive, affective) interrogation of such an issue (the living nature within which death must make some sort of sense, must be confronted and borne) and the discursive interrogation carried on in the monologues. By implication, we sense, too, that we need both these modalities of intelligibility, even if they can be difficult to think together.

VIII

There is much to say about that counterpoint, but the relation to the main monologues also occasionally suggests another kind of question, at least for Train. Train *also* wants to know, and Welsh is sure that he does know, whether *what there is*, in whatever weighty sense in which the question of life can be said to be posed by the photography, *is good*. The question of a kind of natural theodicy emerges. Given what there is, especially the "war with itself" that is nature, according to Train, and given the crushing human awareness of ever-impending death, given the need to kill to stay alive, and given that one needs some orienting attitude toward it all, especially when the primary issues are forced on one by war, what should that attitude be? *How* valuable is mere life?

The different possibilities — never really resolved; everything remains suspended in an interrogative mode — that we are given in the film as responses to such a question are presented mostly in the dialogues between Witt and Welsh. A major focus of the contrast concerns the existence of "another world." The first extended exchange between them sets the terms of the contrast. Welsh says, "In this world . . . a man himself is nothing. And there ain't no world but this one." Witt counters, "You're wrong there, Top. I seen another world. Sometimes I think it was just . . . my imagination." Welsh responds, "We're living in a world that's blowing itself to hell as fast as everybody can arrange it. In a situation like that all a man can do is shut his eyes and let nothing touch him. Look out for himself."

We already know that Witt is not talking about a separate world, heaven, or the afterlife. (Train's monologues — Train believes only in "dying and the

Lord"—*are* often posed in the second person, as if to someone: "Who are you to live in all these many forms?" "This great evil. Where does it come from? Who's doin' this to us? Who's killin' us?" But even his inclinations seem pantheistic even if Manichean, not transcendent.) The "immortality" Witt seeks is in *this* life, *in* his mother's calm acceptance of her own death, as if she has made some sense of it and so peace with it. It is as if he is saying that the interrogative framing of living nature that we see does (despite Welsh's skepticism that it does not) open some sort of possibility that can be realized, even if not discursively justified. *Who can see what*, in these terms, is a frequent theme. After the last, and now touching, dialogue between Witt and Welsh, we hear another voice-over by Train that marks the arbitrariness of who can see anything in the light of whatever question a reflective attentiveness can raise. "One man looks at a dying bird and thinks there's nothing but unanswered pain. But death's got the final word. It's laughing at him. Another man sees that same bird, feels the glory. Feels something smiling through him."

But things are hardly clear-cut even for Witt, who clearly aspires to a kind of goodness, and who even dies in an act of sacrifice, altruism. In a striking scene, he looks at a partially buried face of a Japanese soldier. (This immediately follows a dialogue with no visual place, a dialogue just heard, as if floating from nowhere, between Storm and Fife, unattributed as such, about dead people. We are told that the dead are "no different than dead dogs, once you get used to the idea." And "they're meat, kid.") We hear the imagined voice of the dead Japanese soldier, addressed to Witt as if a kind of indictment: "Are you righteous? Kind? Does your confidence lie in this? Are you loved by all? Know that I was, too. Do you imagine your sufferings will be less because you loved goodness? Truth?" Whatever will be seen or not seen, it will not be redemptive, not be justifying in any sense, at least that Train could recognize. This strange, imagined dialogue in effect rejects the whole premise of Train's speculative questions and makes even less likely that Train's monologues, far and away the most frequent that we hear, are in any way representative of the film's point of view, if we can ever say that about any film, especially one by Malick.

IX

Appropriately, all the monologues and dialogues never resolve anything, and we are left at the end with what amount to two sorts of poems, or perhaps prayers, as if the artwork that is the film is a sort of poem or prayer. Welsh, after he yet again remarks that the only possible orientation in this world is to make oneself an island, nevertheless addresses a prayer or an invocation to some "you," as if addressed to Witt or what Witt saw, some dimension of meaning he envies: "If I never meet you in this life, let me feel the lack. A glance from your eyes, and my life will be yours." This (again, revealingly, a glance, a *look*) is the most Welsh can manage, and we have seen enough of him to know it is nevertheless a considerable achievement, opened up by Witt.

After this, we find ourselves on a landing craft leaving the war, and, as we do, the language of a kind of thoughtless every day, the world of the quotidian bourgeoisie, returns, as Train prattles on in a banal aspiration for a successful life. (In a last, visual emphasis on the lack of community, only Train is talking with someone. The hundreds of other men mill about silently for several minutes.) But we hear one last time what sort of reflection the experience of war has occasioned, at least for Train, whoever he is. Astonishingly, as one last refusal of what, conventionally, we think we know about a character like Train, a simple country boy, afraid to die, his banal everyday voice blends seamlessly with the metaphysical voice-over voice, one last time confounding our settled expectations of what is in or out of character for an individual. In an apostrophe to his own soul (or the World-Soul),[33] Train says:

> Where is it that we were together? Who were you that I lived with? Walked with? The brother. The friend. Darkness from light. Strife from love. Are they the workings of one mind? The features of the same face? Oh, my soul, let me be in you now. Look out through my eyes. Look out at the things you made. All things shining.

This apostrophe suggests a last inflection on the reflective nature of the moving picture we have just seen, as well as returning us to the concerns of the opening monologue. For we *have* been looking through the "eyes" of the film, and what is "made" in and by the film, but whether we can hear the question Train poses (*all* things shining, genuinely illuminated by the light of this reflective interrogation) seems a matter of grace, a dispensation of one's soul that one can only hope for, perhaps occasionally inspired by a work of art. Appropriately, the film closes with three silent images of life (more accurately it ends

---

33. This mode of address to a personalized soul might be an invocation of mystical literature—perhaps St. John of the Cross, where such a dialogue with one's soul is prominent.

with three photographs), no voice-over, no music; whatever is to be intelligible will be so (if it is) primarily visually: human, animal, and plant; three natives in canoes, two tropical birds, and a single somewhat forlorn but living plant, a leaf, growing out of a coconut in the water. Or, the film ends with the question of what it is that we "see" or can see; what it is that we have seen (fig. 9.8).

TEN

Psychology Degree Zero?
The Representation of Action in the Films
of the Dardenne Brothers

I

Since 1996, the Belgian team of Luc and Jean-Pierre Dardenne have made eight theatrical fictional feature films for which they are willing to claim authorship. There are other fiction films—*Falsch* (1987), the short film *Il court, il court, le monde* (*He's Running, They're All Running*) (1988), and in 1992 *Je pense à vous* (*You're on My Mind*)—but they have in one way or another distanced themselves from these. In the case of the last, they have disowned it, furious at studio interference with the final cut. Their recent films, *Deux jours, une nuit* (*Two Days, One Night*; 2014) and *La fille inconnue* (*The Unknown Girl*; 2016) were released to enthusiastic reviews.[1]

All of the films revolve around a basic moral question usually having to do with responsibility; they often involve some sort of recovery from a wrong committed by the wrongdoer against the one wronged; and they all manifest a heightened sense of the complexity of how we might come to understand the characters dealing with such a question. In several films, part of that complexity has to do with the fact that our attention is constantly drawn to the connections between a character's psychological turmoil, stress, and confusion, on the one hand, and the quite distinctive characteristics of the social

---

1. For an especially lucid and helpful account of the brothers' history and their project, see Mosley 2013: 1–75. See also Luc Dardenne's comments in Andrews 2006.

world in which they live, on the other. More to the point of the following, I will claim that various cinematic properties of their films involve ways of rethinking and challenging basic issues in our conventional understanding of the relation between agent and deed in ordinary action and in explanation of action, and so they intimate an unusual picture of human subjectivity.[2] This bears on another issue: what we need to understand in understanding another and how we might come to understand another in a new way. This of course involves a very big question: What is it to call these aesthetic objects "ways of rethinking"? In the present context, I will limit myself to selected details and hope that a possible form of cinematic intelligibility (or, as in my subtitle, cinema itself as reflective form) will start to emerge.

The basic issue at stake is the following. It would not be unfair or anachronistic to say that, in each case, the Dardenne brothers are trying to represent the motivation and decisions (often momentous) of certain characters, but they proceed under two unmistakable assumptions. First, there is often something very difficult to understand, even mysterious, about such motivations and decisions—the films even seem to encourage the proper humility before such complexities. Second, in many of their films, we are shown that the social context (working class and under- or unemployed) within which these decisions must be made is historically novel, a product of free-trade zones, migrant labor, the common market, and globalized capitalism, all creating a new context for labor and power, the implications of which are not yet fully clear. This is a world where a ruthless form of competitiveness is forced on workers (American-style capitalism, as it is now rightly put), where one person's job is another person's unemployment, and where the two persons often know each other.[3] Or, in another formulation, some characters are migrants

2. These complications in the conventional view are different than those discussed in the treatment of agency in Pippin 2012 and have more to do with the "unknowingness" theme introduced in Pippin 2017. The Dardenne films explore the issue of unknowingness with respect to oneself.

3. See O'Shaughnessy 2008: 73. It is significant with respect to the issue of class analysis and class consciousness in the brothers' view of late capitalism that Rosetta in the film of that same name is not "a working-class woman." She is struggling desperately to enter the working class, however exploited it is on traditional accounts. Wage slavery has become a utopian dream; class membership is at least a mode of being acknowledged and of solidarity. See the account of "normalcy" as "utopia" in Berlant 2007: 289–90 and throughout. This issue is also prominent in *The Promise*, as well as with the classless status of the couple in *The Child*, and in the ambiguous working-class status of Lorna in *Lorna's Silence*.

in a strange land, and therefore they live so far outside the normal cycle of production and consumption that in some way their own relation to their inner lives, their own self-understanding, cannot be understood in ways typical for those who live inside that social world. That and why this is so is clearly what they want to explore. They often have no acknowledged social status whatsoever, and that has a psychological, not just a social, dimension. This all puts added pressure on the problem of struggling and coming to understand another. The Dardennes are also acutely aware of what it means to represent such issues in film and are clearly doing all they can to block or interrupt or prevent conventional assumptions about these issues (and their counterpart in conventional cinematic technique) from coming into play.[4]

This fact is especially important because the acts in question can seem, at first glance, gratuitous, unmotivated, and, in that sense, very hard to understand. A boy, under no pressure, and clearly on the verge of escaping undetected, suddenly confesses to the wife of a man whose death he helped cover up (*La promesse* [*The Promise*], 1996). A girl rendered almost insane by her inability to find work (already a great example of the theme just introduced; unemployment itself can be a form of what could be called objective insanity, objectively incapable or "reality testing"), having informed on a friend to secure a job, suddenly resigns the position (*Rosetta*, 1999).[5] A man decides to take on as an apprentice and help teach a boy—who he knows murdered his own son five years earlier—and, on the verge of vengeance, releases the boy and works with him (*Le fils* [*The Son*], 2002). A street criminal casually and thoughtlessly sells his newborn, but when he sees the overwhelming effect of this on the child's mother, his girlfriend, he immediately retrieves the baby at enormous cost to himself and his future (*L'enfant* [*The Child*], 2005). An immigrant woman from Albania, having secured her own legal residence in

4. The intense focus, often in close-ups, of characters, is something that traditionally suggests insight into their inner lives but in these films is always linked in various ways to outside objects on which we also focus the same kind of close-up attention, as if there really is some link. This can seem a distraction if we do not appreciate the point: a statue (*The Promise*), a pair of shoes (*Rosetta*), a jacket (*The Child*), planks of wood and machines, a leather brace and a pair of glasses (*The Son*), money, many close-ups of money (*Lorna's Silence*), a bike (*The Kid with a Bike*); see Dardenne 2005: 158.

5. Rosetta in the end does not fall apart, but, at the end of *Lorna's Silence*, Lorna has clearly gone insane, lost all hold on an unbearable reality; in political terms, a much darker ending than *Rosetta*, with no path forward. See Schütz 2011: 45.

Belgium, is involved in a plot to live with an addict until he overdoses so that she can then, for money, marry and then divorce a Russian eager to emigrate and also to gain Belgian citizenship. But she begins to help the addict get *off* drugs, ruining the plan, and, in the face of terrifying threats of reprisal, continues to refuse to go along even after the addict is murdered by her accomplices (*Le silence de Lorna* [*Lorna's Silence*], 2008). A woman, who by mere chance happens to be just once in the same place as a troubled boy searching for the derelict father who abandoned him, suddenly involves herself deeply in the boy's life, ruining her own romantic relationship and assuming responsibilities no one would say she owed anyone (*Le gamin au vélo* [*The Kid with a Bike*], 2011).

These are, of course, films, not treatises, so whatever they render intelligible is rendered cinematically intelligible, a topic worthy in itself of several books.[6] The cinematic way must be some sort of sensible-affective modality of rendering intelligible, one that has to do with how we are moved, how some features of a moral landscape are made more salient, how some feature grips us, excites our imagination, how we are surprised or puzzled by events we come to see in some new way because we are so surprised or puzzled. What the Dardenne films have accomplished is all the more remarkable because the principal characters are not well educated or articulate or reflective. Almost everything about what is traditionally thought of as their psychologies must be represented in what we see on-screen, through what the characters do and in their faces.

In sum, the films are made in the light of a clear awareness of the possible visual and dramatic intelligibility of our moral lives, and that this awareness results in a novel cinematic style, the powerful credibility of which begins to challenge philosophical and even commonsense orthodoxy about our explanations of what human beings do and why and, further, what it is to understand another and another's deeds.[7]

---

6. The bearing of pictorial on philosophical intelligibility is discussed in Pippin 2014.
7. That is, there are (at least) two issues here and their bearing on each other is complex. We want to understand another's actions, and we take that to involve being able to explain why she did what she did. But we also speak colloquially of wanting to understand someone as such, and we sometimes think that a singular-action explanation is not possible unless we understand something like what kind of person would do such a thing. Or we can formulate a credible action explanation, but still say, "I don't understand how *she* could have done that. That's not *her*." Both of these are relevant to what Olivier is seeking in *The Son*.

II

It is first necessary to say something about the career of the Dardenne brothers and their relation to other filmmakers. They began as documentary filmmakers, and their approach was from the start decidedly political. They focused on the Belgian labor movement, especially in the grim industrial area of Seraing, and gradually moved from making what might be called activist films, aimed at consciousness-raising, to more historical work, in effect conceding what is now all too obvious: that the labor movement after World War II decisively lost its great battle with the owners of capital. In fact, it would not be an exaggeration to say that the Dardennes' films are the most lucid artistic explorations we have of the quotidian and lived-through consequences of the absence of any organized, principled resistance to the excesses of capitalism after the collapse of any credible form of leftist solidarity. The task now was to try to understand what happened and to document the enormity of what was thereby lost. Most of all, what was lost was any experience of social unity, at least the sort that is possible in a collective struggle or in genuinely cooperative work.[8] So in all the feature films, we see exclusively working-class characters — small-shop owners, laborers, garage mechanics, carpenters, beauticians, dry cleaners — as well as petty criminals, human smugglers, minor racketeers. What we don't see is also important. There is not only nothing in the way of class or politically inspired identification, but also very little in the way of local community or collective life; no circle of friends for anyone, no neighborhood community; families are horribly fractured, parents are grotesquely irresponsible in *The Promise, Rosetta, The Child,* and *The Kid with a Bike,* and the dire consequences for the children is a major theme. (Luc Dardenne has even said that we live "in the time of Cronos who eats his children.")[9] Mostly we sense that each person is radically on his or her own and in that profound zero-sum competition with one another mentioned earlier, such that this feature of life must influence how we try to understand what they do. Normalcy itself, even

8. See the account in Mai 2010: 9.
9. Quoted in Mai 2010: 46. For the nature of the intergenerational failure (a *basic* failure in a society's ability to reproduce itself) and its many consequences, see Berlant 2007: 290, 293, 298. Berlant's commitment, here and elsewhere, on the need to understand the affective character of the bond of sociality, especially the affective attachment to forms of "the 'bad life,'" and at a level that reaches aspects of private intimacy often thought irrelevant to that task (279), is one I share, posed in different terms. See the account of political psychology in Pippin 2010: 1–25.

psychological normalcy, or some fantasy of normalcy, becomes the highest aspiration for some characters.

It has even been said that the brothers are depicting the situation of "ethics in the ruin of politics"[10] or showing us post-social realism. So, in the absence of anything recognizably political,[11] the epiphanic moral moments—the ones that characterize each film and occur in moments of deep, unexpected intimacy—seem inspired by the sheer physical presence of some specific particular other person. These moments of moral acknowledgment do not descend from any principles held; they are ad hoc and are unconnected to any group or class or even neighborhood consciousness.[12] The wrongs depicted are injustices—wrongs always against someone—but the wrongs and the recovery from them (and remorse, forgiveness, or reconciliation) are always intimately personal. The structural features of the social world within which these wrongs are all too likely to occur are not absent, but these wrongs tend to be treated fatalistically or at least not as possible objects for collective redress.

This is not to say that the feature films are simply grim, merely cataloguing the catastrophe. As already noted, there are stirring moments of resistance, even transcendence, in each film, however individualized and isolated

10. See O'Shaughnessy 2008.

11. There is an interesting genre issue relevant to their films. Their work can both be associated with the harder edge of corporeal or neo-neorealism, as in the films of Bruno Dumont or Erick Zonca, or with more traditional social realism, as in the films of Mike Leigh, Ken Loach, and Shane Meadows. That is beyond the scope of this discussion.

12. Predictably, the epiphanic and nonpolitical nature of many endings has attracted criticisms from the traditional left. For example, from Walsh 2006 writing about *The Child* but including all their films up until then: "Moreover, their obsessive attention to the particular (exemplified by the irritating and intrusive camera in *Rosetta*, which hardly leaves the central character for an instant) at the expense of the social and historical context ultimately provides a distorted picture of contemporary life. It diverts attention from the structures responsible for human suffering and creates the impression, inadvertently or not, that the blame for social ills lies at least in part with their victims." Or, writing later: "All that being said, there is still the matter of the artistic quality of their films. The fact remains, in my view, that their dramas are rather uninspired and, ultimately, contrived. Moreover, their chilly, matter-of-fact 'realism' expresses an ambiguous attitude toward the working class characters that borders on the unsympathetic" (Walsh 2008). This is an important issue (that what is, in effect, their reformulation of the inner-outer relation in action ought to allow us to look at the outside in some more detail than we are given), but I do not share the aesthetic criticism. I find the idea that Rosetta, for example, does not provoke sympathy, or that she is portrayed as "responsible" for what happens to her, bizarre in the extreme.

those moments are.[13] These are achievements of a distinct sort, forged inevitably in acts directed against the attempted suppression or marginalization of any robust assertions of their agency. Each of the moments noted above can seem at first gratuitous and inexplicable, but, remarkably, not in a way that is unsatisfying or frustrating—the way hardened criminals in movies sometimes suddenly recant and become saintly. We are somehow prepared for such reversals; understanding that "somehow" and comprehending the status of such moments seem to be the key questions for each and every film.

Second, the influences on the brothers are clear. There are philosophical influences, at least on Luc Dardenne, who has written a philosophy book, *Sur l'affaire humaine* (2012). (Luc Dardenne has also written a kind of journal about the making of three of the films, *Au dos de nos images* [2005]—a title that must be referring to an unusual filming technique used by the brothers, which we shall discuss soon. And together, the brothers have also published many revealing interviews.)[14] The most frequent names mentioned in *Sur l'affaire humaine* are Nietzsche, Heidegger, Levinas (a figure who looms large in what critical commentary there is about the brothers),[15] Kafka, and Freud. The cinematic influences are obvious—for *Rosetta* and indeed for the tone and pace of all their films, Robert Bresson (especially *Mouchette* [1967] and *Au hasard Balthazar* [1966]). (They are especially influenced by Bresson's resistance to psychological acting, as we shall see below.)[16] For the general mise-en-scène in the depiction of Seraing, Roberto Rossellini's *Germany Year Zero* (1948) and neorealism in general are of obvious importance. (The Dardennes also make extensive use of nonprofessional or unknown actors.) In the treatment of adolescents, a frequent theme, François Truffaut's *The 400 Blows* (1959) is important; and in *The Kid with a Bike*, Vittorio De Sica's *Bicycle Thieves* (1948) is obviously an influence. They have also singled out Akira Kurosawa's *Stray Dog* (1949) and Kenji Mizoguchi's *Street of Shame* (1956).

13. See O'Shaughnessy 2008: 60.

14. See Dardenne 2012.

15. Levinas and the primary ethical imperative not to kill figure also in their own thinking about the films; see Dardenne 2012: 42. Two Levinasian readings: Cooper 2007 and Cummings 2009. See also Cardullo's (2002) generally Christian reading.

16. Mosley reports that the brothers admit some influence but now dislike the comparison with Bresson; see Mosley 2013: 35. That said, Mosley goes on to show how many points of comparison are possible.

So much for background. I turn now to my main theme, which could be sum-marized as the problem in general of the cinematic representation of the rela-tion between what is traditionally thought of as a psychological interior and outer bodily movement and other forms of expression in the exercise of agency and subjectivity. As noted, the specific inflection of that relation in the partic-ular world that serves as the context or the horizon for some of the characters' intelligible doings can be said to add to the difficulty of coming to understand their deeds.

Insofar as we can speak of issues being raised in a film, they are raised here most prominently by several striking directorial techniques.[17] I will mention four, and then try to assess the philosophic implications of such an aesthetics. They include (1) a striking lack of congruence between the cuts in the film and the normal beginnings and endings of actions or conversations; (2) the posi-tioning of the handheld camera very close to the characters and from behind, as if the viewer is too close, following the action rather than seeing it; (3) the invocation of the cinematic conventions about close-ups, and then the frustra-tion or refusal of these expectations; and (4) the display of the psychological lives of the characters in ways such that, very often, individual faces appear somewhat blank or empty, without detectable psychological inward motion, let us say, as if we might be at psychology degree zero in the sense in which Roland Barthes spoke of "writing degree zero."[18] All of these features could be described in ways that might fit other ambitious art films, and the last has especially been used to try to understand a kind of new genre of corporeal realism, as in the unnerving films of Bruno Dumont, or as calling to mind the non-psychological acting in Bresson's films (such as Michel's demeanor

17. This is another topic in itself. The Dardenne brothers obviously must realize that the uncon-ventionality of their framing, camera position from the rear and instability, deemphasis on dialogue and exposition, indifference to conventional plot, and so forth are immediately and starkly noticeable to the viewer. This means in effect that each of their films, whatever else it is about, is about itself; each film is a kind of allegory of film, instructing us about what cine-matic representability is, can be (and cannot be), must be now. And they are showing us that that issue is inseparable from the philosophical issue of what it is to represent mindedness and action. And since that, for them, is inseparable from the appropriate representation of the contemporary social world, each film is also a political act.
18. See Barthes 2012.

in *Pickpocket* [1959]). There are such similarities, especially to Bresson and Dumont, but I think that the Dardennes' use of these techniques, the combination of all of them, and the repetition of these unconventional techniques throughout their films amount to an unprecedented, distinctive style. And that style, like many radical innovations in modernist art, is historically indexed, not a mere aesthetic experiment. The assumption is that something about the world as we now understand it would be falsely or not credibly represented if pictured in traditional realist narrative form. Some aspects of such a lived world, especially what are traditionally thought of as psychological aspects, *demand* such stylistic innovations.[19]

So first, the cuts in the film and the selection of detail by the camera do not seem to match what we would conventionally expect to be the natural beginnings and endings of some action, and the camera's focus does not seem to isolate what we would normally consider the salient details, given the action.[20] People do not enter and exit scenes according to normal conventions, and the scenes do not begin and end in a way that corresponds to the beginning and ending of actions or even conversations. This should be understood as a kind of cinematic interrogation of what really *is* a beginning and an end for action.[21] There are many jump cuts. Someone is walking somewhere and we begin to follow with the camera, but suddenly there is a jump cut to the destination, and we experience a kind of gap. Have we missed something, or is what we did not see not really a part of what was being done? The unconventional framing of scenes, what the camera directs our attention to, does not help us distinguish what is of major and what of minor significance. This, too, already suggests that conventional views about what a discrete action is or what the unity of an action consists in, how it is to be explained and thus represented,

19. This claim about stylistic innovation could obviously be challenged. A full case for it would have to involve a study of the details of all seven films, especially *Rosetta* and *Lorna's Silence*. The film I will focus on, *The Son*, is focused so intently on one relationship that this socio-historical context, while visible, is not as prominent. It is visible in Francis's demeanor, lethargy, and status as a product of the juvenile prison system. The inspiration for this approach is Hegelian; see Pippin 2014.

20. See the discussion in Mai 2010: 54. For Mai, these effects have as a result our sense of a "lack of an external point of view" (55). This is true, but I think that this and other techniques are putting under pressure traditional assumptions about the unity of action itself. The point is more radical.

21. So, when does whatever Olivier is intending, by taking on Francis, begin? (I discuss this further below.) When does Igor begin to truly *keep* his promise to Amidou?

are not in force. The films themselves all begin and end abruptly, going straight from or to a black screen.

The Son opens on a conversation between Olivier and an administrator that has already begun, and we hear the sounds of hammering and sawing going on before the film visually begins. (We might say that Olivier's state of mind is represented on the sound track, as we hear the irritating whine of a piece of equipment, a high-pitched aural sign of Olivier's extreme tension in the scene.) What we will learn is that Olivier, a dedicated teacher at a kind of trade reform school for youthful offenders, had been asked to take on Francis as another apprentice. We also learn later that he recognizes the name immediately as that of the boy who murdered his son and declines to accept the boy. We see him (we learn later) somehow *in the process of changing his mind* and accepting Francis (a rather long process; it takes up the first twenty minutes of the film, and the change is occasioned by nothing dramatic or decisive), but he does not seem to be weighing the pros and cons or reflecting on his motives. He looks, throughout, mostly stunned, confused, and anxious. The decision to accept Francis seems at least partially occasioned by a visit from his ex-wife, who comes to tell him that she is getting remarried and is pregnant.[22] (Her understandable view in the face of their trauma is to escape the past and begin anew, something we sense Olivier both cannot and will not yet do.)[23] Olivier rushes after her when she leaves, demanding to know why she visited him on just that day, the day he learns of Francis's release, as if that fact means something (as if *something* about their horrific tragedy should, finally, mean something). And it is shortly thereafter that he accepts Francis.[24]

22. Olivier's first view of Francis is fleeting, in the cafeteria (where he has clearly gone to catch a glimpse) and, significantly in this film, from the rear. This is immediately ominous. Olivier looks slightly crazed, and there is prominence given to a knife he borrows. His second view is of Francis sleeping, completely vulnerable.

23. It is no doubt significant that the moment that Olivier changes his mind and decides to accept Francis is precisely the moment when his wife announces, in effect, that as a woman she can and will *produce* another son, something that seems to suggest that Olivier will try to reconstitute a paternal relation in a male way, eventually as a legal guardian. This reminds us that the film we are watching is not, as the brothers once envisaged, called "The Father," but *The Son*. This forces our attention on the pairing of the dead and absent son with Francis, the (unlikely) candidate for a surrogate son. See also Collin 2008: 213. (This kind of mimetic parental pairing with his wife is one of several instances of such mimetic understanding that I discuss below.)

24. See Schütz 2013.

Moreover, while Olivier seems to have no fixed or determinate idea about what he should do in the future, or even how to think about what he should do, even after he accepts Francis, it is fair to say that he still has no fixed or determinate idea why he did, what he is trying to achieve by accepting him. And early in the film, we know none of this and so are even more in the dark, and we have to imagine for quite a while what might be causing the obvious discomfort in Olivier. Later, when we know who Francis is, we might think that Olivier is planning some sort of revenge, and this gives the film a great tension throughout on the first viewing. (The film is built for the viewer around two sorts of tension—tension about what had happened and then tension about what will happen. What, if anything, is Olivier planning? It takes us a while to appreciate the irrelevance of the notion of planning.) Without other conventional narrative techniques like shot/reverse-shot dialogues or any establishing shot setting out where we are, with so little in the way of exposition, with no reflective characters discussing what is happening, and with so many jump cuts and so many small narrative gaps, where we are, literally and in the narrative, and what Olivier is up to can be very hard to establish.[25]

In the beginning scene, Olivier's anxious pondering is not continuous; it is interrupted by a problem in the woodworking area. A plank that one of the young students is working with becomes stuck and Olivier must release it; an image of blockage and release not unrelated to what has happened, what will happen, to Olivier. The camera, in a non-diegetic turn, shows us his back brace, another sign of the constriction he has had to live under as well as a visible sign of the assistance he needs to bear up under the load he is carrying. And there is again a jump cut as he rushes somewhere down the stairs. (When Olivier releases the stuck plank, he tells the boy how to do this "deux fois!" [two times!], which he repeats for emphasis. It is typical of the brothers' films that there are no throwaway lines. Teaching by imitation—Olivier does something, and then the student tries [a second doing]—is crucial to the film. We will see later that such a mimetic intelligibility, itself central to how realist film narrative works, informs what is in effect a kind of reconciliation at the

25. The most extreme example of such a gap, and subsequent viewer confusion, is, in *Lorna's Silence*, the murder of Claudy off-screen by Lorna's accomplices. We see her shopping for clothes for him after we had seen them become quite close. We assume she is buying him gifts and are shocked when we see her give them to the attendant at the morgue for his burial. We are as shocked as she is by his sudden disappearance from the film and from her life.

end of the film, something learned, some mimetic understanding that is not discursively articulable.)[26]

Such questions (When can an action properly be said to begin and end? What is a part of the action, what not, and why?) are, I have suggested, raised simply by the editing and camera work. What I mean by this is evident in the film's most pressing issue. We conventionally think—and conventional editing invites us to think—that Olivier begins to decide whether or not to take Francis when the film begins, when he sees the paper with Francis's name on it, but because we are also plunged in medias res as well as at the beginning, that convention is subtly challenged. What thing we are also in the middle of is not remarked on but is obvious. We learn that, after the murder of his son and the collapse of his marriage, Olivier stopped working with his brother at the family lumberyard and began working at a school for youthful offenders, all about the age that Francis will be after he serves his five years. It would not be unreasonable to suspect that Olivier even knows that it is *this* school that an offender like Francis will attend. Thus the action, in the most general sense—Olivier's understanding of Francis and working something out with the boy—clearly begins much earlier than the film's beginning with Olivier reading the boy's name, all even though Olivier's view of what he is doing is hardly this determinate.

But questions about the unity of action are not altogether representable visually. They depend on the right act description and the agent's self-understanding. For that we need some dialogue, but there is already something destabilizing or at least interrogative in these unnatural cinematic suggestions about action unity. By destabilizing and interrogative, I mean at this point only that the quite plausible understanding of the form of an action and hence its unity (the account that comes down to us from Aristotle)—that actions

---

26. There are several more doublings in the film. His wife follows him out to a parking lot and challenges him about Francis twice; Francis and Olivier eat together twice; Olivier observes Francis sleeping twice; Francis orders the same food as Olivier, blows the dust off himself the same way; Francis builds a carrying box just like Olivier's; and finally, in the closing scene, Francis imitates Olivier carrying and wrapping the wood (and this time seizes a tiny initiative). The theme is also connected to what some see as Christian elements in the films. Each troubled character comes to a point where they can begin again, start a second life: Rosetta, Igor, Bruno, especially Francis, Lorna (in her case, just a fantasy of regeneration), and Cyril (the kid with a bike). There doesn't seem to me anything inherently Christian about these new beginnings, but they all do depend on some moment of generosity of spirit from another.

are undertaken for the sake of some end, properly begin when we undertake something in order to achieve that end, the parts or elements of which must be related to that end within this "in order to" structure (so that smoking a cigarette while one is building a house is not part of the house-building activity), and are over either when the end is achieved or we give up[27]—does not fit what Olivier is doing when he *accepts* Francis, what Lorna does when she *decides* to help Claudy, not murder him, what Samantha does when she *cares* for Cyril in *The Kid with a Bike*, and so forth. For one thing, such dependence on the agent's self-understanding assumes the possibility of some sort of transparency of the self to itself at least with regard to one's own purposes, and although in ordinary circumstances this is almost always unproblematic, that too, we are being signaled, will be in question, and not in the name of the unconscious or a lack of self-knowledge in principle possible. What is quite credibly shown in the nonstandard representations of the mindedness of many of these characters, especially here with Olivier, is that there is nothing yet to be known, at least (and this is the crucial point) nothing *determinate*, even though he is certainly *acting*; things are not merely happening to him. Besides this very frequent lack of fit between the cinematic composition of scenes and the conventional unity of actions, we have seen something of the second technique in noting the very close-up position of the camera *behind* the character. This manner of filming is probably the most prominent and distinctive feature of the films: the handheld, documentary-style camera position in relation to the characters being filmed. Especially in *The Son*, the camera seems to be literally following Olivier like a person, staying out of his sight, peering around a corner unobserved (fig. 10.1), pursuing him, as if embodying our desire to understand and not to miss anything. The action does not seem to be filmed from outside looking in, but from within the scene of the action, as if a truly external point of view were a comforting delusion.

The most dramatic use of the technique was on display right away at the beginning of the brothers' first two serious feature films, *The Promise* and *Rosetta*. In the beginning of the latter, Rosetta has been fired, not because she

---

27. We want to know what Olivier is doing by teaching the murderer of his son, and of course we mean what he thinks he is doing, but the film does not instruct us to find a mental state (his intention); it asks us to look to what he does, is doing over time, has done, if we want to assess what his purpose could be in taking on Francis. Implicitly, the claim is: that is where *he* must look too.

is a bad worker, but because of the unavoidable tardiness caused by the bus system. We will learn that she is a scrupulously, even ferociously, good worker; having and keeping a normal job means everything to her. But her training period has ended and (we assume) her employer must pay her considerably more if she stays. It is easier for him to cycle through such temporaries. It is also interesting that, as the incredibly intense first-time actress Émilie Dequenne storms toward a confrontation about her dismissal, she closes the door on us, on the unstable, pursuing camera, three times. However close we think we are allowed to get to the character, we are reminded that something is unavailable. The gaps in the editing suggest the same thing—something important to any potential understanding is very often not available, at least not if we make standard assumptions about what there is to be understood.

Hence the appropriateness of the title of Luc Dardenne's *Au dos de nos images*; they film from behind the character (we see a great many backs and backs of heads in their films), very close, and, especially, as noted earlier, as if pursuing the character, hastening after them, trying to catch up, following them somewhat anxiously, as if trying to follow the plot. (For Luc Dardenne, the back is the part of one's body one cannot naturally see, so they are being filmed from a point of view they cannot take, attending to what is hidden from them. The back is also our most vulnerable side.)[28]

In all of their films, our impression is always of being much too close to the character, and this also has something to do with the psychology of deliberation and action. We do not seem to have sufficient distance to assess properly what is going on. (Philosophers often describe our capacity for reflection as a capacity to stop and "step back" from what we were doing, so as to get a sense of things.)[29] And since we are following along so close to the characters, we

28. Filming from behind also gives the depiction the air of realist documentary by eliminating any sense that the characters are before or in front of or for a camera, as well as weakening any possible sense that we, the viewer, are on the outside looking in. We are in the scene by always trying to catch up, and in a way, we begin to realize, that is true of the characters too, as if they are trying to catch up with their own deeds.

29. This is not to say there is *no* distance. In this case, being close, but from the back, establishes a kind of tension: with them but not at all from their point of view. Luc Dardenne (2005: 130) says that this gap establishes the "secret" of the other, and it helps to create a sense of mystery, an unclosable gap, about such otherness. (My suggestion is that this is only so on the misguided assumption that we need to see inside them to know them, know their secrets as if they were contents locked in a box.) Rushton (2014: 312) points out how well this sort of tension maps on to Michael Fried's account of the relation between immersion and specularity in his account

sense that in their experience they, too, are propelled forward in the action in a way that cannot be said to be guided by reflection in the standard step-wise, ex ante/post facto way. They are in effect too close to their own actions as well, without sufficient distance from what they are doing, and the pace of the action is such that isolating moments of inner reflection and outer manifestation appears to be very difficult. There are even occasions when we are so close to the characters, so involved with them, so curious about them, that we cannot properly even see what they see; our vision is obscured by the character him- or herself, or by our unusual closeness to the character, because of some over-eagerness to be so close. For example, when the boy Igor looks at a passport in *The Promise*, we are put in the position of looking at what he sees, but we are blocked by his point of view (fig. 10.2).

Third, as we have been noting, the brothers make extensive use of one of the most potent cinematic techniques, the close-up. It is one of cinema's versions of the famous Wittgenstein maxim from the *Philosophical Investigations*: "The human body is the best picture of the human soul."[30] In the films with the most close-ups, like *The Son* or *Lorna's Silence*, we sense (I want at least to suggest, fully aware that this is the most tentative of the suggestions that I am making) something different from the treatment of the face as a sign or mark of the interior, but that, paradoxically, some attitude or reaction is first of all realized in or inseparable from such a physical dimension—or at least that the putative *isolation* of the psychological as an ex ante determinate inner world (which can be expressed or not, which we see into by looking at a face) is being challenged by an attempt to locate such a putative interiority instead in the world. We see any such inner world taking shape and changing *in* the activities and expressions of the characters, and, in some cases, we see that there is very little determinate or fixed or resolved or even linear going on in such a putative world beforehand. As we shall discuss soon, it can seem that any such putative inner psychology is at almost (but not, I want to say, completely) degree zero.

This is all challenging and difficult enough, but there is another huge dif-

---

of Caravaggio's "discovery" of absorptive techniques. He also offers a compelling example of how this works in a detailed analysis of several scenes from *The Promise* (314). Fried's account is not a psychological one and can be mapped on to different philosophical accounts. For its Hegelian resonances, and so its relevance to this account, see Pippin 2014: 63–95.
30. Wittgenstein 1958: 178.

ference in their use of close-ups compared to the conventions of realist movies. In the cinematic world of the Dardenne brothers, when we get something more of the character than the full back and the back of the head, we rarely get more than half or at best three-quarters of the face. And they are very fond of shooting such unusual close-ups from the rear of an automobile, accentuating again the theme of speed, forward motion always under way (not to mention being driven, carried forward—such as Igor and Francis and Lorna—rather than driving themselves), without much in the way of punctuated moments of reflection or decision, as well as a way of again putting us, almost claustrophobically, in the scene (figs. 10.3 and 10.4).

Throughout all the films, however, what we expect from the close-up is frustrated. We expect some revelation, a mark of some passion or intensity or guilt, but in their films we can't get the best picture of the soul, the front of the face, in view. It is as if, even taking account of how little pure interiority is sometimes suggested in their close-ups, what partial insight we might gain about the character's mindedness is deliberately denied us, as if we are being told that we will have to make do, that one always has to make do, with some incomplete picture of the soul.[31] Their dominant close-up is the profile. A standard view of the meaning of this technique, proposed by Paul Coates and echoed by Richard Rushton, is that such a profile view suggests that something in the characters is hidden or blocked.[32] And there are many other possibilities. Sometimes a profile, looking away from a conversation or an action, can suggest absentmindedness or distraction or daydreaming. But rather than indicating that anything is hidden, it may also mean that our expectation of some punctuated moment of insight is being deliberately frustrated because such an assumption is misleading, looking for the wrong thing, for some hidden content, rather than attentive to a still indeterminate and more temporally extended and socially embedded formation process. The profile can suggest that something is ongoing, not completed, being resolved rather than already resolved, so that our normally assumed time frame for coming to understand another is arbitrarily compressed.

31. I should stress that I mean how little of *pure* interiority there is. This is not a claim that there is no inner life to these characters. Olivier is clearly boiling inside. It is just to challenge the simple location of such mindedness in a pure, private, inner realm, uniquely and only knowable by the subject. It is also to suggest that such turmoil and stress may not yet have an object.
32. See Coates 2012: 29–35 and Rushton 2014: 310.

This is remarkable given what the close-up is famously able to do.[33] Consider for the sake of contrast Carl Dreyer's paradigmatic use of Maria Falconetti in *The Passion of Joan of Arc* (1928) with the more passive and confused face of Lorna. (I am also convinced, but cannot prove, that the Dardennes are thinking of Falconetti in the way they cut the hair and photograph and to some extent heroize the Albanian actress Arta Dobroshi in *Lorna's Silence* [figs. 10.5 and 10.6].)[34]

And for the fourth technique, there is something we have already noted in passing: the related general issue of the representation of psychological states in all the films, and *The Son* in particular. Not only do we not very often simply see much of the face; when we do, what we see is sometimes unreadable, nearly blank.[35] There is a flicker of remorse and concern from Lorna in the scene from which the last image was taken, but there is also a long scene in a single take where Lorna is trying to decide whether to defy her gang and divorce Claudy rather than kill him. She knows that she must show evidence of physical abuse to get the quick divorce that she needs (this will save Claudy's life and, she hopes, still satisfy her bosses), but there is a remarkable *stillness* in this scene of deliberation. We detect very little mental movement, we might say, at least nothing visible in her face. At its conclusion, she seems to have decided nothing, then very suddenly, she acts, and we jump in our seats. She calmly sets a cup down and then violently slams her upper arm against the door frame. We see, at least, no moment of deliberation or even preparation to act. There is almost a pure picture here of, and a deliberately isolated focus on, the *seamless* relation between inner deliberation and bodily movement, almost as if this bodily movement, itself rich in meaning, freighted with both self-

33. For a rousing panegyric, see Epstein 1988: "The close-up, the keystone of the cinema, is the maximum expression of this *photogenie* of movement" (236). "The close-up is drama in high gear. . . . Never before has a face turned to mine in that way. Ever closer it presses against me, and I follow it face to face. It's not even true that there is air between us; I consume it. It is in me like a sacrament. Maximum visual acuity" (238–39). All of this the brothers invite and then refuse.

34. The picture of arrogant men in Dreyer's film deciding the fate of Joan is repeated in the gang's discussions of Lorna. The intensity of Lorna's final (and crazy) belief that she is pregnant is also an echo of Joan's intense commitment (to the point of insanity).

35. This is something that has been noted by several critics. See Rancière 1999: 110–12. I disagree with Rancière that the effect here is Brechtian and am arguing for an alternative, but his point about the confluence of both realist and modernist elements in their films is an important one.

punishment, self-sacrifice, and a strategic deed for the sake of a quick divorce, was going to happen all along, as if the pacing and deliberating did not bear directly on the action. She simply sets her cup down, and then, suddenly, this is what we see (fig. 10.7).

Of course, suspicions about human psychology as a kind of inner citadel of occurrent states and dispositions, uniquely accessible to a subject's mind, have long been a feature of post-Hegelian European philosophy, prominent in very different ways, with different implications, in Marx, Nietzsche, Freud, Heidegger, Merleau-Ponty, and the French structuralist and poststructuralist moment, as well as in the modernist novel. But arguably, to summarize with wild abandon, we still do not have a very good sense of *what it would be to be free* of the grip of such illusory Cartesian or Christian or subjectivist pictures, what it would be to live out a whole form of life, day to day, in complex inter-actions with others, *not* informed (and self-deceived) about itself in such ways, and credibly set in a world that determines what forms such interactions shall take (and may not take). As we have seen in the critical reaction we have been tracking in the notes, the idea that the Dardennes' unusual technique shows us that the characters are mysteriously other—that we are blocked from their inside, that much in them is hidden, and so forth—remains prominent in that literature (as would be attempts to apply the notions of the unconscious or self-deceit). If we give up this sort of mystification, we can see that there are glimmers of such a positive possibility, such a different idea of mindedness itself and therewith possible mutual comprehension, in these films, even in a social world with little room, if any, for such a possibility of such "objective subjectivity." When Wittgenstein spoke of being in "the grip of a picture," and when we ask here what it would be to be free from such a grip, we usually do not mean anything as literal as a picture.[36] But this is exactly what I am sug-gesting. What we need are such new, densely textured pictures, something available uniquely in fine art and film. Since our evaluative judgments are tied to what we have come to understand about a person's deeds, and since such an assessment brings with it different possible assumptions about *what* we need to understand and evaluate, all of these issues are in play as we try to understand what happens between Olivier and Francis (*The Son*), Igor and Assita (*The Promise*), Bruno and Sonia (*The Child*), and Lorna and Claudy (*Lorna's Silence*).

36. Wittgenstein 1958: §115, p. 53; my trans. And see §§422–26.

Moreover, the Dardenne picture is not that of the neutral or affectless subjects of some modernist novels. The chief characters in some Heinrich von Kleist and Franz Kafka and Maurice Blanchot novels are not governed by the conventions of psychological realism. Those conventions have been suspended, and the result is more like fable or parable; whereas characters like Meursault in Albert Camus's *The Stranger* are frightening because something is clearly lacking or missing, something that makes them stand out, like a sociopath but clearly not like the insane.[37] We do not have here, in other words, either a traditional psychological realism or the mere *absence* of such realistic interiority. The films show us that any possible self-relation in view in the films is never divorced from whatever outer relations are possible. They show what possible courses of action are closed or open, and so an intimation of genuine, but not individualist, subjectivity is visibly emergent in (and only in) these personal interchanges and in what they try to do—manifestations of such subjectivity that must therefore be understood in a way not captured by conventional assumptions. This is an intimation, because characters often can only sense something essential to such expression as missing, not allowed, blocked, and so they struggle against it; in effect, they form themselves in the struggle. This is paradigmatically true not only of Rosetta but also in Igor's promise (something only he knows about), in Bruno's hurried reversal about selling his child, in Lorna's resistance to the terrible pressure applied by the gang.[38] And "I" is only an intimation, because it is only with repeated viewings of the films that such a picture begins to come into cinematic focus.

IV

There is one interchange in which this all comes to a very fine point. Whatever else Olivier may want in *The Son*—revenge, closure, perhaps even another son—he also wants what we want: understanding, the capacity to render

37. See Camus 1989.

38. Likewise, just as it would be wrong to infer that these frequent blank or unrevealing faces suggest an absence of any interiority, so it would not be right to say that these characters are unreflective because they are not discursively or linguistically reflective. The form of reflection is a kind of agitated, inchoate, but not chaotic self-sentiment; a much larger topic. The same could be said about any supposed affective blankness. It would be a mistake to think this suggests a lack of emotional depth or affectlessness. See Rushton (2014: 313) again on "empathic projection" and his references to Fried's account.

something more intelligible.[39] In this case, he clearly wants to understand how it is possible for an eleven-year-old boy to commit murder.[40] He seems to realize in some abstract way that he should be having the same violent, passionate, desperate reaction of his ex-wife simply on hearing the news that Francis had been released. He doesn't, and Olivier cannot tell the truth to his ex-wife, so he pretends that he has not taken him on as an apprentice. But after his initial moment of panic, it is clear that he cannot bring himself to give up the chance to observe such a boy close-up, however painful it might be to constantly confront again and again what happened to his son. He follows Francis furtively through town, goes through his things, steals his keys, and slips into Francis's apartment, and in a moving scene even lies down on his bed, as if trying to inhabit his space, as if trying for a form of mimetic understanding of the teenaged boy. (We are thereby shown the striking similarity of Francis's and Olivier's apartments: cold, spare, empty of any external signs of personality or comfort. They both seem to have a kind of stalled life.)

It is not the case though that even this much is clear to Olivier or, at least, that there is much more to what he is doing than he can formulate. He gives his basic answer to this "why" question in a tense scene with his ex-wife, who has followed Olivier because she suspects he was lying and that he did in fact take on their son's murderer as an apprentice. Yet again the cut ends before the scene does; there is a radical jump cut before anything in the parking lot has ended. The genuineness of Olivier's answer in the scene is at the heart of what the film is attempting to work out. She asks, "Who do you think you are? Nobody would do this. So why you?" There is a long pause and he says simply, "I don't know." (As in the closing scenes, Olivier's heavy breathing is unusually

39. Olivier has a remarkable ability to estimate distances intuitively. He has a passion for such precision in his work, and we sense that he brings that passion to this question, that he is after something far more determinate and specific than will be possible. He will have to learn somehow to accept this, and it appears that he does. This theme is also a reference to a kind of intuitive, nondiscursive knowledge. Olivier says he knows how to do this "d'habitude," from practice or out of habit.

40. One of the reasons I am somewhat hesitant about Levinasian categories in understanding the film is that Olivier's attempt is not something like an attempt to subsume Francis under Olivier's regime of meaningfulness, let us say, by contrast with a supposedly purer encounter with Francis's wholly other status, a status that breaks through rather than is incorporated in such a regime. That would just mystify what Olivier quite understandably wants to understand, not encounter. This still leaves open the question of what, if anything, he does ultimately understand.

prominent on the sound track. This both reminds us of what was extinguished in the strangulation murder of his son, the burden of memory he must carry, and provides us with another powerful image of the inner-outer relation criterial for action.) We want immediately to say to ourselves, he means "I don't know *yet*," that he has a reason, an end, that he just cannot now formulate. Or we want to say that he means his action is multiply motivated, and he can't isolate his chief motive, what would still move him to act, even if he had none of the others. There is no sense that this "I don't know" is simply the best Olivier can do, as if someone more articulate or reflective could do better. So while it is true that Olivier might retrospectively be able to make some sort of sense of what happened between him and Francis, it is not by way of discovery. To insist on forcing the narrative into such a standard form is again to miss both the power and the point of the film.

Further, in another convention, we would normally say that Olivier is trying to understand what is and was inside Francis; especially what he was thinking and feeling when he killed Olivier's son during a robbery gone bad.[41] That, we think, is how we explain what people do, by reference to their purpose in doing it, to what they had in mind, as if, again, we could isolate such content. Once we know that, we think, we might go on to ask, whatever that internal makeup was, how it got to be that way, what brought it about. Perhaps that would excuse or mitigate blame. But given that answer to his wife, Olivier could just as well be said to be trying to find out why *he* is doing what he is doing, and to do so simply by doing it. More generally, however conventional and familiar, such a way of understanding—access to the hidden inner of another—is denied us by the film, and the suggestion is that the problem is not uniquely true of Francis (that his psychological interior is rather minimal or medicated away), but that the assumption of determinate interiority is bound to lead us astray in all cases.[42]

At any rate, Olivier never finds out anything determinate as to why Francis did what he did. He gets a chance to ask Francis point-blank, but the response is like most of the other psychological indicators in the film: flat, minimal.

41. For more discussion of this persistent but false picture of mutuality, see chapter 7.
42. Again it is the repetition of this theme—the unavailability of any pure interiority for characters in *The Promise*, *Rosetta*, and *The Child* especially—that establishes that something of larger significance is at issue than the personal history of the individuals involved. Readers of Cavell will recognize that this illusion, and the implications of avoiding it, are central issues in his work; see the discussion of Cavell in chapter 7.

They are on a trip to Olivier's family's lumberyard so that Francis can learn about different kinds of wood. The preparation for the trip has been quite ominous, and there is a moment when Olivier stops the car suddenly, throwing the sleeping Francis forward violently. Olivier at one point refuses to shake Francis's hand. There is a definite sense of possible violence in the air. So Olivier finally asks the decisive question: "Why did you kill?" He clearly means, "What made you think it was all right to kill someone for a car radio?" But Francis assumes he is just asking for details and explains that he was surprised that there was someone in the car, that the son grabbed him and wouldn't let go, so he tried to break free by grabbing him by the throat and ended up strangling him. (Francis in effect gives the same kind of non-answer answer ["He wouldn't let go, that's why I strangled him"] that Olivier gave to his wife, when she first asked Olivier why he was even considering taking Francis on, "To teach him carpentry." And, in effect, both of them also give a version of the "I don't know" answer when they are being straightforward. The phrase *deux fois* resonates again.)

We see no remorse from Francis; on the contrary, he exhibits a dogged, adolescent self-justification (the son was killed simply because "he wouldn't let go"). Remorse, we can postulate, would require considerably more understanding of what he did and its consequences than Francis can muster. Of course, he doesn't know who is interrogating him and why, but we don't get the sense that he understands much more of what happened to him and because of him than this. He barely remembers how old he was when he went to prison. He has never heard the word "initials." And there is no real forgiveness from Olivier either (now or ever) and no real way to understand what happened from Francis's point of view. There is *barely* a detectable point of view there, at least as it would be traditionally understood. The same camera technique (what we might call the refusal of the revelatory close-up) and the same signs of minimalist, not yet fully determinate, psychological interiority are characteristic of the treatment of Rosetta in *Rosetta*, Igor in *The Promise*, Bruno in *The Child*, and Lorna in *Lorna's Silence*. It is here in the question of why this is so that the similarities among these characters arise, as does the question of their distinctive sociohistorical world.[43]

---

43. It would take a separate and lengthy study to establish with any credibility that there is at work here an attempt to understand the link between an ever more radical absence of *any* standing or status, *any* recognitive respect, and the altered, reduced psychological determi-

In *The Son*—in many ways a much more intimate, narrowly focused film than most of the others—we get a glimpse of such missing possibilities for social connectedness and the difference such connectedness might make in mutual comprehensibility. (Francis seems to have no family that cares for him. His mother's boyfriend doesn't want him around. He has no contact with his father. And he is a product of the juvenile prison system, one result of which is that he has clearly been overmedicated.) But especially in *The Son*, we see that there is the hint of a mode of mutual understanding that has nothing to do with punctuated moments of insight into the other but is the result of a variety of longer-term, complex diachronic development and interactions, much of which are public, action-based, worked out in a variety of different contexts that seem to have nothing to do, initially, with the issue. (Eating together, playing a Foosball table game together, working together on Francis's carpenter's box, helping the boy carry his load [his "burden"] and much else.) Even the moments when Francis reacts with abject fear when he learns who Olivier is and Olivier chases Francis down and begins to throttle him are made to seem relevant to a form of mutual understanding or acknowledgment that cannot be summarized discursively or driven forward by dialogue or reflection. (This is the last instance of a form of mimetic understanding in which Olivier finds himself to have assumed the position of Francis with respect to his son.)

V

I note in conclusion that we have produced sufficient reason to believe that the Dardennes are in their own way quite sensitive to the implications of this way, a socially mediated way, of thinking about what is involved in trying to understand what people do. The conditions in which such agency exists—or let us say, in general, the possibility of leading a life in a way that can be understood by themselves and others—are, for some, profoundly threatened. In the films where the social conditions under which the characters live are quite prominent and clearly assumed to be relevant to understanding what happens—*The Promise, Rosetta, The Child, Lorna's Silence*—persons are not

nacy in the portrayal of these characters (as opposed to working, recognized characters like Olivier and Samantha). Moving away from a conventional view about inner-outer relations is certainly important for such an issue, and that is all that can be suggested here. A future study of the issue in *Rosetta* is planned.

externally constrained. But the limited sphere of social possibilities and social mobility, and the pathological nature of the socially formative influences on Igor, or Rosetta, or Bruno, and the inhumanity and falseness of the world Lorna is locked in to, do not just mean that the situation of these characters is unjust and that we should perhaps take that into account in assessing whatever wrongs they may have committed. Something fundamental in even their relation to themselves—their ability to understand and evaluate themselves as conventional candidates for standard intentional explanation—is put in question. The possibility of self- and other-understanding is shown to be, in such a world, a kind of luxury, one made possible by the leisure and security these characters do not have, cannot ever expect to have. The consequences of not having it are on view in those films. (We cannot easily, or even with difficulty, imagine what happens after the ending of a Dardenne film, because *the characters* can't. This is not a sign of some flaw or absence in their character, some lack of sufficiently stable dispositions to project into the future. Or it is that, but not merely that. It is at bottom an objective problem.)

The most telling case is that of Rosetta, who—unrecognized, ignored, and in an economy with no place for her—is reduced by her marginalized status to a hunter-gatherer or almost animal level of existence. People so reduced, so far outside the world of production and consumption that confers whatever status is available in a modern world, or who are "illegal" and have no standing to call on authority to address wrongs committed, do not just passively suffer and remain as they were.[44] The strange neutrality and near-blankness of expression that we see in Igor, Rosetta, Bruno, Lorna, and Francis reflects, then, another implication of taking seriously the notion that the relation between inner and outer in our understanding of others and of what they do is dialectical, not cleanly separable. In more fully recognized and socially integrated characters like Olivier and Samantha, the non-isolability of the agent as possessor of an inner world means a kind of provisionality and instability in their initial self-understanding and thereby in our possible understanding. Conventionally, we see what they do as *the exteriorization of something interior*, and that is not wrong, but such states are not something fully determinate and identifiable except as exteriorized and thereby in a domain where *what* has been exteriorized is contestable as well as recognizable. So whatever stops Olivier from harming Francis when he has his hands around his neck is not something we

---

44. In the case of Rosetta and Bruno, their relation to the natural world seems like evolution in reverse, so reduced are their circumstances.

are invited to tie to some conclusion he has reached or decision he has made about Francis, even though it is obviously not unrelated to how he feels, to what is going on in his mental life, to some mode of comprehension in which his view of Francis changes. The change is marked by the first expression of intense emotion in Francis's face and in Olivier's torment as he releases the boy, after which they both revert to their neutral, stern demeanor. (As noted, perhaps finding himself doing to Francis what Francis did to his son gives Olivier some form of mimetic understanding. See the striking look of amazement on Francis's face; his wonder that he is not being killed [fig. 10.8].)

This indeterminacy is due to the fact that what he is doing, "teaching Francis," is not complete, the event in the world that he is bringing about cannot yet be determinately specified. (This is indicated again by the typical way the film ends so abruptly, without any "natural" fulfillment of their joint deed.) Their final scene of reconciliation—when Francis walks slowly back to where Olivier is loading planks, begins to help, and, with Olivier's quiet acquiescence, joins him in tying down and wrapping up the load—is silent, played out *in what they do*; and in that action, what Olivier is doing is not driven by any thought about what he ought to do, yet nor is it mindless or unintentional. Their joint action seems to suggest that they have *silently* found some way to wrap up or tie together—tentatively—what they have jointly achieved with respect to the past.[45] It is also obviously of major importance to the filmmakers (and the mark of another huge difference between *The Son* and most of their other films) that that way involves meaningful work (and non-alienated craftsman labor at that), the possibility of which is wholly absent in *The Promise*, *Rosetta*, *The Child*, and *Lorna's Silence* (fig. 10.9 and 10.10).

By contrast, in the unrecognized and marginal characters, we see evidence

---

45. Everything is different between them, a mode of understanding has been reached, with nothing articulated, no words of regret or forgiveness; no words at all. Luc Dardenne has said that Olivier has become Francis's father, fulfills the role of father, by *teaching* him, but what he has taught him is extremely simple: "I didn't kill you." That is all they have at this point, and it seems decisive in a way that is hard to state. See West and West 2009: 126. As Collin 2008 points out, the transition from a kind of state of nature, out in the forest, with living trees, where Olivier's passion for revenge seemed close to getting out of control, to the scene with manufactured planks of wood, and so an "established" paternity or at least legal patronage, is significant. They leave "l'ombre des arbres vivants pour attacher à la voiture ces arbres morts et débité en planches qu'ils doivent ramener à l'atelier. La loi du travail donne une limite à l'illimité de la passion. . . . La lutte à mort a été jouée jusqu'à sa limite" (213). Collin is aware of the resonances with Hegel in the relationship between this struggle and a self-liberation from the natural.

of a kind of deep interiorization of the minimal exterior possibilities and the limitations of their social world, but not in a way that simply reduces them to victims of such objective conditions and certainly not to objects. We return again to the moments of resistance mentioned earlier, but in the limited, restricted ways objectively possible in the world they inhabit. I mean such moments as when Rosetta, while going to sleep at her friend's place, reflectively determines in a bravely hopeful way who she is and what she will do. As one of the most pathos-filled moments in any of the Dardennes' films, the scene's minimality and simplicity is painful to watch. As Rosetta falls asleep, she manifests in what she says a form of dissociation that, we have been shown, is clearly no individual pathology. She is preparing to tell herself good night, assuming the role of the only recognizing other she can imagine in her world: herself. (She becomes her own "outside" for the realization of her "inside" [fig. 10.11].)

"Your name is Rosetta." "My name is Rosetta." "You found a job."
"I found a job." "You've got a friend." "I've got a friend."
"You have a normal life." "I have a normal life."
"You won't fall in the hole." "I won't fall in the hole."
"Good night." "Good night."[46]

46. *Rosetta*, dir. Jean-Pierre Dardenne and Luc Dardenne (1999; New York, 2012, DVD). This is not the closing scene of that movie. And she says she will not fall into a "trou" (a hole). (I have altered the subtitle translation.) In English, to "fall into a rut" is to be numbed by routine and repetition. Rosetta would welcome that; she is afraid of *disappearing*.

ACKNOWLEDGMENTS

Three of these chapters—6, 9, and 10—first appeared in *Critical Inquiry*; chapters 7 and 8 first appeared in nonsite.org; chapter 5 in *The New Hollywood Revisited*, edited by J. Kirshner and Jon Lewis (Ithaca, NY: Cornell University Press, 2019); chapter 3 in *Talk to Her*, edited by A. Eaton (New York: Routledge, 2008). Chapters 1, 2, and 4 appear here for the first time. I am grateful to all the editors for allowing retention of copyright to publish in a collection of essays. I am especially grateful to Michael Fried for conversations about all the chapters, and to Dan Morgan, Richard Neer, Tom Gunning, Jonathan Kirshner, Jon Lewis, and Mark Wilson for conversations about individual chapters and directors. The dedication is an inadequate expression of gratitude to George Wilson for his pioneering work on film, and to Mark Wilson for many comments, suggestions, and advice about film over the last thirty years.

WORKS CITED

Adorno, T. 1951. *Minima Moralia, Reflexionen aus dem beschädigten Leben*. Frankfurt: Suhrkamp.

Adorno, T. 2016. *Minima Moralia, Reflections on a Damaged Life*. Translated by E. F. N. Jephcott. London: Verso.

Almodóvar, P. 2006. *Almodóvar on Almodóvar*. Edited by Frederic Strauss. New York: Faber and Faber.

Andrew, G. 1991. *The Films of Nicholas Ray*. London: BFI.

Andrew, G. 2006. "Luc and Jean-Pierre Dardenne." *Guardian*, 11 February 2006. www .theguardian.com/film/2006/feb/11/features.

Barthes, R. 2012. *Writing Degree Zero*. Translated by Annette Lavers and Colin Smith. New York: Hill and Wang.

Belton, J. 1991. "The Space of *Rear Window*." In *Hitchcock's Rereleased Films*, edited by W. Raubicheck and W. Strebnick. Detroit: Wayne State University Press.

Bennett, J. 1995. *The Act Itself*. Oxford: Oxford University Press.

Berlant, L. 2007. "Nearly Utopian, Nearly Normal: Post-Fordist Affect in *La Promesse* and *Rosetta*." *Public Culture* 19 (Spring): 273–301.

Bersani, L., and U. Dutoit. 2004. *Forms of Being: Cinema, Aesthetics, Subjectivity*. London: BFI.

Biskind, P. 1994. "The Low Road to *Chinatown*." *Premiere*, June.

Brooks, P. 1976. *The Melodramatic Imagination: Balzac, Henry James, Melodrama, and the Mode of Excess*. New Haven, CT: Yale University Press.

Cameron, I., ed. 1992. *The Movie Book of Film Noir*. London: Studio Vista.

Cameron, I., and D. Pye, eds. 1996. *The Movie Book of the Western*. London: Studio Vista Books.

Camper, F. 1971. "The Films of Douglas Sirk." *Screen* 12, no. 2 (1 July): 44–62.

Camus, A. 1989. *The Stranger*. Translated by M. Ward. New York: Knopf.

Cardullo, B. 2002. "Rosetta Stone: A Consideration of the Dardenne Brothers' *Rosetta*." *Journal of Religion and Film* 6, no. 1 (April).

Cardullo, B., ed. 2009. *Committed Cinema: The Films of Jean-Pierre and Luc Dardenne; Essays and Interviews*. Newcastle: Cambridge Scholars.

Cavell, S. 1979. *The World Viewed: Reflections on the Ontology of Film*. Cambridge, MA: Harvard University Press.

Cavell, S. 1982. "Politics as Opposed to What?" *Critical Inquiry* 9, no. 1 (September): 157–78.

Cavell, S. 1984. *Pursuits of Happiness: The Hollywood Comedy of Remarriage*. Cambridge, MA: Harvard University Press.

Cavell, S. 1991. *Conditions Handsome and Unhandsome: The Constitution of Emersonian Perfectionism*. Chicago: University of Chicago Press.

Cavell, S. 1996. *Contesting Tears: The Hollywood Melodrama of the Unknown Woman*. Chicago: University of Chicago Press.

Cavell, S. 1999. *The Claim of Reason: Wittgenstein, Skepticism, Morality, and Tragedy*. Oxford: Oxford University Press.

Cavell, S. 2002. *Must We Mean What We Say?* Cambridge: Cambridge University Press.

Cavell, S. 2002a. "The Avoidance of Love: A Reading of *King Lear*." In *Must We Mean What We Say?*, 267–356. Cambridge: Cambridge University Press.

Cavell, S. 2002b. "Music Discomposed." In *Must We Mean What We Say?*, 180–212. Cambridge: Cambridge University Press.

Cavell, S. 2002c. "Must We Mean What We Say?" In *Must We Mean What We Say?*, 1–40. Cambridge: Cambridge University Press.

Cavell, S. 2003. *Disowning Knowledge in Seven Plays of Shakespeare*. Cambridge: Cambridge University Press.

Cavell, S. 2013. *This New Yet Unapproachable America: Lectures after Emerson after Wittgenstein*. Chicago: University of Chicago Press.

Chabrol, C. 1985. "Serious Things." In *Cahiers du Cinéma: The 1950s, New Realism, Hollywood, New Wave*, edited by J. Hiller. Cambridge, MA: Harvard University Press.

Chion, M. 2004. *The Thin Red Line*. Translated by Trista Selous. London, BFI.

Clark, T. J. 1996. *The Painting of Modern Life: Paris in the Art of Manet and His Followers*. Princeton, NJ: Princeton University Press.

Coates, P. 2012. *Screening the Face*. New York: Palgrave Macmillan.

Collin, F. 2008. "*Le Fils*." In *Jean-Pierre et Luc Dardenne*, edited by Jacqueline Aubenas. Brussels: CGRI.

Comolli, J.-L., and P. Narboli. 1971. "Cinema/Ideology/Criticism." Reprinted from *Cahiers du Cinéma* in *Screen* 12, no. 1 (1 March): 27–38.

Cooper, S. 2007. "Mortal Ethics: Reading Levinas with the Dardenne Brothers." *Film-Philosophy* 11, no. 2: 66–87.

Critchley, S. 2002. "Calm—On Terrence Malick's *The Thin Red Line*." *Film-Philosophy* 6, no. 1.

Cummings, D. 2009. "The Brothers Dardenne: Responding to the Face of the Other." In *Committed Cinema: The Films of Jean-Pierre and Luc Dardenne; Essays and Interviews*, edited by B. Cardullo, 55–68. Newcastle: Cambridge Scholars.

Dardenne, L. 2005. *Au dos de nos images: 1901–2005*. Paris: Contemporary French Fiction.

Dardenne, L. 2012. *Sur l'affaire humaine*. Paris: Le Seuil.

Douchet, J. 1960–61. "Hitch et son public." *Cahiers du Cinéma* 19–20, no. 113.

Dufrenne, M. 1973. *The Phenomenology of Aesthetic Experience*. Translated by E. Casey. Evanston, IL: Northwestern University Press.

Durgnat, R. 1971. *Film as Feeling*. Cambridge, MA: MIT Press.

Dyer, R. 2000. "Introduction to Film Studies." In *Film Studies: Critical Approaches*, edited by J. Hill and P. Church Gibson, 3–10. Oxford: Oxford University Press.

Eaton, M. 1997. *Chinatown*. London: BFI.

Eisenschitz, B. 1993. *Nicholas Ray: An American Journey*. London: Faber and Faber.

Elsaesser, T. 1987. "Tales of Sound and Fury: Observations on the Family Melodrama." In *Home Is Where the Heart Is: Studies in Melodrama and the Woman's Film*, edited by C. Gledhill, 43–69. London: BFI.

Epstein, J. 1988. "Magnification," translated by S. Liebman. In *French Film Theory and Criticism*, translated by R. Abel et al., edited by R. Abel, 235–41. Princeton, NJ: Princeton University Press.

Evans, R. 1994. *The Kid Stays in the Picture*. London: Aurum Press.

Fawell, J. 2001. *Hitchcock's "Rear Window": The Well-Made Film*. Carbondale: Southern Illinois Press.

Frampton, D. 2006. *Filmosophy*. London: Wallflower.

Fried, M. 2002. *Menzel's Realism: Art and Embodiment in Nineteenth-Century Berlin*. New Haven, CT: Yale University Press.

Fried, M. 2010. *The Moment of Caravaggio*. Princeton, NJ: Princeton University Press.

Girard, R. 1961. *Deceit, Desire, and the Novel: Self and Other in Literary Structure*. Translated by Y. Freccero. Baltimore: Johns Hopkins University Press.

Gledhill, C., ed. 1987. *Home Is Where the Heart Is: Studies in Melodrama and the Woman's Film*. London: BFI.

Halliday, J. 1971. *Sirk on Sirk: Conversations with Jon Halliday*. London: Faber and Faber.

Harvey, J. 2001. *Movie Love in the Fifties*. Cambridge: Da Capo Press.

Hegel, G. W. F. 1975. *Aesthetics: Lectures on Fine Art*. Translated by T. M. Knox. 2 vols. Oxford: Clarendon Press.

Hegel, G. W. F. 1991. *The Encyclopedia Logic*. Translated by T. F. Geraets, W. A. Suchting, and H. S. Harris. Indianapolis: Hackett.

Hegel, G. W. F. 2018. *The Phenomenology of Spirit*. Translated by T. Pinkard. Cambridge: Cambridge University Press.

Heilman, R. B. 1968. *Tragedy and Melodrama: Versions of Experience*. Seattle: University of Washington Press.

Hitchcock, A. 1937. "Why I Make Melodramas," *Film and Stars*. https://the.hitchcock.zone/wiki/Film_and_Stars_(1937)_-_Why_I_Make_Melodramas.

James, D., and R. Berg. 1996. *The Hidden Foundation: Cinema and the Question of Class*. Minneapolis: University of Minnesota Press.

James, H. 1984. *Literary Criticism: French Writers, Other European Writers, The Prefaces to the New York Edition*. New York: Penguin.

Klinger, B. 1989. "Much Ado about Excess: Genre, Mise en Scène and the Woman in *Written on the Wind*." *Wide Angle* 11, no. 4: 4–22.

Klinger, B. 1994. *Melodrama and Meaning: History, Culture, and the Films of Douglas Sirk*. Bloomington: Indiana University Press.

Livingston, P. 2009. *Cinema, Philosophy, Bergman: On Film as Philosophy*. Oxford: Oxford University Press.

MacDowell, J. 2016. "Interpretation, Irony, and 'Surface Meanings' in Film." *Film-Philosophy* 22, no. 2: 261–80.

MacDowell, J. 2018. *Irony in Film*. London: Palgrave Macmillan.

Mai, J. 2010. *Jean-Pierre and Luc Dardenne*. Urbana: University of Illinois Press.

Mercer, J., and M. Shingler. 2004. *Melodrama: Genre, Style, Sensibility*. London: Wallflower.

Miller, D. A. 2016. *Hidden Hitchcock*. Chicago: University of Chicago Press.

Moran, R. 2011. "Cavell on Outsiders and Others." *Revue internationale de philosophie* 2, no. 256 (September): 239–54.

Mosley, P. 2013. *The Cinema of the Dardenne Brothers: Responsible Realism*. New York: Columbia University Press.

Mulhall, S. 2008. *On Film*. 2nd ed. New York: Routledge.

Mulvey, L. 1987. "Notes on Sirk and Melodrama." In *Home Is Where the Heart Is: Studies in Melodrama and the Woman's Film*, edited by C. Gledhill, 75–82. London: BFI.

Mulvey, L., and J. Halliday, eds. 1972. *Douglas Sirk*. Edinburgh: Edinburgh Film Festival.

Naremore, J. 1988. *Acting in the Cinema*. Berkeley: University of California Press.

Neer, R. 2011. "Terrence Malick's New World." *nonsite*, no. 2 (June). nonsite.org/issues /issue-2/terrence-malicks-new-world#foot_src_4.

Nietzsche, F. 2001. *The Gay Science*. Edited by B. Williams and J. Nauckhoff. Translated by A. Del Caro. Cambridge: Cambridge University Press.

O'Shaughnessy, M. 2008. "Ethics in the Ruin of Politics: The Dardenne Brothers." In *Five Directors: Auteurism from Assayas to Ozon*, edited by Kate Ince. Manchester: Manchester University Press.

Peebles, S. 2003. "The Other World of War: Terrence Malick's Adaptation of *The Thin Red Line*." In *The Cinema of Terrence Malick: Poetic Visions of America*, edited by Hannah Patterson, 152–63. New York: Wallflower Press.

Perez, G. 2014. "Hitchcock's Family Romance: Allegory in *Shadow of a Doubt*." In *Understanding Love: Philosophy, Film, and Fiction*, edited by S. Wolf and C. Grau, 251–70. Oxford: Oxford University Press.

Perkins, V. S. 1963. "The Cinema of Nicholas Ray." *Movie* 9 (May): 5–10.

Perkins, V. 1972. *Film as Film: Understanding and Judging Movies*. New York: Penguin.

Perkins, V. 1992. "*In a Lonely Place*." In *The Movie Book of Film Noir*, edited by I. Cameron, 222–31. London: Studio Vista.

Perkins, V. 1996. "*Johnny Guitar*." In *The Movie Book of the Western*, edited by I. Cameron and D. Pye. London: Studio Vista Books.

Perkins, V. 2013. "Action on Objects." *Cine-Files* 4 (Spring).

Pippin, R. 2005. "Authenticity in Painting: Remarks on Michael Fried's Art History." *Critical Inquiry* 31, no. 3 (Spring): 575–98.

Pippin, R. 2008. *Hegel's Practical Philosophy: Rational Agency as Ethical Life*. Cambridge: Cambridge University Press.

Pippin, R. 2010. *Hollywood Westerns and American Myth: The Importance of Howard Hawks and John Ford for Political Philosophy*. New Haven, CT: Yale University Press.

Pippin, R. 2012. *Fatalism in American Film Noir: Some Cinematic Philosophy*. Charlottesville: University of Virginia Press.

Pippin, R. 2013. "Le grand imagier of George Wilson." *European Journal of Philosophy* 21, no. 2 (Summer): 334–41.

Pippin, R. 2014. *After the Beautiful: Hegel and the Philosophy of Pictorial Modernism*. Chicago: University of Chicago Press.

Pippin, R. 2017. *The Philosophical Hitchcock: "Vertigo" and the Anxieties of Unknowing-ness.* Chicago: University of Chicago Press.

Pippin, R. Forthcoming. *The Cambridge History of Philosophy, 1946–2010*, edited by I. Thompson and K. M. Becker. Cambridge: Cambridge University Press.

Polan, D. 1993. *In a Lonely Place.* London: BFI.

Power, S. P. 2003. "The Other World of War: Terrence Malick's Adaptation of *The Thin Red Line.*" In *The Cinema of Terrence Malick: Poetic Visions of America*, edited by Hannah Patterson, 148–59. New York: Wallflower Press.

Rancière, J. 1999. "Le Bruit du peuple, l'image de l'art: a propos de *Rosetta* et *L'Humanitié.*" *Cahiers du Cinema*, no. 540.

Rodowick, D. 1987. "Madness, Authority and Ideology: The Domestic Melodrama of the 1950s." In *Home Is Where the Heart Is: Studies in Melodrama and the Woman's Film*, edited by C. Gledhill, 268–82. London: BFI.

Rohmer, E., and C. Chabrol. 1992. *Hitchcock: The First Forty-Four Films.* Translated by S. Hochman. New York: Unger.

Rothman, W. 1982. *Hitchcock — The Murderous Gaze.* Cambridge, MA: Harvard University Press.

Rushton, R. 2007. "Douglas Sirk's Theatres of Imitation." In *Screening the Past*, no. 21.

Rushton, R. 2011. *The Reality of Film: Theories of Filmic Reality.* Manchester: Manchester University Press.

Rushton, R. 2014. "Empathic Projection in the Films of the Dardenne Brothers." *Screen* 55, no. 3 (1 September): 303–16.

Scharff, S. 1997. *The Art of Looking in Hitchcock's "Rear Window."* New York: Limelight.

Schatz, T. 1981. *Hollywood Genres: Formulas, Filmmaking, and the Studio System.* New York: Random House.

Schütz, M. 2011. *Explorationskino: Die Filme der Brüder Dardenne.* Marburg: Schüren Verlag.

Schütz, M. 2013. "Begreifen wollen: Bewegende Begegnung mit dem Mörder in *Le Fils* (Der Sohn, 2002)." *Film-Konzepte* 31: 70–89.

Shetley, V. 1999. "Incest and Capital in *Chinatown.*" *MLN* 114.

Shuster, M. 2017. *The New Television: The Aesthetics and Politics of a Genre.* Chicago: University of Chicago Press.

Silverman, K. 2003. "All Things Shining." In *Loss: The Politics of Mourning*, edited by D. L. Eng and D. Kazanjian, 323–42. Berkeley: University of California Press.

Sinnerbrink, R. 2006. "A Heideggerian Cinema? On Terrence Malick's *The Thin Red Line.*" *Film-Philosophy* 10 (December).

Sinnerbrink, R. 2011. *New Philosophies of Film: Thinking Images.* New York: Continuum.

Sirk, D. 1977–78. "Interview with Douglas Sirk." *Bright Lights* (Winter).

Smith, M. 2006. "Film Art, Argument, and Ambiguity." In *Thinking through Cinema: Film as Philosophy*, edited by M. Smith and T. Wartenberg, 33–40. Malden, MA: Blackwell.

Stam, R., and R. Pearson. 1986. "Hitchcock's *Rear Window*: Reflexivity and the Critique of Voyeurism." In *A Hitchcock Reader*, edited by M. Deutelbaum and L. Poague. Ames: Iowa State University Press.

Strawson, P. F. 1974. "Freedom and Resentment." In *Freedom and Resentment and Other Essays.* London: Methuen.

Toles, G. 2001. "*Rear Window* as Critical Allegory." In *A House Made of Light: Essays on the Art of Film.* Detroit: Wayne State University Press.

Trilling, L. 1973. *Sincerity and Authenticity.* Cambridge, MA: Harvard University Press.

Walsh, D. 2006. "The Dardenne Brothers' *L'Enfant*: An Argument for a Far More Critical Appraisal." World Socialist Web Site, 30 June. https://www.wsws.org/en/articles
/2006/06/dard-j30.html.

Walsh, D. 2008. "The Dardenne Brothers: But What about the 'Extenuating Circumstances'?" World Socialist Web Site, 29 September. https://www.wsws.org/en
/articles/2008/09/tff5-s29.html.

Wartenberg, T. 2007. *Thinking in Screen: Film as Philosophy*. New York: Routledge.

Wartenberg, T. 2015. "Philosophy of Film." In *The Stanford Encyclopedia of Philosophy*
(Winter 2015 ed.), edited by E. N. Zalta. http://plato.stanford.edu/archives/win2015
/entries/film/.

West, J., and D. West. 2009. "Taking the Measure of Human Relationships: An Inter-
view with the Dardenne Brothers." In *Committed Cinema: The Films of Jean-Pierre and
Luc Dardenne; Essays and Interviews*, edited by B. Cardullo. Newcastle: Cambridge
Scholars.

Willemen, P. 1971. "Distanciation and Douglas Sirk." *Screen* 12, no. 2 (1 July): 63–67.

Wilmington, M. 1974. "Nicholas Ray's *Johnny Guitar*." *Velvet Light Trap*, no. 12.

Wilson, G. 1986. *Narration in Light: Studies in Cinematic Point of View*. Baltimore: Johns
Hopkins University Press.

Wilson, G. 2008. "Interpretation." In *The Routledge Companion to Film and Philosophy*,
edited by P. Livingston and C. Plantinga, 162–72. New York: Routledge.

Wilson, G. 2011. *Seeing Fictions in Films: The Epistemology of Movies*. Oxford: Oxford
University Press.

Wittgenstein, L. 1958. *Philosophical Investigations*. Translated by G. E. M. Anscombe.
Oxford: Blackwell.

Wood, R. 1989. *Hitchcock's Films Revisited*. New York: Columbia University Press.

Yacavone, D. 2015. *Film Worlds: A Philosophical Aesthetics of Cinema*. New York: Columbia University Press.

INDEX